Mind Reeling

THE SUNY SERIES

HORIZONS OF CINEMA

MURRAY POMERANCE | EDITOR

Mind Reeling
Psychopathology on Film

Edited by

Homer B. Pettey

Cover: Conrad Veidt as Cesare in *The Cabinet of Dr. Caligari* (1920; dir. Robert Weine).

Published by State University of New York Press, Albany

© 2020 State University of New York

All rights reserved

No part of this book may be used or reproduced in any manner whatsoever without written permission. No part of this book may be stored in a retrieval system or transmitted in any form or by any means including electronic, electrostatic, magnetic tape, mechanical, photocopying, recording, or otherwise without the prior permission in writing of the publisher.

For information, contact State University of New York Press, Albany, NY
www.sunypress.edu

Library of Congress Cataloging-in-Publication Data

Names: Pettey, Homer B., editor.
Title: Mind reeling : psychopathology on film / Homer B. Pettey, editor.
Description: Albany : State University of New York Press, [2020] | Series: SUNY series, horizons of cinema | Includes bibliographical references and index.
Identifiers: LCCN 2020018466 | ISBN 9781438481012 (hardcover : alk. paper) | ISBN 9781438481005 (pbk. : alk. paper) | ISBN 9781438481029 (ebook)
Subjects: LCSH: Mental illness in motion pictures.
Classification: LCC PN1995.9.M463 M56 2020 | DDC 791.43/6561—dc23
LC record available at https://lccn.loc.gov/2020018466

10 9 8 7 6 5 4 3 2 1

For Melissa
and
to Jennifer, as always

Contents

List of Illustrations   ix

Acknowledgments   xi

1 Introduction: A Very Brief History of Psychopathology in Cinema   1
   Homer B. Pettey

2 Adèle H., Camille Claudel, and Margot de Valois: Isabelle Adjani's Real "Mad" Women? Costume Drama and the Disruptive Female   37
   Susan Hayward

3 Musical Madness on Hangover Square   65
   Murray Pomerance

4 Screening Multiple Personality Disorder in the Age of Kinsey: *Lizzie* and *The Three Faces of Eve*   79
   R. Barton Palmer

5 The Cine-Telescopic Psyche: 1950s Serial Killers and Sexual Psychopathology in *The Sniper* and *While the City Sleeps*   101
   Robert Miklitsch

6 Pathologies of Pedagogy in Midcentury Melodrama: *The Miracle Worker* and *A Child Is Waiting*   129
   Jennifer L. Jenkins

7 Passion and Delirium: Representing Madness in *Spider*
   and *Asylum*   155
   Jim Leach

8 Scorched: Landscape, Trauma, and Embodied Experience
   in *Incendies*   173
   Tarja Laine

9 Ghostly and Ghastly Desires and Disorders in *Young Adult*:
   KenTacoHuts in Mercury   191
   Julie Grossman

10 Criminal Biographies and Visual Culture   207
   Homer B. Pettey

Contributors   235

Index   239

Illustrations

1.1 Jim (Stuart Whitman) trying to resist temptation at a schoolyard in *The Mark*. 26

1.2 Walter (Kevin Bacon) tempted by Robin (Hannah Pilkes) in *The Woodsman*. 27

2.1 Adèle (Isabelle Adjani) holding her father's book as her identity becomes known in *L'Histoire d' Adèle H*. 51

2.2 Margot's nightly escapade to look for sex in *La Reine Margot*. 59

3.1 George (Laird Cregar) mounting the Guy Fawkes bonfire with Netta's (Linda Darnell) disguised body in *Hangover Square*. 67

4.1 Lizzie (Eleanor Parker), Elizabeth's other self, at a piano bar looking for men in *Lizzie*. 87

4.2 Eve Black (Joanne Woodward) ready for a night on the town in *The Three Faces of Eve*. 95

5.1 Suspect gazing at a "Fill-In-the-Face" newspaper drawing he's filled in, in *While the City Sleeps*. 107

5.2 Sniper Eddie Miller (Arthur Franz) takes aim on the object of his hatred in *The Sniper*. 114

5.3 Eddie's target. 114

6.1 Breakthrough moment with W-A-T-E-R for Helen Keller (Patty Duke) with her teacher, Annie Sullivan (Anne Bancroft), in *The Miracle Worker*. 139

6.2	First-day polite nerves of Jean Hansen (Judy Garland) as she enters a classroom of mentally challenged children in *A Child Is Waiting*.	143
7.1	Spider (Ralph Fiennes) at the window envisions a scene from his own family's past in *Spider*.	162
7.2	Stella (Natasha Richardson), after plummeting through the glass of a hothouse, to get away from Dr. Cleave (Ian McKellen) in *Asylum*.	165
8.1	Nawal within the ruins in *Incendies*.	181
8.2	Landscape as prison.	184
8.3	Face as landscape.	186
8.4	Landscape as face.	187
9.1	Mavis (Charlize Theron) in bed with insignificant lovers in *Young Adult*.	196
9.2	Mirroring warped feminine personalities of Aileen Wuornos (Charlize Theron) and Mavis.	197
9.3	Empty hallways as visual metaphors for Mavis.	201
9.4	Day and night at the BUY BUY BABY mart.	203
9.5	A world-weary, beaten down hotel clerk who could have been Mavis.	204
10.1	Fake copilot, con man Frank Abagnale (Leonardo DiCaprio), follows the objects of his desire in *Catch Me If You Can*.	224
10.2	Bonson's (Tom Hardy) stage profile as himself arguing for his release in *Bronson*.	225
10.3	Bronson, reverse profile, as the nurse who denies his request.	226
10.4	Steven Russell (Jim Carey) walking toward the prison exit as a vice cop in *I Love You Phillip Morris*.	230

Acknowledgments

Homer B. Pettey would like to thank Melissa Alice Pettey, to whom this collection is dedicated. His sister has not only been an inspiration for joy and devotion throughout his life, but, even more, she has also given him insights into real-world, not the academic, issues affecting individuals with mental disabilities. Moreover, her life and occasional struggles have provided him with an understanding of the social, economic, and political problems facing those citizens among us who endure the hardships of their psychological conditions, whether biological or environmental in nature. While she has faced ignorant and disdainful comments, while she has lived through decade after decade of public shunning and derision, while she and her fellow friends with disabilities have endured obnoxious, prejudicial, and far too often socially acceptable jokes, especially from so-called comedians, "social justice" academics, films, and supposedly morally high-ground television and internet personalities, she has never, because of her nature, expressed any feelings other than acceptance of others, no matter their race, religion, ethnicity, disability, or sexual orientations. Her love has never wavered, her warmth has never diminished, and her playful humor has never ceased. Homer B. Pettey owes his sister more than he can ever repay.

Additionally, he would like to thank R. Barton Palmer and Susan Hayward, two admirable scholars and good friends who have supported his efforts for years. To his old pals in high crimes and misdemeanors, Allan J. Arffa, Carter B. Burwell, and Chip Johannessen, he continues to owe debts, although some repayment on their parts would be accepted. As always, he would like to thank that great American institution and its publication, the *Harvard Lampoon*, for its continued work to achieve humor in this often all-too-serious world.

1

Introduction

A Very Brief History of Psychopathology in Cinema

HOMER B. PETTEY

THE HISTORY OF CINEMA REVEALS a fascination with psychopathology. No matter the psychological classification, in the main, cinema has willingly portrayed these psychic dimensions, symptoms, and perversions. The stages of the history of psychopathology onscreen accord with general public perceptions and misperceptions of mental illness. Early cinema treated what was called at the time insanity, rather than specific ailments, as a cause for bizarre behavior and criminality. The late 1920s and 1930s, with the introduction of sound, gave voice to horrific crimes of so-considered demonic madmen. In the postwar period, however, public sentiment leaned toward a more clinical, diagnostic view of mental incapacity. The new era of therapy, of psychoanalyzing everyday life, of psychosuggestive advertising, of personality, IQ, and Rorschach tests—all transformed and informed the public about the dimensions, distinctions, and degrees of mental abilities and disabilities. By the late 1960s and throughout the 1970s, psychopathology in mass media became categorizable into discrete patterns of recognizable misbehavior with nomenclature now understood by police, jurors, judges, teachers, editors, and anchormen. Universities required psychology majors to learn the differences among types of symptoms of abnormal psychology and the theories about their etiologies. The stigma of seeking therapy gradually ebbed away and a more accepting mass media turned to narratives of social responsibility for persons with mental illness. Of course, a simultaneous dissolution of mandatory institutionalization, either through exposure of corrupt management and horrific conditions or through removing state legislative economic support, produced an influx of mentally impaired people on urban streets. In contemporary cinema, shifts in attitudes toward afflicted people have now created a need for new social problem films, ones dealing with a variety of abuses and disorientations of the self. New awareness of disorder has become common parlance, so much so that news media, talk shows, and successful television comedy and dramatic series focus upon protagonists with anxiety and obsessive-compulsive behavior (*Monk*), manic-depressive bipolarity (*Homeland*), and even homicidal sociopathy (*Dexter*). Cinema continually expands its depictions of mental illness, almost as though with each new disorder, a film waits to be made. In the main, cinema holds up a mirror, no matter how dark or cracked, to reflect the public's continual fascination with these typifications—still regarded by many as pathologies.

Much of the silent era treatment of mental illness accords with Oliver Sacks's concept of the asylum:

> Finally, coming back to the original meaning of asylum, these hospitals provided control and protection for patients, both from their own (perhaps suicidal or homicidal) impulses and from ridicule, isolation, aggression, or abuse so often visited upon them in the outside world. Asylums offered a life with its own special protections and limitations, a simplified and narrowed life perhaps, but with this protective structure, the freedom to be as mad as one liked and, for some patients at least, to live through their psychoses and emerge from their depths as saner and stabler people. (2)

The popular view of the asylum as the residence for the marginal figures of society, the insane, befit their Victorian and oppressive structures. These hospitals provided shelter, mostly for society, from the inmates who suffered social diseases, syphilis in particular, and mental dysfunctions, paranoia being quite common. Professional interest in insanity certainly reached its initial stage in the nineteenth century with the founding of the *American Journal of Insanity* in 1844, whose organization, by the end of the century, would change its name to the American Medico-Psychological Association (1892), then to the American Psychiatric Association (1921) (Freedheim 32). While skeptics had predicted that moving pictures would cause nervous problems among their audiences, several asylums, including the Nebraska State Institute for the Insane, installed minitheaters in order to soothe patients "without the exciting effects of other forms of diversion" (Keil and Singer 29). Insanity appears in significant silent films, especially among those revealing the interiors of institutions for madness through visual hallucinations: Robert Wiene's *The Cabinet of Dr. Caligari* (1919), Benjamin Christensen's *Häxan* (1922), Roland West's *The Monster* (1925), and Teinosuke Kinugasa's *Kurutta ippeji* (*A Page of Madness*, 1926). Modernist art movements enhanced the sense of delirium experienced by residents of the asylums, ranging from expressionist mise-en-scène to surrealistic psychosexual imagery. Milos Forman's *Amadeus* (1984), based on Peter Shaffer's 1979 play, employs the concept of the voiceover narrator, Antonio Salieri (F. Murray Abraham), being the resident of an eighteenth-century asylum driven to murderous thoughts out of envy. Often forgotten about this tale of musical rivalry is that Alexander Pushkin first wrote a short play, *Mozart and Salieri* (1830), which begins with Salieri's demented soliloquy against justice and the heavens for anointing Mozart with artistic genius:

> Where, where is justice, when the sacred gift,
> When deathless genius comes not to reward
> Perfervid love and utter self-denial,
> And toils and strivings and beseeching prayers,
> But puts her halo round a lack-wit's skull,
> A frivolous idler's brow? . . . O Mozart, Mozart! (Clark 430)

Forman's film begins with Salieri's failed suicide and his shout of "Mozart!" the source of his severe melancholy. Pushkin's play concludes with Salieri unrepentant about his crime, but also adds his own mad elevation to a kind of suspect greatness:

> So villainy and genius are two things
> That never go together? That's not true;
> Think but of Buonarotti . . . Or was that
> A tale of the dull, stupid crowd—and he
> Who built the Vatican was *not* a murderer? (436)

Forman's film concludes in a somewhat similar fashion, with Salieri showing no regret for his murderous intent, but elevating himself to being the patron saint of all mediocrities as an attendant wheels him past dismally treated residents in irons or sitting amongst straw and dung. Mental institutions proved to be a perpetual subject of cinema; among the numerous films with all or portions set in asylums, excluding more contemporary horror films, are these: *Spellbound* (1945); *Bedlam* (1946); *The Snake Pit* (1948); *Harvey* (1950); *The Three Faces of Eve* (1957); *David and Lisa* (1962); *Captain Newman, M. D.* (1963); *Lilith* (1964); *King of Hearts* (1966); *One Flew over the Cuckoo's Nest* (1975); *Girl Interrupted* (1999); *Spider* (2002); *Gothika* (2003); *The Jacket* (2005); *Asylum* (2005); and *Shutter Island* (2010).

Three months before the release of *The Cabinet of Dr. Caligari*, Robert Reinert released in Munich *Nerves* (1919), whose aesthetic reflects the processes of nervous conditions spreading throughout the social classes: "Digressive and fragmentary, Reinert's film follows a group of people whose nerves have been shattered by war and revolution; traumatized and racked with guilt, they exist on the edge of madness. The film's own perplexing narrative structure imitates the liminal mental states it portrays, ranging from despondency to suicide, from agitation to delirium, from mental breakdowns to hallucinations of a harmonious life in nature" (Kaes 39). Key aesthetics for early cinema of madness required the perceptual experience of madness to be conveyed onto the screen. A fine example remains the hallucinations and misperceptions that drive a jealous husband to the brink of madness in Arthur Robison's *Warning Shadows* (1923). Physicians and alienists often viewed criminality as symptomatic of extreme mental derangement: "As a symptom instead of a disease, the homicidal impulse became identified with two distinct mental conditions. In constitutional psychopathic states, a name given to the conditions brought about by a degenerating nervous system, the homicidal impulse, and impulses in general, were believed to be stigmata of degeneracy. In dementia praecox, alienists saw the homicidal impulse as evidence of the emotional indifference, deterioration of the will, and the impulsive as well as purposeless behaviors that were often destructive and dangerous" (Colaizzi 84). Anthony Asquith's *A Cottage on Dartmoor* (1929) relies upon the prison escape of a love-obsessed, emotionally unstable man (Uno Henning). Louis Feuillade's crime serials suggest transgressive acts among the underworld gangs of *Les vampires* (1915–16), particularly the vicious, sadistic Apache Irma Vep (Musidora). Silent horror films mix the macabre with touches of insanity; cases in point include

John Barrymore's film version of his sensational stage production of *Dr. Jekyll and Mr. Hyde* (1920); Lon Chaney's remarkable performance in *The Phantom of the Opera* (1925); and Jean Epstein's dark, disorienting film of Luis Buñuel's adaptation of Edgar Allan Poe's *The Fall of the House of Usher* (1928). The dual personalities of many of these early films can be attributed to Robert Louis Stevenson's tale of Jekyll and Hyde, as well as to Morton Prince's detailed study *The Dissociation of Personality* (1908), which dealt with descriptions of dual behavioral personality.

Duality certainly became a visual trope for Dada and surrealist cinema. In *Anémic Cinéma* (1926), Dadaist Marcel Duchamp created "rotoreliefs," spinning conical-within-conical figures that were interspersed with spinning French phrases filled with puns and dual meanings. Significantly, Duchamp concluded this six-minute film with a copyright signed by Rrose Sélavy, or *eros c'est la vie*, his gender-split alter ego as a woman, of whom Man Ray took several portraits. Of course, such dual personality intrigued Luis Buñuel and Salvador Dali and influenced their *Un chien andalou* (1929), which also flirts with psychosexual fixation, fetishism, and sadism as the underpinnings for surrealism. Specifically, Dali and Buñuel reveal this duality as an expression of film aesthetics, with "dislocations and disruptions of space and of narrative continuity" presented in a way that seems to be matter-of-fact reality: "In their script the young woman's lack of surprise as she turns around and sees the absent cyclist—whose frills, box, and collar she has just arranged on the bed—standing in another corner of the room" (Finkelstein 85). It is the subverting of cinematic conventions, along with the almost slapstick, silent film aesthetic, that contribute to the disturbing images that thwart the viewer's expectations, but in an "unassuming way" (85). Buñuel in particular was fascinated with the cinema of Harry Landon and other silent comedians. Consequently, during the first showings of *Un chien andalou* at Studio 28, it featured "on a double bill with a Harold Lloyd comedy" (Adamowicz 72). In this way, the Surrealism of Dali and Buñuel eschews techniques of modernist films in order to reveal the banal workings of the popular psyche, best represented by the nonchalance in the face of a mad and chaotic world characterized by silent comedy, particularly Lloyd and Keaton.

By the 1930s, psychopathy, often associated with dangerous scientific experimentation and criminality, became commonplace in the era of great horror films. If, as Jack Shadoian has claimed, the rise of 1930s gangster films was "a paradigm of the American dream," then, also during this same period, the rise of horror films was a paradigm of the American nightmare, the abhorrent psyche that repels as it compels audience attention (3). Horror subject matter involves the grotesque, the deformed, the demented, and the pathological; the worst fears of the institutions for the insane become realities in these films. Angela M. Smith shows a close relationship in 1930s horror films between medical science, often of the brain, and disability, a societal fear of the other, the ab-normal:

> Their formulaic tropes and plots focus on characters/monsters who are clearly bodily, cognitively, or psychologically deformed or impaired; they engage the ethical dilemmas of scientific and medical "advances"; they explicitly mobilize the power dynamics of the medical gaze; and they repeatedly trouble any easy distinction between health professionals and the problematic bodies that they survey, interpret, diagnose, and seek to fix. To that extent, they indicate a popular anxiety about the powers wielded by medical men, a concern that eschews faith in eugenic principles and their proponents and, using the visual rhetoric of disability, transfigures doctors into monsters and monster-makers. (165)

Often, mad scientists have figures of physical disability surround them, as the classical horror films allegorize the physical with the mental instability of the mad doctor. In *The Island of Lost Souls* (1932), demented Dr. Moreau (Charles Laughton) uses biological-anthropomorphic surgeries to transform animals into humans. Of course, James Whale's *Frankenstein* films associate the not-so-good doctor with a kind of mental pathology, displayed admirably by Colin Clive's frenetic, campy exclamation, "It's alive!" Frankenstein's hunchbacked assistant Fritz represents a clearly allegorical physical marker for the not-so-good doctor's mental state. Of course, the numerous cinematic retellings of the mentally and emotionally disturbed doctor have been part of film history since Edison Studio's 1910 adaptation, but so too has the mad concept of reanimation and creating human life from base materials. In Michael Curtiz's *Doctor X* (1932), Dr. Wells (Preston Foster) attempts to create artificial flesh by using a scalpel to remove body parts after first murdering his victims, making the crime scenes appear as though a mad cannibal now terrorizes New York City. Megalomanical Dr. Fu Manchu, based upon Sax Rohmer's novels, began his cinematic criminal career in the 1923 British serial *The Mystery of Dr. Fu Manchu*, and debuted in the United States with Warner Oland as the infamous doctor in *The Mysterious Dr. Fu Manchu* (1929), *The Return of Dr. Fu Manchu* (1930), and *The Dragon's Daughter* (1931).

Perhaps the most well-known remains Boris Karloff's insidiously mad and evil portrayal in Charles Brabin's *The Mask of Fu Manchu* (1932). Experimenting with invisibility by using the drug "monocane," Dr. Jack Griffin (Claude Rains) in *The Invisible Man* (1933) becomes increasingly madder and madder, eventually becoming an outrageous murderer who derails a train and thereby kills hundreds of passengers. In *Night of Terror* (1933), mad scientist Dr. Arthur Hornsby (George Meeker), in reality the homicidal maniac, fakes his own death, only to return to exterminate all of his relatives in order to secure his uncle's fortune. The ending cannot be discussed, since the crazed doctor warns the audience that he will haunt them if they reveal the plot to a single soul. As campy as these films appear in retrospect, their significance still lies in how they depict not so much gothic terror, but rather societal phobias about the demented and deranged, in short, the mentally afflicted.

By the 1940s, the mad criminal morphs into figures with much deeper and more explicit psychopathological syndromes and symptoms, particularly in film noir. In *Raw Deal* (1948), mob boss and sadistic pyromaniac Rick Coyle (Raymond Burr) spends his birthday playing poker and losing to an equally vicious henchman Fantail (John Ireland). Rick achieves a kind of sexual fulfillment watching a flaming dessert, until he receives bad news. Then, in retaliation for his girlfriend accidentally spilling her drink on his jacket, he hurls the flaming contents of the saucepan on her (off-screen). She screams, returns on camera, covering her face as she flees the room. Similarly, in *The Big Heat* (1953) misogynistically sadistic Vince Stone (Lee Marvin), upon concluding that his girlfriend Debby Marsh (Gloria Grahame) has betrayed him to police sergeant Dave Bannion (Glenn Ford), hurls a pot of scalding coffee in her face (off-screen). In *Kiss of Death* (1947), searching for the perceived police informant Rizzo, sadistic killer Tom Udo (Richard Widmark) interrogates Rizzo's wheelchair-using mother (Mildred Dunnock). She lies that Rizzo will return later that night, Udo discovers that his clothes are gone and harangues Ma Rizzo with his maniacal laughter, "Squealers. Both of yous." Taking a standing lamp's electrical cord, Udo straps Ma Rizzo into her wheelchair, then pushes her out the apartment door and down the stairs (on-screen)! Much of this psychopathic display of violence derives from the egomaniacal, often sadistic gangsters of the 1930s, among them Edward G. Robinson's narcissistic death scene at the end of *Little Caesar* (1931). In *White Heat* (1949), oedipally challenged, sociopathic armed robber Cody Jarrett (James Cagney, veteran of 1930s gangster films), tries to escape from the police, led by undercover gang infiltrator Vic Pardo (Edmond O'Brien), by running through a field of gas storage tanks. Climbing the spiral stairs to the top of one of the gas tanks, Cody taunts the police, only to be hit by three of Vic's rifle shots. Wheeling and laughing, Cody fires his pistol into the tank and as flames shoot up, he shouts, "Made it, Ma, top of the world!" Then, explosive fireballs end the film. While these famous male psychopaths certainly represent a strain in film noir, female sociopaths—femmes fatales—also abound in this genre and mete out cruel murder primarily to men: among them, serial murderess Brigid O'Shaughnessy (Mary Astor) of *The Maltese Falcon* (1941); mariticidal Phyllis Dietrichson (Barbara Stanwyck) of *Double Indemnity* (1944); child killer Ellen Berent (Gene Tierney) of *Leave Her To Heaven* (1945); narcisstic murderess Kathie Moffat (Jane Greer) of *Out of the Past* (1947); and parricidal Diane Tremayne (Jean Simmons) of *Angel Face* (1953). Prescient about gender maladies, film noir understood not only the psychopathological behavior of men, but also the equally distributed sociopathy among women.

From the 1940s onward, cinema began to present serious psychological conditions in a more sympathetic light. Numerous films dealt with forms of amnesia. In Mervyn LeRoy's *Random Harvest* (1942), Charles "Smithy" Rainier (Roland Coleman) suffers from severe post-traumatic stress from his trench fighting in World War I that induces long memory gaps, and then, after marrying sympathetic stage singer Paula Ridgeway/Margaret Hanson (Greer Garson), an automobile accident induces yet another bout of amnesia. Smithy recovers only at the film's conclusion, when he inserts a key into the couple's former cottage door and unlocks his memory, allowing him to turn and recognize the ever-patient Paula once again. Alfred Hitchcock's *Spellbound* (1945) has Dr. Constance Peterson (Ingrid Bergman) treating a psychologically impaired victim of serious childhood and adult traumas, Anthony Edwardes/John Ballantyne (Gregory Peck), with the help of dream symbolism, word association, and her old teacher, Dr. Brulov (Michael Chekhov), who looks remarkably like Sigmund Freud. Hitchcock's film treats mental disorders—from nymphomania to the oedipal complex—with a kind of empathy that is not to be found in his tale of the vampiric widow killer, Uncle Charlie (Joseph Cotten) of *Shadow of a Doubt* (1943). Of course, Hitchcock explored a number of psychopathologies in his directorial career: severe depression in *The Wrong Man* (1956), paralyzing acrophobia in *Vertigo* (1958), dual personality, cross-dressing, and sexual murder in *Psycho* (1960), kleptomania, sexual dysfunction, hyposexuality, and trauma in *Marnie* (1964), and predatory serial sexual murder in *Frenzy* (1972). Hitchcock certainly saw how cinematic language could represent amnesia in flashbacks, distorted dreamscapes, and sudden editing of moments of trauma. In *The Snake Pit* (1948), Anatole Litvak also saw the filmic potential for the element of mystery in a narrative about amnesia, as well as its moments of recovered memory. Virginia Cunningham (Olivia de Havilland), a schizophrenic in a sometimes oppressive state asylum for women, experiences electroshock therapy, hypnosis, and the padded cell and straitjacket as she gradually regains some of her memory about her former life. These scenes of disturbing clinical treatment and their effects upon Virginia in *The Snake Pit* would garner Olivia de Havilland the Best Actress Oscar.

Rare comic versions of amnesia include *Clean Slate* (1994), with Dana Carvey as a private investigator who cannot remember anything from the previous day and so keeps tape recordings and notes to remind him once he wakes up. *Clean Slate* was released six years before a very similar plot formed the basis of *Memento* (2000). In both *Clean Slate* and *Memento*, moments of amnesia take the form of dark comedy. In *Overboard* (1987), "rich bitch" Goldie Hawn falls from her yacht, suffers amnesia from the shock, finds herself the wife of the same handyman (Kurt Russell) she has previously verbally abused aboard the ship, and now must cook, clean, and care for her new household, which includes mothering the handyman's unruly sons. Amnesia in melodramas affords directors several aesthetic elements that allow for a coherent restructuring of past events, flashbacks and montages in particular. Amnesia as a mental restriction corresponds well with these types of experimental editing.

Socially relevant films about mental disorders abound in postwar cinema. With the expansion of suburbia and the idealization of new modern family life, the psychopathology of the family became an industry. The nuclear family became the etiological space for that fine line between mental stability and insanity, due to bad parenting, especially *momism*, and divorce. Family therapeutics looked at interrelations as potential indicators for disease. Marriage counseling began in the United States with Paul Popenoe, and was aligned with his previous racial eugenics for institutionalization and sterilization of "defectives," especially the mentally retarded. Popenoe made marriage counseling socially acceptable: "Popenoe also popularized marriage counseling through a 1954 *Ladies' Home Journal* series, 'How to Be Marriageable,' which featured cases from the files of his American Institute of Family Relations; a syndicated newspaper column titled 'Modern Marriage' (1947–57), later renamed 'Your Family and You' (1958–72); and a television show, Divorce Hearing (1957–60), on which Popenoe and other 'judges' listened to the problems of couples on the verge of divorce and tried to help them reconcile" (Weinstein 17). The rise in television shows about family life, advertising campaigns about family normalcy as both emotionally stable and chaotic (Anacin's "Mother, please, I'd rather do it myself!"), and the explosion of advice columns on topics from home decorating to becoming a happy homemaker—all contributed to a new American lifestyle. Crucially, mental illness narratives would adopt this concentration on familial and partnership relations.

Perhaps due to the aging of boomers, public interest in and concern about Alzheimer's disease and its effects upon family members has continued to increase:

> In mass media, literature, and film, Alzheimer's disease offers a cunning demotic for late life because it magnifies what people fear most about how age could manifest itself—that is, in an apparent loss of sense and self. The erosion of memory feeds well into stories of both loss and regret—especially when what one begins to forget is what one sought to ignore in the past. Alzheimer's thereby becomes a quick way to symbolize not just other forms of dementia but also old age more generally. . . . This is not to deny the incredible life-changing devastation this disabling illness can wreak on patients, their family, friends, and care workers. Witnessing a relative become demented has its physical horrors, but also equals witnessing a loss of cultural memory, of family history, and ultimately of a past as well as of a future. The general public—with or without personal experience—frequently connects Alzheimer's with the most horrifying possible loss of self. (Chivers 60)

Alzheimer's disease melodramas have found welcoming audiences, considerable box-office success, and Oscar nominations. Black chauffeur Hoke (Morgan Freeman) discovers Miss Daisy (Jessica Tandy) in the early stages of dementia, but continues to be her closest friend, attending to her in the rest home at the conclusion of *Driving Miss Daisy* (1989). Iris Murdock (Judi Dench) falls into slow mental disintegration, while her caretaker-husband John Bayley (Jim Broadbent) recalls their, and especially her, sexual past in *Iris* (2001), a past Iris can no longer hold on to. Woody Grant (Bruce Dern) dementedly heads to Lincoln to collect his nonexistent sweepstakes prize money, disrupting his son's life and his family's life in *Nebraska* (2013). In *Still Alice* (2014), the serious progressive memory loss of Alice Daly Howland (Julianne Moore), a Columbia

University professor of linguistics, from early onset of the disease ruins her life, breaks up her family, and leaves her without much verbal ability. These Alzheimer's disease melodramas rarely pull punches as they depict demoralizing conditions for sufferers whose worlds transform before their unacknowledging eyes. The sufferers also rarely evoke pity, since their anger, frustration, and impatience wears on family and audiences alike. Here, the psychopathology encompasses the process of familial breakdown and often marital dysfunction as symptomatic of the disease's advancement. From a psychopathological viewpoint, these films do not spend considerable time on etiology and prognosis, but rather work out the melodramatic narratives that resemble disability films. The crucial difference, however, remains that no cure occurs, no overcoming obstacles, and no awaiting a bright future, unlike so many disability films that wish to reinforce a false ending offering normalcy for the protagonist.

Similar to the social relevance of Alzheimer films, America's century-long involvement in warfare sparked numerous films about the psychological problems facing returning soldiers. *The Best Years of Our Lives* (1946) recounts the social-psychological integration of three World War II veterans, Al Stephenson (Frederic March) as a former bank officer, Fred Derry (Dana Andrews) as a newly divorced returning officer, and Homer Parrish (Harold Russell) an armless combatant, all of whom suffer different social and economic problems of reintegration into American postwar culture. Clearly, each man stoically endures both these new hardships and moments of war memories, and never succumbs to a breakdown. Since the Korean conflict and the Vietnam War, posttraumatic stress disorder (PTSD) has served as a central psychoanalytical pretext for the lives of returning military men. Some of that reason has to do with the American psychiatric establishment finally recognizing an ailment that has persisted since World War I. In *Captain Newman, M.D.* (1963), Newman (Gregory Peck) heads a psychiatric ward for veterans with mental afflictions from serving in World War II. Two of the film's main cases in particular point to PTSD: Colonel Bliss (Eddie Albert), whose guilt over sending men to their deaths drives him to adopt a schizoid personality and eventually to take his own life; Jim Thompkins (Bobby Darin), whose experiences as an airborne gunner have shattered his nerves. Michael Cimino's *The Deer Hunter* (1978) follows the postwar lives of three blue-collar Pennsylvania men who suffered physical and psychological torture, particularly their being forced to play a sadistic game of Russian roulette for the amusement of their Viet Cong captors. Most devastated of the three remains Nick Chevotarevich (Christopher

Walken), who exists in a nearly comatose mental state after surviving the sadistic game. His long-time friend Mike Vronsky (Robert De Niro) tries to bring Nick home from blandly continuing to play Russian roulette in Saigon for money, but fails when Nick loses his final game; still, the film concludes with Nick's funeral, so that no matter the trauma, a soldier makes it back home. Hal Ashby's *Coming Home* (1978) and Oliver Stone's *Born on the Fourth of July* (1989) both skirt around fairly obvious PTSD issues afflicting, respectively, paraplegic Luke Martin (Jon Voight), as a Ron Kovic–like disgruntled returning Vietnam veteran, and Ron Kovic (Tom Cruise). Instead of confronting this disorder in depth, both films politicize mental breakdowns and reward their heroes with, in one, a coming-home romance to Jane Fonda and, in the other, a film-closing, trite preachy biopic celebration of Kovic's oration at the Democratic National Convention in 1976. While generally limited to Vietnam and now Middle East war experiences, PTSD occupies contemporary Holocaust survivor films like *Sophie's Choice* (1982) and, more recently, *Sarah's Key* (2010). PTSD also afflicts survivors of airplane crashes, as in *Fearless* (1993), which returns PTSD to its original meaning for symptoms following horrific train accidents, a condition known as "railroad spine," coined by John Erichson in his 1867 work *On Railway Spine and Other Injuries of the Nervous System* (see Young).

Substance abuse and addictive personality disorder have a long history in film, with memorable scenes of the pain of addiction. The propaganda film *Reefer Madness* (1936) really begins the lengthy cycle of substance abuse films, which often lend themselves to moralizing about potential physical dangers and often overt sexual perversions associated with addiction. In *Reefer Madness*, marijuana abuse leads to numerous social and psychological problems, such as DUI accidents, sexual assault, and murder, all stemming from increasing symptoms of cannabis poisoning and hallucinations. Hallucinatory effects from abuse frame cinema narratives concerning dipsomania, chemical dependence, and withdrawal. Often, these films cast crucial scenes of terrifying hallucinations, personality distortions, and physical suffering by employing animation, intensified lighting, and other worldly soundscapes. In *The Lost Weekend* (1945), Ray Milland hallucinates a bat grotesquely eating a mouse on his apartment wall. Frank Sinatra goes through grueling cold turkey withdrawal from morphine in *The Man with the Golden Arm* (1955). James Mason experiences medicinal megalomania from cortisone abuse in *Bigger than Life* (1956). Twice straitjacketed Jack Lemmon suffers delirium tremens in *Days of Wine and Roses* (1962) before reaching sobriety. In *Valley of the Dolls* (1967), Patty Duke incessantly binges on Seconal and alcohol, a psychologically lethal combination that produces self-aggrandizement, debilitating social malfunctions, and, eventually, near psychotic breakdown. The downward spiral of heroin addiction by small-time hustler Al Pacino and his prostitute girlfriend Kitty Winn form the urban narrative of dismal junkie existence in *The Panic in Needle Park* (1971). Matt Dillon cannot escape the pervasive culture of drugs and its leeching lowlifes in *Drugstore Cowboy* (1989). In *Flight* (2012), Denzel Washington plays an alcohol- and cocaine-ridden commercial airline pilot whose lack of control leads to a stewardess's death and eventually his own imprisonment. In *The Wolf of Wall Street* (2013), Leonardo di Caprio's twisted world of overconsumption of drugs and money stands as an allegory for a demented, American dream. In the novel, Jordan, after putting six drops of Visine in each eye, comically reflects upon the absurdity of his drug habit:

> In that very instant, an odd thought came bubbling up into my brain, namely: What kind of man abuses Visine? And, for that matter why had I taken six Bayer aspirin? It made no sense. After all, unlike Ludes, coke, and Xanax, where the benefits of increasing the dose are plain as day, there was absolutely no valid reason to exceed the recommended doses of Visine and aspirin. Yet, ironically, that was exactly what my very life had come to represent. It was all about excess: about crossing over forbidden lines, about doing things you thought you'd never do and associating with people who were even wilder than yourself, so you'd feel that much more normal about your own life. (Belfort 33)

Clearly, the film reveals excess of speed, danger, and ludicrous drug taking at every turn, even turning the suburban kitchen into a repulsive den of iniquity. This pattern of accelerating abuse characterizes the demented devolution of addicts in these films. So numerous are these addiction films that they constitute their own genre, having similar plots of the descent into drug or alcohol dependency, resultant debilitating errors and miscalculations caused by intoxication, usually concluding either in a painful recovery or an unnecessary death, usually by suicide.

Suicide in cinema also has a long film history, with the American Film Institute listing "over 1,600 films that deal with suicide" and among the mental disorders that psychiatrists categorize associated with suicidality, major depression and bipolar disorder with a risk of suicide are "15.1 times that of the general population," and substance abuse is involved in anywhere from "19 to 63% of the suicides," depending upon the clinical study (Stack and Bowman 13, 34, 37). In cinema's history, suicide is accounted for by a number of reasons, but it often stems from implicit psychological disorders, such as openly facing one's death in a heroic act during war, often to mitigate previous cowardice. For example, Kirk Douglas flies a stolen reconnaissance plane in a suicide mission to report Japanese fleet positions as a way to assuage his rape of Navy nurse Jill Haworth and her subsequent suicide in *In Harm's Way* (1965). In *The Slender Thread* (1965), Sidney Poitier plays a volunteer for a new suicide prevention hotline in Seattle, who helps rescue Anne Bancroft from the lethal dose of pills she has just consumed. This tense procedural drama has the telephone company's tracing techniques heighten the suspense as Poitier keeps Bancroft on the line for the entire film. As with so many mental disorder films, flashbacks fill in the chronology of events that led to the victim taking her own life. In Robert Redford's *Ordinary People* (1980), guilt-ridden over his brother's death, Conrad (Timothy Hutton) attempts suicide, but eventually works through therapeutic recovery as he observes the dissolution of his parents' (Mary Tyler Moore and Donald Sutherland) marriage. Teenage suicide, a national problem in the media, becomes the resolution for angst and alienation in Peter Weir's *Dead Poets Society* (1989). Combining addiction and suicide, Mike Figgis's *Leaving Las Vegas* (1995) provides a dark portrait of Hollywood and contemporary America, with Nicolas Cage as a fired screenwriter ending his life through excessive alcohol abuse. The epidemic of young women committing suicide becomes the social problem at the center of several successful films, among them *Girl, Interrupted* (1999), *The Virgin Suicides* (1999), and *Black Swan* (2010).

In the 1980s, the media served its own Jekyll and Hyde function for an ambiguous public, by simultaneously promoting a body type from the rail-thin sixties through the heroin-chic 1980s for models and denouncing, mostly through daytime television, the sometimes excessive body-image culture in America. Public awareness of eating disorders, particularly the supposed pandemic occurrence of anorexia and bulimia among young women, led filmmakers to tackle this latest psychosocial problem, particularly on television: Jennifer Jason Leigh has both syndromes in Aaron Spelling's *The Best Little Girl in the World* (1981); Meredith Baxter Birney binges and purges in *Kate's Secret* (1986); and Tracey Gold's own experience with anorexia adds to the reality of *For the Love of Nancy* (1994). Most famous of celebrities to suffer from this mental malady was Karen Carpenter, whose disorder Todd Haynes parodied in the now cult classic *Superstar—The Karen Carpenter Story* (1987), in which Haynes disturbingly employed Barbie and Ken dolls instead of actors and a soundtrack of songs by the Carpenters. Almost assuredly, cult and independent films spring up as mockeries of the media concentration on particular psychopathological conditions.

Bipolar disorder and obsessive-compulsive disorder, also coming to public recognition through talk shows and media service announcements, become the subject of contemporary family melodramas. In Scott Hick's biopic *Shine* (1996), Geoffrey Rush portrays the manic life of pianist David Helfgott, whose story focuses primarily upon his father's intolerance and abuse of the young musician, even as David wins major competitions. As a consequence, David develops extreme manic behavior that eventuates in his receiving shock therapy: after years of hospitalization, as in so many disability films, David recovers sufficiently to find love and to return successfully to professional performances. In David O. Russell's *Silver Linings Playbook* (2012), after leaving the hospital, a still manic, bipolar Pat (Bradley Cooper) returns to his parents' home, where his equally manic, sports-betting father (Robert De Niro) compulsively and superstitiously looks to Pat as a kind of charm to help the Philadelphia Eagles continue to win. Pat's obsession with his ex-wife serves as an allegory for America's disturbing, delusional mania for sports and gambling. As with so many mental disability films, Pat finds love with a kindred spirit, Tiffany (Jennifer Lawrence), who introduces him to another kind of sport, professional dancing. In the end, manic states decline as love triumphs.

Obsessive-compulsive disorder films equally rely upon the family as the way to resolve behavior by degrees. In *What about Bob?* (1991), obsessively phobic, yet almost childlike Bob Wiley (Bill Murray) relentlessly plagues egotistical pop psychiatrist Dr. Leo Marvin (Richard Dreyfuss) by following his best-seller's protocol "baby steps," all the while insinuating himself into the doctor's family and consequently ruining his vacation, threatening his career, and alienating his ties to family. Here, mental illness proves to be comedic gold: the more outrageously phobic Bob reveals himself to be (unable to exit his apartment, afraid of water and sailing), the more empathetic the shrink's family feels toward him. They soon draw away from the good doctor, as he has newly developed compulsions about ridding himself of Bob. OCD comedies follow an aesthetic of repetition in order to reveal, often in a slapstick fashion, the physical barriers to avoid and behavior rituals that recur. Of course, what helps the comedy along remains not one specific, identifiable disorder, but a closet full of fears, anxieties, tics, and avoidance rituals. In *As Good As It Gets* (1997), successful author Melvin Udall (Jack Nicholson) finds his obsessive daily routine abruptly interrupted as his familiar, yet hardly sympathetic, waitress Carol Connelly (Helen Hunt) must deal with a seemingly incurable disease plaguing her son. This romantic comedy recasts mental illness as a kind of male personality problem and social disease that can be overcome only when Udall comes to understand the humanity in those around him, a homosexual artist neighbor and an independent woman—except that Carol does rely upon Udall's money and his physician to cure her son. *As Good As It Gets* follows a now classic misandric formula of contemporary cinema, but carried to a psychoanalytical, social imperative: the heterosexual male is the disorder, his view of the world is tainted by his mental obsession with being a heterosexual male, and his cure can occur only when he recognizes this social and mental illness and submits to the healing power of the feminine. Even in the end, Nicholson's character still avoids the superstitious cracks in the sidewalk, signs of his persistent inadequacy, and he can progress, physically and spiritually, only if he is led by Carol. As Paul Nathanson and Katherine K. Young reveal in *Spreading Misandry*, this formula pervades popular cultures, especially in film narratives: "In short, the only good man is either a corpse or a woman. After annihilating, or 'deconstructing,' everything distinctive to men, whether physical or otherwise, what is left? Only whatever affirms women and honorary women. There is no room in this universe for *men per se*" (8). In *Matchstick Men* (2003), Nicolas Cage's con man character shares similar inadequacies with Nicholson's character, with the exception that Cage opens himself up to the possibility of his supposed daughter's love, no longer hiding in his private obsessive world, only to be fooled by the con girl and humiliated in the end. Elaine Davis sees the connection between these two OCD films in terms of character traits, not so much pathology:

> Occasionally, OCD has taken center stage in the entertainment industry's products. Unfortunately, many of the characters are portrayed as "unlikable." Jack Nicholson won an Academy Award for his over-the-top portrayal of an author with OCD in *As Good As It Gets*. Despite guidance by an OCD advocacy group, this depiction had little basis in reality. His symptoms became the reason that he was socially inept rather than the underlying fact that the character himself was not a particularly nice guy. The con man portrayed by Nicholas Cage in

> *Matchstick Men* did have more redeeming qualities despite his chosen life style. This movie also did a better job of showing the compulsive behavior as occurring behind closed doors. Only those closest to him were aware of these activities but, even then, exhibited little compassion or understanding of the underlying pathology. While ultimately portrayed as a victim, at least the film did not base the victimization on the mental illness. (Davis 167)

While Davis points out the difference in the depiction of mental illness, maleness, particularly bachelor, heterosexual maleness, seems to be the primary affliction in both films. The most curious thing about OCD films remains the public acceptance of the pathology as comic and satiric, so long as the butt of the joke, like so many dads, bosses, and boyfriends in television sitcoms, is masculine. Gendering psychopathology does not simply rely upon the conventions of romance, but rather takes the narrative strategies of 1930s screwball comedies and replaces the eccentric female with the afflicted male.

Films about depression, particular atypical depression, abound in Hollywood. *Prozac Nation* (2001) chronicles the familial alienation, substance abuse, and eventual recovery of Lizzie Wrutzel (Christina Ricci) as she negotiates loss of virginity, writer's block, and therapy in her first years at Harvard. Steven Soderbergh's *The Informant!* (2009) follows the severely depressive moments and manic ups-and-downs of FBI whistleblower Mark Whitacre (Matt Damon), who initially claims evidence of price-fixing at his biotech company, but who turns out to have been embezzling funds for a considerable time, and that, along with radical behavior shifts, lands Whitacre in prison. Samuel Byck (Bicke in the film), a maniac-depressive on lithium carbonate, failed to hijack an airplane, which he hoped to fly into the White House and assassinate Richard Nixon in *The Assassination of Richard Nixon* (2004). The camera follows Bicke (Sean Penn) through several manic episodes, his failed marriage, his dismal salesmanship, and even his trying to join the Black Panther Party. Cinema tends to treat many extreme psychopathological conditions not as single syndromes, but usually and for dramatic effect as comorbidity, as with the example of manic depression, for which even clinicians have difficulty limiting characteristics: "The boundary between unipolar depression and bipolar disorder also remains unclear, as clinical presentations such as agitated depression and mixed mood states defy attempts at neat categorization" (Youngstrom and Van Meter 269). For film, such blurred distinctions allow for greater expansion in the range of performances of mania. Indeed, methodological studies, while inconclusive in pandemic analysis, still point to an association of violence with severe mental disorders: "In other words, aggression may not be specific to personality pathology per se, but may be characteristic of psychopathology in general" (Blonigen and Krueger 290). In the final days of his delirium, Bicke undergoes several mood episodes from excessive mania to hypomanic collapse. An extended montage depicts his frenetic messages to conductor Leonard Bernstein (whom he much admires), seemingly triggered by Nixon's appearance on television, especially Nixon's economic and business analogies in his speeches; as well as his construction of a miniature White House and a plane flying into it. At the Baltimore airport while waiting to board a plane, Bicke undergoes an episode, which the film captures as delusions, fainting, disorientation, and auditory displacement. Cinematic aesthetic conveys an interpretation of Bicke's beleaguered and demented consciousness. Finally, Bicke rampages onto the aircraft, makes insane demands of the pilots, eventually shooting both, before he holds a female passenger hostage. An officer shoots Bicke through the entry door window, and he collapses, murmuring before killing himself.

Unlike American culture's despicable history of neglect for and prejudice toward those who have been called "mentally retarded" (the current *DSM* term is "persons with intellectual disabilites") cinema has in general shown them in a humane light. Tod Browning's *Freaks* (1932) treats the microcephalic siblings Zip (Jenny Lee Snow) and Pip (Elivra Snow) with compassion by allowing their sweetness and bashful natures to appeal to audiences. Fortunately for cinema, long gone are the days of corrupt institutions like Willowbrook with its inhumane conditions and cruel abuses, the eugenic policies of sterilization, criminalization, and then forced custodial asylums for the mentally disabled. To be fair, films about mentally challenged individuals, even when exaggerating the characters' normalcy and eschewing major difficulties facing most intellectually disabled people, have also shared considerable box-office appeal. In *To Kill a Mockingbird* (1962), shy, yet heroic Arthur "Boo" Radley (Robert Duvall) saves Atticus Finch's children from a drunken, homicidal bigot, Bob Ewell (James Anderson). *Charly* (1968) garnered Cliff Robertson the Best Actor Oscar for his performance as a mentally retarded man who undergoes a surgical operation to advance his IQ, only to return after a brief spell of superior intelligence and violence to his childlike, kind state of wonder. In the biopic of *Radio* (2003), Cuba Gooding, Jr., plays a mentally challenged young black man who becomes the source of inspiration for a high school football team, because of the kindness of their football coach (Ed Harris) who practically adopts Radio, despite familial and social intolerance. Types of retardation in cinema that have also proven to be box office gold include the Sean Penn vehicle *I Am Sam* (2001), which quadrupled its studio outlay and garnered Penn an Oscar nomination, and *Forrest Gump* (1994), earning six times its budget and sweeping the Academy Awards. These sensitive portrayals of the mentally disabled recur with some frequency in contemporary cinema, usually following a similar narrative structure wherein the disabled protagonist faces social obstacles, often from despicable, insensitive individuals who berate them with "retard" and other abhorrent terms, only to overcome them in the end, either through self-motivated perseverance or with the assistance of a compassionate surrogate parental figure, or both. Perhaps the elimination of "retard" from socially accepted speech, like that of "nigger," might be a justifiable outcome for these unrealistic, yet humanely oriented films.

According to the first published edition of the *Diagnostic and Statistical Manual of Mental Disorders*, the American Psychiatric Association classified homosexuality as a "sociopathic personality disturbance" and a decade and a half later, in the *DSM-II* of 1968, homosexuality had been rediagnosed as "sexual deviation," still under the category of a mental disorder (Drescher 569). Its misclassification and reclassification are relevant to cinema history. Of course, such maligning designation for sexual conduct remains a throwback to the fin-de-siècle, particularly the criminal trial of Oscar Wilde and his sentencing to hard labor in films: *The Trials of Oscar Wilde* (1960), starring Peter Finch, with mixed receptions about Finch's subtle portrayal, but critics denigrating Wilde's character; *Oscar Wilde* (1960), with Robert Morley in a less than sympathetic role; and *Wilde* (1997), with Stephen Fry in a very intelligent, witty, and ultimately tragic performance. These films also register legal decisions about gay rights as addressed in US Supreme Court decisions, among them, *One, Inc. v. Olesen* (1958), which reversed both lower and appellate rulings that the gay magazine *One* was obscenity. However, in *Bowers v. Hardwick* (1986), the 5–4 decision ruled against any constitutional guarantee of the right to privacy for homosexual activity, since that right belongs to married couples; that ruling was later overturned by the court in *Lawrence v. Texas* (2003).

Ridding the *DSM* of homosexuality as a mental-disorder category from the sixth printing of the *DSM-II* in 1974 did not completely remove it from psychiatric scrutiny. Instead, homosexuality became a "sexual orientation disorder" (SOD), a term replaced in the 1980 *DSM-III* with "ego-dystonic homosexuality," a term that lost favor among the psychiatric profession and was removed entirely from the 1987 *DSM-IIIR* (Drescher 571). The shifts in psychiatric diagnoses came about due to a number of events in popular culture, among them the Stonewall riots of 1969, disruptions at annual psychiatric meetings, and portrayals in cinema. John Schlesinger's *Midnight Cowboy* (1969) had depictions of homosexual prostitution by a sympathetic Joe Buck (Jon Voight) and was the only X-rated film to win the Best Picture Oscar. His *Sunday, Bloody Sunday* (1971) focused upon Dr. Daniel Hirsh (Peter Finch), an upscale, mentally normal physician with a bisexual younger lover, whom he unknowingly shares with Alex Greville (Glenda Jackson). Mart Crowley's *The Boys in the Band* shocked audiences in its 1968 off-Broadway seriocomic portrayal of catty, outlandish, and campy gay men at a birthday party. In 1970, William Friedkin directed a film adaptation of Crowley's play that included members of the original cast, and its reception, while somewhat cautious, found favorable reviews for the most part. While both the play and especially the film allowed for some normalizing of homosexuality, Michael, the central character, exhibits complex personality problems, including alcoholism, narcissism, and antisocial behavior, that point to a self-destructive lifestyle. In 1971, Wakefield Poole's sexual, explicit *Boys in the Sand*, an obvious pun on Crowley's title, became the first gay pornographic film to include credits, to receive advanced publicity in the *New York Times* and *Variety*, and to earn commercial success. Under "Picture Grossers," *Variety* in 1972 included "Boys in Sand" in a headline of successful New York runs that also listed "Fiddler" (*Fiddler On the Roof*), "Harry" (*Dirty Harry*), "Orange" (*Clockwork Orange*), and "Garden" (*The Garden of the Finzi-Continis*), settling the indie porno firmly within acceptable cinema (9). Clearly, the social acceptance that had begun to replace much of the mental disease taint that had plagued the gay community was attributable in large part to empathetic portrayals in film.

Cinema has also had a penchant for sexual offense as a way to identify despicable characters, while still allowing for a form of sexual exploitation. A curious psychopathology finds its way into cinema, a kind of visual deviancy that compels as it repels viewers. Films about rape remain numerous in cinema's history, generally with the psychopathology of the rapist and the crime's effects upon the victim as central to the narrative. Cecil B. DeMille's *The Cheat* (1915) has several lurid moments of seduction, adulterous behavior, sadistic flesh branding, and, ultimately, attempted rape. At times, victims become unsteady, even sadistic aggressors, as in rape-revenge films: *Lipstick* (1976), *Extremities* (1986), *Eye for an Eye* (1996), the various *I Spit on Your Grave* films, *Irréversible* (2002), and, most recently, *Elle* (2016). So pervasive is this reversal of victim-avenger formula in cinema that *Monster* (2003) erroneously portrayed Aileen Wuornos's first killing of a viciously brutal john as an act of self-defense, even though Wuornos herself confessed in prison that there never was any self-defense.

The sexual child abuse film also fits into this larger genre of sexual assault and occasional retaliation cinema. Fritz Lang's disturbing look into the action of a child murderer (Peter Lorre) in *M* (1931) ends with societal retribution against this monster. Stanley Kubrick's *Lolita* (1962), like Nabokov's novel, deflects the monstrosity of pedophilia onto social satire on American sexuality. Kubrick's film is a very rare portrayal of this type of crime and criminal, with Dolores being as invested in Humbert at times as he is in her. Otto Preminger's tale of a missing child, an ignored mother (Ann Lake), and an incestuous brother/uncle (Keir Dullea) reveals the British sense of arrested childish madness as the etiology of this crime in *Bunny Lake Is Missing* (1965). The incest/child rape serves as the hard-boiled detective's epiphany in the accused pederast Roman Polanski's *Chinatown* (1974). Louis Malle's scandalous *Pretty Baby* (1978) reveals the exploitation of a twelve-year-old prostitute (Brook Shields) in a fin-de-siècle New Orleans brothel. A teenaged girl (Reese Witherspoon) runs off to find her real father only to hitch a ride with the I-5 killer of young girls (Kiefer Sutherland) in *Freeway* (1996). Barry Levinson's *Sleepers* (1996) recounts the sadistic sexual rape of young boys at a 1960s New York juvenile correction facility, with two of the four boys (Billy Crudup and Ron Eldard) becoming part of the Irish outlaw gang, the Westies, who accidentally discover their main abuser (Kevin Bacon) in a Hell's Kitchen diner and kill him. Wrongful accusations of child abduction, child abuse, and murder form the basis of Clint Eastwood's very dark *Mystic River* (2003), which culminates in the execution-style killing of the wrong man. In *Hard Candy* (2005), a vigilante fourteen-year old (Ellen Page) takes revenge on a predatory participant (Patrick Wilson) in a local young girl's violation, offering either death or castration as the only possible escape. Most recently, *Spotlight* (2015) chronicled the *Boston Globe*'s investigation in scores of Catholic priests' repeated pedophilic crimes. *Mystic River* received Oscars for Best Actor (Sean Penn) and Best Supporting Actor (Tim Robbins); Jerry Wexler's music was nominated for an Oscar for *Pretty Baby* and the film won a Grant Technical Prize at Cannes; Ellen Page was a nominee for numerous independent film awards for *Hard Candy*; and Tom McCarthy's *Spotlight* won Best Picture. In terms of earnings, *Mystic River* won back over five times its outlay, and *Spotlight* received more than four and one-half times its production costs. Clearly, film producers understand the box-office value of exhibiting films about the most loathsome of criminal and psychologically twisted behavior. The psychopathology of obsession, if not a prurient attraction, then, extends beyond the perpetrators to film studios and audiences.

Two significant films concerning child sexual predators span the 1960s to the present day, garnering similar accolades from film award-giving bodies; they are Guy Green's *The Mark* (1961), for which Stuart Whitman received an Academy Award nomination for Best Actor; and Nicole Kassell's vehicle for Kevin Bacon as a newly released child molester in *The Woodsman* (2004). In general, pedophile films follow narrative patterns similar to crime films, whereby the audience has the opportunity to experience with some fascination a rigidly taboo topic and also to experience relief that the perpetrator does not offend again or is severely punished. Even though a growing body of evidence supports the claim that women are as likely as men to commit acts of child sexual abuse, as Julia C. Davidson demonstrates, these films maintain the antiquated societal misperception of this crime being perpetrated only by dirty old men (60). Citing a study by Warren and Hislop, Davidson lists six categories for female sexual abusers: facilitators (aiding men's access to children), reluctant partners (going along with abuse out of fear of abandonment), initiating partner (the sole or accompanying abuser), seducer/lover (particularly toward adolescent males), pedophiles (same distinction as a male), and psychotics (severe mental illness that causes the crime). Jacqui Saradjian corroborates data on the numbers of female child molesters in her study in order to understand "the prevalence of female-perpetrated sexual abuse and the impact of that abuse on victims." Significantly, as taboo as child sex abuse remains, for cinema an even greater taboo exists for having a female lead as the sexual psychopath.

Karen A. Duncan, in *Female Sexual Predators*, examines another misleading stereotype that women do not commit institutional sexual abuse at a rate similar to men. Duncan reports alarming statistics from numerous countries—among them, the United States, Great Britain, Canada, Australia, and South Africa. In South Africa, a 2008 study to protect boys from rape found that nearly fourteen thousand school-aged boys experienced forced sex and that "42 percent of the sexual offenders were female and that 32 percent were male, while 27 percent of the boys identified that both male and female perpetrators had sexually offended against them" (Duncan 3). A 2007 study of Vancouver, British Columbia, street youth discovered that 79 percent of the sexual exploiters of boys were females; in Australia, Child Wise, an organization for youths with female caretakers, showed in 2006 that sexual abuse of both genders occurred by female workers; and United States Department of Justice in 2008 reported that in juvenile facilities forty-six percent of substantiated sexual abuse came from females (Duncan 3–5). These school and facility female sexual crimes recast the stereotype of such films as *Summer of '42* (1971) and *Tea and Sympathy* (1956), while *To Die For* (1995) reveals the female sexual abuser in a satiric, darkly comic light. In Richard Eyre's complex study of fixation and misconduct in *Notes on a Scandal* (2006), a teacher (Cate Blanchett) has sex with a fifteen-year old student, all the while under the voyeuristic, lesbian gaze of her colleague (Judi Dench). For this very rare account of female pedophilic behavior, both Judi Dench (Best Actress) and Cate Blanchett (Best Supporting Actress) got Oscar nominations. Of course, made-for-TV movies have recently taken up the predatory female sexual abuser for increased network ratings: such as, *Murder in New Hampshire: The Pamela Wojas Smart Story* (1991) and *The All-American Girl: The Mary Kay Letourneau Story* (2000). Mass media coverage of female teachers' sexual aggression and exploitations often take on a prurient, libidinous approach, which only adds more to the stereotypes. While the media immediately label male teachers who sexually abuse teenaged girls as predators, the female teacher who sexually abuses is often considered lonely, vulnerable, somewhat confused, or in a loveless marriage. The sentencing for this double-standard bears out in harsher and lengthier prison terms for males as opposed to females. Even with the rising firestorms of female predatory teacher coverage, films have yet to be made of Debra Lafave (victim, fourteen years old), who received three years of house arrest, Abbie Jane Swogger (victims' range, fourteen to seventeen years old), who pled guilty to eleven of thirty-nine charges and received a three-to-six year sentence, Melinda Deluca (victim, sixteen years old), who faked an assault on herself for sympathy that worked and received only a ninety day sentence, or Pamela Rogers Turner (victim, thirteen years old), who received a nine-month sentence, but after sending naked photos to her victim received a total of nine years behind bars.

Equally silent, mainstream media and especially feminism almost ignore the harsh reality of lesbian domestic and partnership violence. Researcher Claire Renzetti distributed a lengthy questionnaire about abusive relationships to one hundred lesbians and discovered that physical, sexual, and psychological abuse occurred at the same rate or more in comparison with heterosexual relationships. In fact, as Janice L. Ristock reports these findings, the rate of combined psychological and physical abuse affected 87 percent of the lesbian respondents, which included threats, humiliation, being restrained, and, even more violent, although rarer, acts of stabbing, shooting, and vaginal insertion of weapons occurring (9). Ristock confirms other researchers' rates of violence among lesbian couples to be staggering: Valerie Coleman's 46 percent, Gwat-Yong Lee and Sabrina Gentlewarrior's 52 percent from a survey at the Michigan Womyn's Festival, and Waldner-Haugrud, Vaden Gratch, and Magruder's 47.5 percent of lesbians having been victims of relationship violence (10–11). Several studies extend sexual and physical aggression to over 50 percent for lesbian domestic relationships (Nathanson and Young, *Legalizing* 244). These alarming rates reveal lesbian relationship violence at a rate nearly one and one-half times more prevalent than for heterosexual couples, according to the Center for Disease Control (Glass). Yet, feminists and Hollywood have yet to attend to this epidemic and its root psychosociological problems, instead opting to ignore it or blame it on misogyny and the "patriarchy," two ponderously absurd causes for *lesbian* violence. Still, from the 1980s onward, the film and television industry has produced well over one hundred and seventy films about domestic abuse, all of which have female victims and male perpetrators. A National Intimate Partner and Sexual Violence survey, according to the Center for Disease Control, indicates that 35 percent of heterosexual women and 29 percent of heterosexual men "experience rape, physical violence" from an intimate partner (*Preventing Intimate Partner Violence*). Those percentages are far too close to be ignored. Still, social politics and constructed narratives outweigh the needs of real victims in the news media and Hollywood, as evidenced by the lack of representation of female sexual predators and female domestic abusers.

Child molestation law changed in progressive stages of additional definitions from the late 1920s to the late 1950s. Initially, enactment of new laws aimed to curtail a new legal offense, carnal abuse of a child, meaning a female child. This new offense defined both abuse to the body or immoral practices with sexual organs of the female child. Age limitation initially targeted the crime perpetrated on girls ten years old and younger. Lawmakers and the courts continued to refine this offense by practices—object or genital—and by age of the victim. By the 1930s, such legal definitions began to include male children. In his admirable history of this and other offenses, Stephen Robertson reveals the swift lawmaking nation-wide against these immoral acts, especially during the midcentury "sex crime panic":

> In drawing on understandings of psychosexual development to craft a genderblind law targeted at men who committed genital acts other than intercourse, New York was at the forefront of a nationwide wave of legislative action to expand definitions of sexual violence against children. Nevada, North Dakota, and Minnesota had enacted similar laws in the late 1920s, and Vermont followed suit in 1937; another twenty-one states passed laws of a comparable nature between 1948 and 1958, in the midst of the sex crime panic. Seven states joined New York in using the term "indecent and immoral practices"; seven others persisted with the "lewd and lascivious" language that was popular early in the century; and another seven combined the two definitions. A new, even more explicit vocabulary of fondling and touching distinguished the laws of the remaining four states. . . . By the late 1950s, the blunted impact of new ideas of psychosexual development was reflected in a new label applied to sex crimes against children: "child molestation." (Robertson 162–63)

The Mark offers insight into postwar psychotherapeutic treatment for pedophilia. Jim Fuller (Stuart Whitman), a newly paroled child sexual offender, works with his appointed psychiatrist Dr. McNally (Rod Steiger) to uncover the roots of his pathology. While Fuller did abduct a young girl, he did not molest her, but instead returned her unharmed. Unlike most pedophile films in which the sexual psychopath has molested, *The Mark* begins with a man who has had urges, but not fully acted on them. In doing so, then, *The Mark* makes Fuller a sympathetic character, a rarity for pedophile films. Still, the stigma of the label follows Fuller as he tries to reenter society, eventually leading to his being fired from his white-collar job. *The Mark* allows for the audience to witness the urges and Fuller's conscious repression of them, most notably as he stands and watches schoolgirls playing in a schoolyard near his apartment. His relationship with his psychologist remains cooperative throughout the film, although Fuller's frustrations do emerge as he faces social stigma. Fuller even has a girlfriend, Ruth Leighton (Maria Schell), in whom he confides his problem, but who, even though representing a forgiving society, cannot so easily dismiss this tabooed desire. When her young daughter rushes to

Figure 1.1. Jim (Stuart Whitman) trying to resist temptation at a schoolyard in *The Mark*.

embrace Fuller as a gesture of good-bye, Ruth screams for her to stop, thereby letting Fuller know her (and society's) true feelings. Of particular interest remains the film's message that a kind of cure potentially exists for these offenders.

The Woodsman, like *The Mark*, deals with a newly paroled pedophile, Walter (Kevin Bacon), who has a job, meets social resistance, and even has a coworker girlfriend (Kyra Sedgwick), who admits to Walter her own abuse as a child. Unlike *The Mark*, this narrative provides the pedophile with several supporters and enemies. Knowing Walter to be a very fine carpenter, Walter's employer (David Allan Grier) protects him from his fellow workers. Office secretary Eve (Mary Kay) whose overt advances Walter has ignored, delves into his past and discovers his dark secret, which she promptly distributes to the company. Even though Walter's sister refuses to see him, his brother-in-law (Benjamin Bratt) checks in on Walter, updates him about his sister and his nephew. Sergeant Lucas (Mos Def) hounds Walter in an almost stereotypical cop-to-ex-con manner.

Pauline Greenhill and Steven Kohm situate *The Woodsman* within the narrative patterns of many pedophile films, which rely to some extent on variations of *Little Red Ridinghood*. Walter observes a young girl, Robin (Hannah Pilkes), bird-watching in a park and begins a process of grooming her for molestation, taking on a dual role in the process: "We locate this same doubling and overlapping of figures as an essential element of 'Little Red Riding Hood'/pedophile films, and *The Woodsman* exemplifies this strategy. The viewers' familiarity with fairy-tale characters helps to complicate their potential knee-jerk reactions to Walter as pedophile. His most obvious parallels are with the eponymous woodsman and wolf" (Greenhill and Kohm 48). At the moment that Walter could molest Robin, she tells him that her father has been violating her. Walter recoils in horror and self-recognition, and then tells Robin to "go home." Morally ambiguous as this moment remains, *The Woodsman* proposes to give awareness about the real danger of pedophilia, not the woods (the outside world), with lurking wolves (monstrous predators), but the home and family.

In a form of self-empowerment and self-hatred simultaneously, Walter severely beats "Candy" (Kevin Rice), a pedophile Walter has recognized for his grooming of young schoolboys. When Sergeant Lucas finds out about the assault, he refuses to charge Walter, but admonishes him: "There ain't no fucking woodsman in this world." Yet, the only woodsman may well be Walter himself, who must protect young girls from himself. *The Mark* and, even more so, *The Woodsman* end without closure, since pedophilia has no sudden cure, as is the case with most profound mental disorders. Clearly, cinema has its own obsession with aberrant behavior as a spectacle and a diagnosis of societal ills. Cinema plays therapist to numerous forms of mental illness and sympathetic observer of mental incapacitation. The history of psychopathology in cinema, then, not only appeals to public interest, but also to the corporate bottom line.

Figure 1.2. Walter (Kevin Bacon) tempted by Robin (Hannah Pilkes) in *The Woodsman*.

Psychopathological Cinema Studies

Considerable ink has been spilt over the past few decades on psychoanalytical, psychofeminist theoretical approaches to film. These works have provided both pathways for and controversies about psychoanalytical approaches to cinema, often relying upon reinterpretations of Freud, extensions, sometimes jargon-filled repetitions, of Lacan, reconceptualizations and appropriations of Deleuze's employment of Bergsonian taxonomy, and Zizek's frequent admixtures of Hegel and Lacan. Of course, extensive feminist theories have had impact upon film studies, often employing and then repurposing psychoanalytical theorists whose methods Laura Mulvey, Mary Ann Doane, E. Ann Kaplan, and Joan Copjec have sustained and critiqued. This collection, however, does not add to that already significant volume of monographs and anthologies orientated along those theoretical lines. Instead, it offers readings of films within the history of the representation of psychopathology onscreen. It explores, through specific film examples, the history, narrative structures, cultural expressions, popular and often erroneous assumptions, and aesthetics of representations of mental disorders and the mentally challenged in cinema. As such, this collection concerns itself not with the critical diagnosis of symptoms of psychopathology in film and not with an overarching theory about psychopathology; instead, the contributors are concerned with psychological manifestations as expressed in film narrative and cinematic techniques. This collection of new essays offers close analyses of single and multiple films that elucidate how pervasive narratives and imagery of psychopathology have been in the history of cinema. In short, this collection wishes to open up the discussion to expand the approaches to psychopathology onscreen, but not by imposing an overarching theory on this complex history.

These chapters investigate how cinema displays and even mirrors psychological disorders. The range of psychopathological conditions in the introduction and in these essays includes manic depression, amnesia, psychotic delusions, obsessive compulsive behavior, schizophrenia, trauma, paranoia, substance addiction, borderline personalities, and mental disabilities. Moreover, these essays explore a range of genres, among them biopics, romantic comedies, film noirs, satires, contemporary dramedies, thrillers, gothic mysteries, and docufictions. This collection, however, does not endeavor to uncover the etiology of mental conditions, but rather the etiology of their representations in film history, aesthetics, and genres. The essays open up critical approaches to reveal audience fascination with film depictions of serious disturbances within the human psyche. These distinct approaches in this collection mirror the history of diagnoses for the varieties of psychopathological conditions. Many films examined in this collection have had little scholarly attention and commentary, especially in terms of how the narrative device of psychopathology determines film construction. The scholars pay particular attention to how cinematic techniques contribute to popular culture's conception of mental dysfunction, trauma, and illness. This book, then, aims to reveal the complex artistic and generic patterns that produce images of psychopathology in cinema.

In the proliferation of scholarly texts devoted to psychology and psychoanalysis in cinema, few works directly address psychological disorders and their filmic representations. In general, psychological issues in film studies fall into distinct categories: 1) psychoanalytical history, theory, and application; 2) general diagnosis of mental disorders that are represented in film; 3) general discussions of psychological symptoms and the public and commercial views of specific illnesses; and 4) cognitive sciences and cinema.

Psychoanalytic criticism has focused upon the convergence and divergence within the history of theoretical psychoanalysis and broader issues of gender, the apparatus, and power. Two insightful and path-breaking works on psychoanalytical theory and film are Janet Bergstrom's *Endless Night: Cinema and Psychoanalysis, Parallel Histories* and E. Ann Kaplan's *Psychoanalysis and Cinema*. These exemplary collections remain standards in the field for the history, application, and critique of psychoanalytical processes in relationship to cinema. Most often, psychoanalytical studies negotiate advantages and distortions produced by applications of specific theoretical approaches to cinema. Steven Jay Schneider's *Horror Film and Psychoanalysis: Freud's Worst Nightmare* defends psychoanalytic criticism as a means to explore the cinematic expressions of voyeuristic pleasure, the uncanny, transference, and violence. Todd McGowan's *The Real Gaze: Film Theory after Lacan* expands upon the concept of the gaze in film studies from ideological, cultural, and existential perspectives. Kristyn Gorton's *Theorizing Desire: From Freud to Feminism to Film* pursues the concept of screen desire and attempts new explications of shame, hysteria, and melancholy. Some notable works of psychoanalytic criticism delve into traditional issues of social construction, feminism, and spectatorship. Constance Penley's *The Future of an Illusion: Film, Feminism, and Psychoanalysis* explores sexual difference by forging feminist and Lacanian theories with cultural constructions as represented in film and television. Vicky Lebeau's *Lost Angels: Psychoanalysis and Cinema* relies upon Freudian categories and

Laura Mulvey's gaze theory for its examination of portrayals of fantasy, narcissism, and social conditions. Still, some works resist such academic theorizing. Harvey Roy Greenberg's *Screen Memories: Hollywood Cinema on the Psychoanalytic Couch* critiques overtly theoretical studies of cinema, mostly based upon Lacan, for being too jargon-filled, too rigid in interpretation, and for a lack of clarity in content and expression that the author attributes to a lack of pleasure and style: "As their joy in cinema has withered, so has their prose" (14). While this current collection acknowledges these psychoanalytical theories and approaches to cinema as having had sway over film studies for considerable time, it aims to move the discussion of mental disorders into new, interdisciplinary fields.

Occasionally, specific mental disorders have been catalogued in psychology books typically focused on the diagnosis of characters within film. In general, these texts discuss many films in brief synopses in order to provide almost encyclopedia entries of disorders. These texts, however, offer some limited analysis of film narrative, technique, and aesthetics. Of course, their purpose is primarily a cinematic registry equivalent of the *Diagnostic and Statistical Manual*. Examples of the disorder indices include Michael Fleming and Roger Manvell's *Images of Madness—The Portrayal of Insanity in the Feature Film*, Glen O. Gabbard's *Psychoanalysis and Film*, Jacqueline Noll Zimmerman's *People like Ourselves—Portrayals of Mental Illness in the Movies*, and Danny Wedding and Ryan M. Niemiec's *Movies and Mental Illness: Using Films to Understand Psychopathology*. These books serve as solid, general reference sources for those who wish to have an initial glimpse into the array of psychological conditions presented in film.

Societal construction of and responses to psychological symptoms and syndromes form the basis for several film studies. Otto Wahl's *Media Madness: Public Images of Mental Illness* analyzes and critiques negative portrayals of mental illness in film and other media. Emily Fox-Kales's *Body Shots: Hollywood and the Culture of Eating Disorders* explores how Hollywood contributes to the development of eating disorders in the general population. John Markert contextualizes social portrayals of addicts in *Hooked in Film: Substance Abuse on the Big Screen*. While these symptomatic examinations have relevance to shaping public opinions of psychological disorders, their social agendas do not correspond to the generic and aesthetic analysis in this collection.

Cognitive and affective studies of films use psychopathology as a means to designate and evaluate responses in viewers. Among the contributors to this burgeoning field are Carl Plantinga and Greg Smith's *Passionate Views: Film, Cognition, and Emotion*, Torben Grodal's *Embodied*

Visions: Evolution, Emotion, Culture, and Film, Carl Plantinga's *Moving Viewers: American Film and the Spectator's Experience*, Arthur Shimamura's *Psychocinematics: Exploring Cognition at the Movies*, and Jeffrey Sacks's *Flicker: Your Brain on Movies*. Taking their cue from earlier spectatorship studies and critiques, these works explore overarching emotional, rhetorical, and cognitive affects, but offer only peripheral discussions of specific mental disorders in film.

Many of the contributors to this collection are already known for their commentary on and examination of psychological issues and theories in relationship to film. Murray Pomerance's study *Hitchcock's Marnie* and his analysis of *Spellbound* in *An Eye for Hitchcock* challenge a number of received critical opinions about psychological conditions and their portrayals. R. Barton Palmer's numerous excellent collections on adaptations of drama and novels to screen, as well as his books on Hitchcock and film noir, often engage with psychological elements, but always with a reference to material history and film techniques. Tarja Laine has analyzed disorders in terms of affective resonance and dynamic emotional responses in *Feeling Cinema: Emotional Dynamics in Film Studies* and *Bodies in Pain: Emotion and the Cinema of Darren Aronofsky*. French cinema scholar Susan Hayward's admirable analysis of Henri-Georges Clouzot's *Les Diaboliques* offered profound insights into the technical, aesthetic, and psychological structure of this dynamic thriller. Julie Grossman's *Rethinking the Femme Fatale in Film Noir: Ready for Her Close-Up* critiques and modifies the tone of feminist psychoanalytical approaches to the femme fatale in order to contextualize and to call attention to filmic elements and social contexts that move women beyond the status of objects. In many ways, these contributors' reconfiguring of the critical discourse of film led in part to the initial idea for this collection.

Many of these filmic examinations will be conducted at the level of film narrative and aesthetics, not the application of theoretical psychoanalytical paradigms or their critiques of film. Specifically, this collection will investigate underexamined, if not neglected, films in order to demonstrate correlations between generic, aesthetic, and psychoresponsive content and the psychopathological disorder represented in the films. To do so, then, the contributing scholars approach these underrated films from a variety of new critical and theoretical perspectives for articulating the prevalent representation of psychopathological conditions onscreen. Overall, the general chronological order of the introduction and chapters indicates the complex unfolding of psychopathology in the history of film. As evident from the table of contents that follows, we embrace new and varied approaches to the representations of mental dysfunction in cinema. We have solicited a variety of textual and interpretive approaches, whether examining single films or several topical films, so that the numerous types of psychic disorders could be addressed. Gender, sexuality, class, and social conventions become fundamental issues for many of the interpretations of these films, as do relevant contexts—technological, narrative, and aesthetic—for determining methods of investigating texts. We find the multiplicity of these scholarly approaches mirrors the complexity and diversity of this subject in popular culture.

Several chapters examine specific psychological manifestations in cinema as serving to define subgenres within genres. In film history, the most common genre associated with mental disorder remains the psychotic serial killer film. While this collection includes films about murderers, it does not take the psychological model or profiler approach so common in contemporary films. Instead, chapters dealing with murderers concentrate upon cinematic techniques for the portrayal of disturbed mental conditions. A key feature throughout this collection remains the cinematic connection between aesthetic and narrative techniques and psychopathological conditions. Several chapters are devoted to specific aesthetic elements that contribute to the expression and affective sense of particular and peculiar psychopathologies, such as neurosis and sound, female repression and costuming, and trauma and landscape cinematography. Other chapters concentrate upon narrative patterns that correspond to the development of or popular conception of mental disorder, such as for *The Three Faces of Eve*, *While the City Sleeps*, and *Young Adult*. Another feature of this collection is the range of psychopathologies discussed, including amnesia, manic depression, compulsive behavior, borderline personalities, mental retardation, and symptomatic trauma. Our intent, then, is to present those *other* psychopathological disorders so often neglected in film studies, but that constitute a significant portion of international, popular film culture. This collection has been conceived to fill a need for contemporary discussions of diverse depictions of mental disorders in film and popular culture. The essays in this collection look at a variety of psychopathologies, disorders, and traumas represented in film not only as phenomena for investigation in themselves, but also as how film portrays them aesthetically and thematically. We endeavor to reveal how cinema represented these conditions, often in less enlightened times. This collection hopes to open up film studies to regard the numerous depictions of mental instability and disease as constituting a field. In short, we hope to break new ground here.

Works Cited

Adamowicz, Elza. *Un Chien Andalou*. I. B. Tauris, 2010.
Belfort, Jordan. *The Wolf of Wall Street*. Bantam, 2007.
Bergstrom, Janet, editor. *Endless Night: Cinema and Psychoanalysis, Parallel Histories*. U of California P, 1990.
Blonigen, Daniel M., and Robert F. Krueger. "Personality and Violence; The Unifying Role of Structural Models of Personality." *The Cambridge Handbook of Violent Behavior and Aggression*, edited by Daniel J. Flannery, Alexander T. Vazsonyi, and Irwin D. Waldman, Cambridge UP, 2007.
Center for Disease Control. *Preventing Intimate Partner Violence across the Lifespan: A Technical Package of Programs, Policies, and Practices*. National Center for Injury Prevention and Control, Center for Disease Control, 2013.
Chivers, Sally. *The Silvering Screen: Old Age and Disability in Cinema*. U of Toronto P, 2011.
Clark, A. F. B. *Mozart and Salieri*. In *The Poems, Prose and Plays of Alexander Pushkin*, edited by Avrahm Yarmolinsky, Modern Library, 1964.
Colaizzi, Janet. *Homicidal Insanity, 1800–1985*. U of Alabama P, 1989.
Davidson, Julia C. *Child Sexual Abuse: Media Representations and Government Reactions*. Routledge-Cavendish, 2008.
Davis, Elaine. "Community Support and Societal Influences." *Clinical Obsessive-Compulsive Disorders in Adults and Children*, edited by Robert Hudak and Darin D. Dougherty, Cambridge UP, 2011, pp. 152–71.
Drescher, Jack. "Out of DSM: Depathologizing Homosexuality." *Behavioral Sciences*, vol. 5, no. 4, 2015, pp. 565–75.
Duncan, Karen A. *Female Sexual Predators: Understanding Them to Protect Our Children and Youths*. Praeger, 2010.
Finkelstein, Haim. *Salvador Dali's Art and Writings, 1927–1942: The Metamorphoses of Narcissus*. Cambridge UP, 1996.
Fleming, Michael, and Roger Manvell. *Images of Madness: The Portrayal of Insanity in the Feature Film*. Associated UP, 1985.
Fox-Kales, Emily. *Body Shots: Hollywood and the Culture of Eating Disorders*. State U of New York P, 2011.
Freedheim, Donald K. editor. *History of Psychology*. *Handbook of Psychology*, editor-in-chief, Irving B. Weiner, vol. 1, Wiley, 2003.
Gabbard, Glen O., editor. *Psychoanalysis and Film*. Routledge, 2001.
Glass, J. D. "2 Studies That Prove Domestic Violence Is an LGBT Issue." *Advocate*, Sept. 4, 2004.
Gorton, Kristyn. *Theorizing Desire: From Freud to Feminism to Film*. Palgrave, 2008.
Greenberg, Harvey Roy. *Screen Memories: Hollywood Cinema on the Psychoanalytic Couch*. Columbia UP, 1993.

Greenhill, Pauline, and Steven Kohm. "Little Red Riding Hood and the Pedophile in Film: *Freeway, Hard Candy,* and *The Woodsman.*" *Jeunesse: Young People, Texts, Cultures*, vol. 1, no. 2, 2009, pp. 35–65.

Grodal, Torben. *Embodied Visions: Evolution, Emotion, Culture, and Film.* Oxford UP, 2009.

Grossman, Julie. *Rethinking the Femme Fatale in Film Noir: Ready for Her Close-Up.* Palgrave Macmillan, 2009.

Hayward, Susan. *Les Diaboliques.* U of Illinois P, 2005.

Kaes, Anton. *Shell Shock Cinema: Weimar Culture and the Wounds of War.* Princeton UP, 2009.

Kaplan, E. Ann, editor. *Psychoanalysis and Cinema.* Routledge, 1990.

Keil, Charlie, and Ben Singer, editors. *American Cinema of the 1910s: Themes and Variations.* Rutgers UP, 2009.

Laine, Tarja. *Bodies in Pain: Emotion and the Cinema of Darren Aronofsky.* Berghahn, 2015.

———. *Feeling Cinema: Emotional Dynamics in Film Studies.* Bloomsbury, 2011.

Lebeau, Vicky. *Lost Angels: Psychoanalysis and Cinema.* Routledge, 1995.

Markert, John. *Hooked in Film: Substance Abuse on the Big Screen.* Scarecrow, 2013.

McGowan, Todd. *The Real Gaze: Film Theory after Lacan.* Albany: State U of New York P, 2007.

Nathanson, Paul, and Katherine K. Young. *Spreading Misandry: The Teaching of Contempt for Men in Popular Culture.* McGill-Queen's UP, 2001.

———. *Legalizing Misandry: From Public Shame to Systemic Discrimination against Men.* McGill-Queen's UP, 2006.

Penley, Constance. *The Future of an Illusion: Film, Feminism, and Psychoanalysis.* U of Minnesota P, 1989.

"Picture Grossers." *Variety*, January 12, 1972, p. 9.

Plantinga, Carl. *Moving Viewers: American Film and the Spectator's Experience.* U of California P, 2009.

Plantinga, Carl, and Greg M. Smith, editors. *Passionate Views: Film, Cognition, and Emotion.* Johns Hopkins UP, 1999.

Pomerance, Murray. *An Eye for Hitchcock.* Rutgers UP, 2004.

———. *Hitchcock's Marnie.* British Film Institute, 2014.

Ristock, Janice L. *No More Secrets: Violence in Lesbian Relationships.* Routledge, 2002.

Robertson, Stephen. *Crimes against Children: Sexual Violence and Legal Culture in New York City, 1880–1960.* U of North Carolina P, 2005.

Sacks, Jeffrey. *Flicker: Your Brain on Movies.* Oxford UP, 2014.

Sacks, Oliver. "Asylum." *Asylum: Inside the Closed World of State Mental Hospitals,* photographs by Christopher Payne, MIT P, 2009.

Saradjian, Jacqui. "Understanding the Prevalence of Female-Perpetrated Sexual Abuse and the Impact of That Abuse on Victims." *Female Sexual Offenders: Theory, Assessment, and Treatment,* edited by Theresa A. Gannon and Franca Cortoni, Wiley, 2010, pp. 9–30.

Schneider, Steven Jay, editor. *Horror Film and Psychoanalysis: Freud's Worst Nightmare*. Cambridge UP, 2004.
Shadoian, Jack. *Dreams and Dead Ends: The American Gangster Film*. 2nd ed., Oxford UP, 2003.
Shimamura, Arthur P., editor. *Psychocinematics: Exploring Cognition at the Movies*. Oxford UP, 2013.
Smith, Angela M. *Hideous Progeny: Disability, Eugenics, and Classic Horror Cinema*. Columbia UP, 2011.
Stack, Steven, and Barbara Bowman. *Suicide Movies: Social Patterns, 1900–2009*. Hogrefe, 2012.
Wahl, Otto F. *Media Madness: Public Images of Mental Illness*. Rutgers UP, 1997.
Wedding, Danny, and Ryan M. Niemiec. *Movies and Mental Illness: Using Films to Understand Psychopathology*. 4th ed., Hogrefe, 2014.
Weinstein, Deborah. *The Pathological Family: Postwar America and the Rise of Family Therapy*. Cornell UP, 2013.
Young, Allan. "Making Traumatic Memory." *The Harmony of Illusions: Inventing Post-traumatic Stress Disorder*. Princeton UP, 1995, pp. 13–42.
Youngstrom, Eric, and Anna Van Meter. "Comorbidity of Bipolar Disorder and Depression." *The Oxford Handbook of Depression and Comorbidity*, edited by C. Steven Richards and Michael W. O'Hara, Oxford UP, 2014, pp. 268–86.
Zimmerman, Jacqueline Noll. *People like Ourselves: Portrayals of Mental Illness in the Movies*. Scarecrow, 2003.

2

Adèle H., Camille Claudel, and Margot de Valois

Isabelle Adjani's Real "Mad" Women? Costume Drama and the Disruptive Female

SUSAN HAYWARD

FEW FRENCH FEMALE STAR BODIES have been so frequently attached to the concept of "mental disorder" as Isabelle Adjani; unfairly, as it transpires. Contrary to myth, we need only consider her filmography to note that her association with disruptive, liminally insane characters is not a constant. Apart from the three films that are the focus of this chapter, we are hard-pushed to find more than four other films in which Adjani has played in this context of mental disorder: *Possession* (1981); *Mortelle randonnée* and *L'été meurtrier* (both 1983); and *Toxic Affair* (1993) (all based in fiction and set in contemporary times). But, leaving aside the pigeon-holing of Adjani's characterizations, what is of interest here— beginning with her first major film *L'histoire d'Adèle H* (Truffaut, 1975), through *Camille Claudel* (Nuytten, 1988) to *La reine Margot* (Chéreau, 1994)—is that these films are based on real people, and more specifically women who purportedly went mad thanks to their obsession with their male lover. The selection of these three films is also guided by the fact that they are costume dramas. A genre not necessarily associated with madness, but certainly one that normatively allows for a more fulsome representation of female repression, including sexual repression (merely to consider the costumes and mise-en-scène of their environs makes this point self-evident). Grand narratives, swashbuckling cloak-and-dagger stories, lives of great men, romantic passion (whether requited or not) are the stuff of costume dramas. However, unruly women, as goes the trope of narrative cinema (whatever the genre), must be punished for their disorderly conduct (we need only consider the femme fatale of the film noir genre). With regard to the three films under consideration here, in two instances (Adèle Hugo and Camille Claudel), the women are deemed mad and ultimately interred in asylums by a patriarchal figure (i.e., silenced and severely punished). In the third film, Margot, despite her defiance, is nonetheless the instrument of her mother's (Catherine de Medici) obsessive scheming to install her second son as king—first, she is forced to marry against her faith and, second, unable to prevent the brutal torture and beheading of her lover, she is banished from court out into the wilds of Navarre (exile being an alternative form of silencing). Contrary to popular myth, however, of these three personages, Margot is the one who maintains her sanity. She is, if anything, caught in a maelstrom of political violence that, in itself, borders on madness. This chapter will investigate these distinctive cinematic representations of (mental) disorder, first, through the optic of gender and genre, and, second, through the optic of narrative construction and film aesthetics.

Gender and Genre

The starting point here surely has to be the cultural construction of these three women. By that I mean the various narratives spawned around their "real" stories that have left us with an "imaginary" truth of their trajectory as represented in the films we have before us. We begin with *L'histoire d'Adèle H*. If, as we are told by Truffaut (in the rolling credits), his film about Adèle Hugo is the true story and is based on her journals, then we would naturally expect the story to unfold from Adèle's point of view. Such is the case, *but* only insofar as Adjani's embodiment of Hugo's second daughter dominates the screen (she is in almost every shot). Yet, here lies the paradox: because these journals began when Adèle was held a virtual captive by her self-exiled father, for twelve years (from1851 to 1863) on the islands of Jersey and later Guernsey, we should naturally expect to learn more about the circumstances that led her to pursue her tragic adventure. However, at no instance are we supplied with a back story that serves to explain her condition—that of a woman obsessed by her passion for the British soldier Lieutenant Pinson, which apparently developed into a psychotic disorder of erotomania. We merely witness Adèle's physical and mental decline over the nine years during which she pursues him, first to Halifax in Nova Scotia and subsequently to Barbados, with barely enough money to survive. Indeed, Truffaut's film serves to endorse the myth, first set in place by her famous father, Victor Hugo, that she had gone mad because of her hopeless romantic attachment to a man who rejected her—a condition for which he, the father, "sadly" had to have her interned at Saint-Mandé (a mental institution just outside Paris), where she remained interned for forty-two years, until her death in 1915, despite evidence that, over time, her neurosis had dissipated and that she most certainly was not mad. However, it suited Hugo to expunge her from the family (so as to ensure his own greatness as a writer, a greatness achieved despite the *terrible tragedies* he had had to endure as a patriarch and a father of the Republic). Furthermore, to preserve the great man's name, this myth of her madness was sustained after his death in 1885, when Adèle could have been released. Instead, she was moved to another institution, Suresnes. As we shall see, Truffaut's film does nothing to disrupt this gothico-romantic reading of the unfortunate Adèle H.

The narrative construction for Camille Claudel is far more nuanced and is based upon the novel written by her great-niece (Reine-Marie Paris), which endeavours to develop the complex story of the woman whose genius undoubtedly led to her changing the course of sculpting history, but whose passionate temperament contributed so dramatically to her undoing. The film offers up the whole trajectory of Camille's sculpting trajectory, from her early days as a student until her internment. Thus, it traces her emergence (with all the difficulties of being a woman sculptor notwithstanding) into a brilliant sculptor who had very little to learn from Auguste Rodin, for whom she was both muse and lover. Indeed (and as Rodin readily acknowledged), if anything, it was she who taught Rodin how to sculpt in a new and modern way: from the inside out (that is to say, by bringing the emotional, inner being into movement; *sculpture intérieure*/sculpture of the soul). The initial great love story subsequently turned sour as Camille realized that, by becoming Rodin's assistant, she had lost sight of her own aesthetic practice. The film portrays her struggle between her love for Rodin and her deep conviction that she must separate from him for her art to survive. She craved recognition for her work in its own right, resenting the fact that she was mostly perceived as "Rodin's assistant," and that it was assumed her work derived from his, whereas the opposite was truer (again, this Rodin recognized). The ending of their ten-year relationship, in 1893, was triggered also, it has to be said, by Rodin's refusal to leave his common-law wife, Rose, and by Camille's choice to abort their child (one of several pregnancies she is presumed to have had with Rodin). Many things, therefore, pushed her to make this break, a decision that came at a terrible cost. First, her physical health declined because of her progressively indigent state. Commissions failed to come her way (her rupture with Rodin meant that many investors lost interest in her work). She refused to accept any monetary help from Rodin (breaking definitively from any contact with him in 1898) and received but a measly sum from her family (by now her father had very little to spare and her successful diplomat brother, Paul, contributed very little). Second, as her condition of penury continued, her mental health began to deteriorate. Camille's original realization of what she had brought to Rodin, in terms of sculpturing aesthetics, turned into a paranoid delusion that he had stolen and continued to steal from her work. Moreover, she was convinced that he was responsible for her lack of success. In fact, the reverse is true. He did as much as possible to help her, as did a handful of others, as a result of which she managed to have some of her most memorable pieces in several major exhibitions as late as 1905.

After 1905, however, the cumulative effect of indigence and delusion served to push Camille into a state of temporary paranoia. She gradually became a total recluse in her studio and, in 1912, destroyed nearly all of her work as an act of vengeance against her (perceived) enemies, including Rodin. Rodin may have been weak-willed, but he was not the enemy in the final analysis. Rather, it was her brother Paul who, in collusion with their mother (who had no empathy for Camille), had her interned just one week after the death of her beloved father (who had protected her and believed in her throughout her career). With him out of the way, Paul and his mother could step in and do as they saw fit. This was to bury her alive, as it were, first, at the Ville-Evrard Mental Institution until the outbreak of World War I, when she was moved to the Montfavet Asylum in Montdevergues (near Avignon). Doctors who treated Camille told the family she did not need to be institutionalized, but they insisted she remain (Kerri Mahon 279). As with Adèle Hugo, she remained in the insane asylum until she died (in 1943). Unlike Adèle, who lived out her years in asylum in relative physical comfort, Camille spent the rest of her life in the most appalling conditions: freezing cold in the winter, dreadful food, and surrounded by demented screeching women (Delbée 347). During her thirty years of internment, she was visited no more than a dozen times by her brother, by her mother not at all. Paul's cruelty towards his sister is a complex affair. Neither child was really loved by their mother, who was particularly critical and distant towards Camille. Their father (whose work meant he was mostly absent from family life) adored Camille and saw her great potential, which he did everything to foster, at the expense (it could be said) of Paul and their other sister, Louise (for money was tight). However, Paul also had conflicting feelings about his sister, whom he loved deeply, yet also resented. A conservative and repressed individual (who found faith in his late teens), he was troubled and attracted by her free spirit (something he was incapable of) and frustrated at his lack of success as a poet during her great days as a sculptor. Only once his own greatness was assured (as a poet and playwright) did he finally acknowledge her real importance (in 1953, he at last allowed her work to be exhibited alongside Rodin's).

The film *La reine Margot* is ostensibly based on Alexandre Dumas's novel of the same title. Set in the period of the Wars of Religion (in the second half of the sixteenth century), the novel, which was published in serial form in *La Presse*, is a fast-action, dialogue-ridden narrative (to keep the readers hooked). Although somewhat risqué in its allusions to Margot's love affairs, it is, nevertheless, very clear in its depiction of her intelligence, her political astuteness, and her full awareness of her role as a member of the royal Valois family, including her obligations, in terms of personal sacrifice, to the state. Cloak-and-dagger tropes run throughout the novel. The Louvre itself, with its labyrinthine passages, secret boudoirs, spy-holes, and hidden exits into the streets of Paris is a central personage to the unravelling tale of deceit, murder, trysts, and treason that Dumas has constructed in his novel about the days leading up to Margot's wedding to the Protestant Henri de Navarre, the subsequent Saint Bartholomew's Day Massacre, and the various (unsuccessful) attempts to murder her husband by her mother, Catherine de Medici, amongst others. Patrice Chéreau's adaptation, however, unlike the more respectful 1954 film version by Dréville, chooses almost exclusively to focus on the political machinations *through* the optic of the sexualized bodies of his main protagonists. Thus, Margot, far from being revealed as the rounded royal woman of court that she was, is represented as a lustful whore, her close confidante Henriette de Nevers as a potential lesbian lover and equally salacious when it comes to beautiful young men. In Dumas's novel (as in Dréville's film), Margot is instrumental in saving lives, helping endangered people escape, thwarting her mother's schemes and those of her younger brother François. Finally, she is a true ally to her husband, Henri de Navarre. Very little of this remains in Chéreau's version. The purported incestuous relationships (Margot and her brothers, Catherine and her middle son, Henri d'Anjou), all of which were part of the contemporary gossip-mongering put about in an effort to discredit Margot, are only vaguely hinted at in Dumas, but they come fully to the fore in Chéreau's film, to the point where in one scene Margot is gang-raped by her brothers. In short, sexuality is the centerfold of Chéreau's film. Affairs of the state become visceral engagements between different fluids: blood, semen, and the excrement of the torture chamber. There is no point of entry to enjoy these characters, whereas in Dumas we admire Margot, we enjoy observing the relationship that develops between Coconnas and La Môle, and we like the measured nature of Henri de Navarre and admire his survival tactics, caught as he is in the machinations of the Medici/Valois household. Finally, the significance of the Louvre, so present in Dumas's novel as a metaphor for the labyrinthine political intrigues of the times, is nowhere to be seen.

What remains true within these three brutal narratives is that each of these historical personages encountered very similar sets of circumstances. In all instances, their sense of personal worth was undermined by the forces of patriarchy; all three suffered familial rejection, whether by the mother (as with Camille and Margot), the father (as with Adèle), or a patriarchal force (as with Camille in the form of her brother). In all cases, these women were the progeny of dysfunctional families. Adèle was victim of the exigencies of her tyrannical father, Victor Hugo, who would brook no opposition and found it perfectly natural that his entire family (his wife and adult children) should remain by his egocentric side (while in exile) so that his own myth construction could be forever preserved. Adèle's youthful years (twenty-two to thirty-three) were sacrificed to his own needs. Hugo also feared madness as a genetic flaw in the family; his own brother, Eugène, having been hospitalized for psychotic disorders. In time, Adèle, as Eugène before her, would be all but erased from family history, with just the single official version that she was mad, a version that has prevailed and that Truffaut's film does nothing to contradict, despite having access to her journals. Recently, however, thanks to Henri Gourdin's excellent study, *Les Hugo*, it has become abundantly clear that, while Adèle was driven by unrequited passion, and while she did indeed suffer a nervous breakdown from her grand unrequited love affair, nonetheless, she was certainly fully capable of managing her affairs. It is also clear that trouble for Adèle in terms of her well-being began only once it became increasingly difficult for her to obtain funding from her father. It is, then, in this respect that, as her falling into a state of indigence began, so her physical decline began, which in turn led to mental disorders that intensified considerably once she established herself in Barbados. So, although it is possible that she suffered from erotomania, she certainly was not mad, as Hugo would have it. However, it suited his purpose (as with the tragic death of his eldest daughter Léopoldine) to reinscribe Adèle's tragedy into his own legend of the exemplary patriarch and head of the family burdened by events in which he played no part (Gourdin 215).

Within this framework of dysfunctional families, interestingly, both Adèle Hugo and Camille Claudel suffered as a result of their parents' inability to process the death of an earlier sibling. In Adèle's case, when her sister Léopoldine died in a boating accident (shortly after "escaping" from her father's tentacles by marrying), Hugo's reaction was to project his love for his dead daughter onto Adèle (only thirteen at the time), often mistakenly calling her by her elder sister's name. This talented daughter's own identity (Adèle, named after her mother) was subsumed into that of her dead sister, herself named in memory of Hugo's first child, a son (Léopold, who died shortly after being born). Hugo writes of how Léopoldine's death deeply affected Adèle and was the beginning of her mental disorders. Yet the evidence points to the fact that it was Hugo who was overcome with grief and that, in projecting his grief onto Adèle and by obliging her to replace the irreplaceable Léopoldine, she became, in turn, depressed (Meurice 6). The precocious scholar, writer, musician, and composer that Adèle was, signified less to Hugo than his need to find in her the ghost of his departed beloved Léopoldine (who, in defying her father and striking out on her own, had lost her life and brought terrible suffering to her father, according to his legend).

In Camille Claudel's case, her mother also lost her first child, a boy, after birth, and Camille was born just over a year later. But her mother was unable to bond with her daughter, calling her "the usurper," or again "the devil incarnate" (Delbée 40, 44). Her mother had no physical contact with any of her children, but Camille bore the brunt of her mother's opprobrium because she was strong-willed and rebellious (characteristics her father admired). By issuing forth from dysfunctional families and as "replacement" children, both Camille and Adèle carried the traumas of loss and rejection (they were not enough as they were, for they were not the loved ones). This inability of the parent to recognize them for their own worth would be a source of deep suffering, which Camille was able to bring into her beautiful but often melancholic sculptures and Adèle into her acts of defiance against her father, her writing and musical composition. There is no doubt that the levels of suffering (through rejection or lack of recognition) endured by these two women led to psychoses expressed in a number of different ways, but firstly through the body. Thus, these unruly bodies, sexually and genderically, challenged patriarchy as materialized in the form of "Great Men," be it Victor Hugo, Paul Claudel, or Auguste Rodin. As to the films that portray these two women, if we grasp a clear understanding of all this trauma in Nuytten's film, *Camille Claudel* (written by a woman; produced by a woman, Adjani; and shot by a director, Nuytten, who was well-known to the lead actor, Adjani, again), such is not the case for Truffaut's *L'histoire d'Adèle H*—essentially a remake of the Hugolian myth of her descent into madness (as we know women-unbridled-passion-madness is a frequent trope in Truffaut's films).

It seems almost self-evident that Margot, our third personage, came from a dysfunctional family. Her mother, Catherine de Medici was the great manipulator, often at the center of all the many intrigues, and most certainly a mother whose obsession for her middle son, Henri d'Anjou, left no room for her other children, whom she quite happily played off against each other. Margot's father died when she was six; her eldest brother (François II) died six months later, leaving her mother as regent of France upon the accession to the throne of Charles IX, who was only ten. Even once Charles officially took the reins of power (at thirteen), Catherine remained the guiding force behind the throne (Charles was weak, sickly, and suffered from tuberculosis). She it was who held in check the ambitions of her other two sons, all the while ensuring the future of her much beloved son Henri d'Anjou (Henri III, after his brother's death in 1574). Catherine saw in her daughter little more than a pawn she could use to obtain the results she wanted. Even before her enforced marriage to Henri de Navarre, Margot was fully aware how little she mattered to her mother: "She consistently diminished me in her favour, making her son (Henri) her idol, wanting to please him in all things and giving in to his every wish" (Margot's memoirs, cited in Bertière 233). And yet this young woman was a cultivated woman and an accomplished linguist; however, her desire to have some kind of political role was persistently thwarted by her mother. That is with the major exception of Margot protecting her husband, whom she saved on several occasions from being assassinated. By becoming his political ally, for a brief while at least, she had the role of queen and protector of her sovereign lord against the murderous schemes of her mother and her acolytes. Dumas's novel covers this period of Margot's coming of age into the political morass of the Valois dynasty; arguably, he covers her strongest moments of defiance. Regrettably, Chéreau's film is more in thrall to the political violence that abounded at this time, and uses Margot/Adjani's body as just one of several major cyphers upon which to play out his narrative.

Let us now turn to genre: the costume drama. The first point to make is that these three films follow in the tradition of French cinema, in that they draw on the nineteenth century or a nineteenth-century novel as their source. For, although Dumas's text refers back to a romanticized interpretation of Renaissance history (a period of particular fascination to nineteenth-century authors and readers), nonetheless, the optic remains that of the nineteenth century. The second point concerns both the genre and that nineteenth-century optic. Traditionally, costume drama displaces issues of sex and sexuality onto decor and costume (thus rich veloured draperies, abundantly rich silk gowns, even cross-dressing, all speak to the textured, sexualized body, however indirectly). As we shall see in the three films we are discussing, the decor is very restrained in both *Adèle H* and *La reine Margot*—the former through its dark tones and lack of ostentation (including the costumes), the latter through its minor focus on environment in favor of a concentration on the physical body and the ostentation of the Valois family's adornments (including costumes). Only *Camille Claudel* sustains a sense of abundance in terms of décor, but this is largely in terms of big buildings (Rodin's various studios, major exhibition halls) and as such directly refers to the industry of sculpture—from its beginnings in the studio space to its end point on display. In terms of decor, there is nothing of the feminine, therefore, in any of these films. And in terms of costumes, only Margot's dresses and her three brothers' attire give any hint of some form of sexuality.

The primary ideological function of the costume drama (at least in the French context) is, surprisingly, not to sell marriage—if anything it exposes the difficulties inherent therein. Rather, it presents us with an ongoing discourse about power relations on both a political and personal level (including marriage)—which at many stages overlap, particularly in relation to masculinity and femininity. Masculinity is revealed as a complex affair: everything is far from straight, sexual relations included, and war is often represented as vainglorious, and so on. This was ever the case with the costume drama genre in France, even at its height in the 1950s (Yves Allégret's *Nez de cuir*, 1952, is exemplary on all of these points). Femininity is often equally interesting, and is not always submissive to the masculine. Madness, however, is not typically at the center of this genre, and certainly not female madness. Which brings me back to the nineteenth century and to our three films.

According to Foucault, the eighteenth and nineteenth centuries took an increasing interest in sexuality, especially those "perverse" manifestations that did not fit into the marital mould (we need only think of some of the late eighteenth-century French novels by Diderot, De Sade, and Laclos). This interest, however, was ambiguously poised in that this "world of perversion" had to be controlled—be it in the form of brothels or, more punitively (if in "excess"), contained in madhouses. Sexuality became a socially managed affair. In a parallel, if not overlapping, way, by the late eighteenth century, madness also became socially controlled. Crucially, madness, or the so-called perception of madness in the form of unreasonable behaviour—be it prostitution, erotomania, vagrancy, blasphemy, or hysteria—was conflated with mental illness, as a result of which deviant (or perverse) sexuality and madness were seen as one and the same and, in turn, defined as mental illness. The national response to the mad (be it sexual, mental or deviancy) was to separate them completely from society into newly created institutions—to bury them alive, as it were. The condition of these outcasts was seen by society as one of moral error and, even if the institutions did succeed in reversing the condition, the social forces driving the confinement, often meant that these "unreasonable, poor demented creatures" (as both Hugo and Claudel referred to Adèle and Camille, respectively) would never be permitted to leave by those who put them there in the first place, namely, the family.

Yet, as Foucault points out, madness is a social construct that is distinct from mental illness (257–78). And so, where Victor Hugo and Paul Claudel are concerned, it is their construction of their "creatures" that constitutes the first *cinematic disorder* in relation to the films based on the lives of Adèle and Camille. In Truffaut's film, we have a virtual reconstruction of Victor Hugo's interpretation of his wayward daughter's adventures and passionate pursuit of Pinson. Conversely, in Nuytten's film, we are guided away from the myths surrounding Camille (whose rehabilitation only began in the early 1980s) towards an understanding of her greatness and the terrible consequences of being a woman of genius well before her time.

Cinematic Disorders:
Narrative Construction and Film Aesthetics

Until Truffaut's film, very little was known about Adèle Hugo. An edited version of her journals was published in 1968, which Truffaut accessed (but appears to have left to one side). He also had discussions with Hugo's great-grandson, Jean Hugo, which may have tempered his approach (Gourdin 248–49). Whatever the case, the fact remains that when Truffaut, in the opening credits to his film writes, "L'Histoire d'Adèle H est authentique/This is the true story of Adèle H," it seems clear that the true story he is referring to is none other than the interpretation imposed by the Hugolian patrimony. Ultimately, therefore, the point of view is not hers (even if, in camera terms, it could be argued it is hers). So we are left with a story about her, but viewed from outside.

As we now know, the truer story is that Adèle's youthful prime adult years (twenty-two to thirty-three) were spent incarcerated on a tiny island in a gloomy house, all designed to correspond to her father's romantic sense of self and space (Adèle writes of this in her journal, begun in 1851). She did indeed meet Lieutenant Pinson, with whom she formed some kind of liaison of which her father disapproved. Her persistence in keeping the affair alive says a great deal about her willfulness; but her resistance to her father's ruling is hardly surprising given his own unruly behavior. Hugo had sexual relations not just with his mistress but also with the housemaids (Gourdin 221). And let us not forget that Adèle was herself an object of his fantasy, as was Léopoldine (147). Thus, her understanding of sex, as she perceived it within her dysfunctional family (in which her father abused his authority), means she may have considered that, for people of genius, nonmarital sexuality was not a taboo, indeed, could be accepted as normative. In any event, the suffocation she felt, the loss of self under his overbearing rule ("le goum"/the tribe/martial law, as she called it) led her eventually to plan and make her escape (as did her sister before her). She chose to follow her heart. It is unclear, if at the time Pinson had already broken off amorous alliances with her, but as a thirty-three-year-old woman, she did not require the permission of her father to leave (under French law, unmarried women, once they had reached maturity at twenty-one, had greater freedoms than married women or minors).

What clearly troubled Hugo was that Adèle had defied him, she had deserted him; what troubled him more was her striking out for her own autonomy—for it assailed his image of perfect fatherhood (Gourdin 228). Adèle's enormous striving for independence, what today might be called acting as a free spirit, was far from acceptable behavior in the nineteenth century. Moreover, despite her controlling father limiting her funds, the evidence is there, in her correspondence with her brother François-Victor Hugo, that she was perfectly able to make complex travel plans and lead an independent life (230). As far as we can determine, she had two moments when she collapsed, or fell into a momentary madness that was subsequently labeled erotomania (bordering on schizophrenia)—but which in fact may have been induced by the alarming effects of indigence upon her person. The first trauma occurred when Pinson set sail for Barbados. By this time, Adèle's finances were in dire straits, since her father sent her barely enough upon which to survive (having been deceived into believing she'd married Pinson, when he discovered the truth, he punished her by withholding funds). The second occurred in 1869 when she heard that Pinson was leaving Barbados, returning to England to marry and rescind his army post. Certainly Pinson rejected Adèle's advances and had no intention of marrying her: however, it is also the case that they continued to see each other intermittently and remained on friendly terms. Furthermore, they were in touch by letter even after he had married (in 1870), and, moreover, he encouraged her to come home to her family. The tone of his letters is one of tender concern (Gourdin 235). Conversely, Hugo never wrote to her the whole time she was away. He dictated his words via the third person of his son (François-Victor). Here is an example: "I long for an answer from our poor lost daughter. It's now been 5 years since, because of her, my heart is broken. Tell her she must return and that my heart will melt and my arms wide open" (Gourdin 232; all translations are mine).

Truffaut's film is constructed of eight main episodes, the first seven of which focus on Adèle's time in Halifax (1 hr., 20 min.) and only one of which deals with her time in Barbados (14 min.). There is a curious temporal imbalance in this reconstruction of her nine year "fugue." She stayed in Halifax for three years (1863–66); and was in Barbados for six (1866–72). Furthermore, contrary to evidence, Truffaut's "true story" has Adèle leaving for Barbados in 1864, merely a year after arriving in Halifax (in fact, she left in 1866). Why this imprecision or falsification of the length of her stay? It pays no regard to the historical truth; moreover, it compresses the narrative line so that we are, from the beginning, witness to Adèle as a deluded personage. As to the foreshortened representation of her time in Barbados, it is almost as if, having documented her first descent into madness, Truffaut could move to shorthand for the second cycle. This is a suggestion that gains weight when we consider how fractured and simplified the eighth episode is, composed as it is of a series of cameo shots, most of which are overlaid by a music score (there is virtually no spoken word or dialogue, and no utterance from Adèle). These cameo shots reveal Adèle wandering through the market place; Adèle fainting; Pinson at a fancy party with his wife; Adèle rescued by Mme. Bâa and nursed by her; and Pinson shadowing Adèle through the back streets of the garrison town, but being unrecognized by her. Finally, we are told (in voice-over by Truffaut), Adèle returns to France and is interned by her father, where she remains until her death. The epilogue to the film almost seals this "true story" of Adèle H within the Hugolian mythology in that we return to Paris to a series of still images (voiced-over by Truffaut) of Hugo's great burial ceremony in 1885, and a recap of his greatness. Only a tiny gap of light or hope for Adèle transpires when this part of the epilogue is followed by a still image of her tombstone and Truffaut's voice-over informing us that her death in 1915 passed unnoticed (as indeed Hugo and his family might have wished), swiftly followed by shots of her as a young woman standing by the ocean and declaring, "I'll do something no young woman has done, walk across the sea from the old to the new continent to follow my lover" (asserting, here, her independence with words she first uttered in an earlier episode when she rejects all parentage to Victor Hugo by declaring that she is born of an unknown father).

Let us look at how Truffaut uses the seven Halifax episodes to construct his mad Adèle. From the very first episode (from arriving in Halifax to her spotting Pinson in the bookshop and spying on him through the window), her delusions are expressed through the word and the body—a graphosomatic erotomania, if you will. She constructs wildly different stories about Pinson ("he is my niece's intended"; "he is in love with me"); and she constructs half-true stories about her dead sister Léopoldine and her father ("she drowned and my father drowned himself from grief"). Her sleep is disturbed and she dreams that she too is drowning, only to awaken sweating and crying out. Thenceforward, with each setback she encounters with Pinson (coming face to face with him at her lodgings, when he rejects her, seeing him with his mistress and spying on them having sex, confronting him in the churchyard), she rewrites the events into a favorable fabulation. Thus, in episode 2 (from going to the bank to the table-turning séance to conjure up the spirit of Léopoldine), she writes to her parents assuring them she and Pinson are together; she writes in her journal, "I'll find a way to convince him to love me, through kindness" and "I am your wife, definitively." In episode 3, having spied on Pinson and his mistress having sex, she writes, "My religion is love," and "I surrender all of me to it"; and yet the effect of her spying leads her to faint in the snow (the body says one thing, the word another). In episode 4, now ill with pleurisy, she writes to her parents to say she and Pinson are engaged; furthermore, she has somehow managed to conceal various love notes into the pockets of Pinson's jacket. By episode 5 (from visiting the bank, to using the subterfuge of cross-dressing to force an encounter with Pinson in the churchyard and making him kiss her, and later building a shrine in her room to her lover), she informs her parents she is now married to Pinson and must be written to as Mme. Pinson. By episode 6 (from going to the bank and receiving her father's angry letter at discovering she had lied about the marriage, to her fury at Mr. Whistler in the bookstore for discovering her true identity and offering her a present of Hugo's *Les Misérables*), the graphosomatic nature of her disorder blends into one single manifestation of nonbeing—there is no more Adèle H. First, by now myopic and wearing glasses, she sends a prostitute to Pinson as a gift from her; a body-offering replacement for herself, therefore. Since she has always been a replacement figure (in her father's eyes), this is a perfectly reasonable gesture (so her unreason, or myopic state tells her). Second, her father's furious letter to her denouncing her for her deceitfulness leads her, at last, to express one of the underlying truths as to the source of her own distress: the crushing effect of being the child of a famous man. As he sought to erase her identity by making her a replacement child, as he sought to bury her

Figure 2.1. Adèle (Isabelle Adjani) holding her father's book as her identity becomes known in *L'histoire d'Adèle H.*

alive in Halifax ("my poor mad daughter"), as he sought to punish her by restricting her allowance, so now Adèle rejects him: "I am born of an unknown father, a completely unknown father," she proclaims. She is no longer Adèle H, no longer recognizable as the daughter of Victor Hugo. Small surprise, therefore, that by episode 7 (from her destroying Pinson's engagement to Agnes Johnson by claiming she is pregnant by him, to ending up in the poor house, and later arriving, totally unkempt, at the bank where she is not recognized), Adèle has finally tumbled into a state of anonymity and dereliction. Her former physical attire, in elegant albeit predominantly dark, earth-colored silk-taffeta dresses and hair neatly tied up in a bun, is now in total disarray. Her hair is loose and wild, her dress torn and dirty. Penury and delusion have done their work. So too has Truffaut.

In terms of film aesthetics, with the exception of the last episode (set in Barbados, but actually shot on the island of Gorée, off Senegal), the entire film is shot on a palette of brown hues. Although filmed in EastmanKodak color (a fast-stock film process well known for its pastel-like tones and its great sensitivity to light), the gloomy darkness of interiors and exteriors merely echoes the romantic-gothic aesthetic

Truffaut undoubtedly wished to achieve. It is as if we have entered an illustrated version of one of Hugo's own novels and the fact that the film's opening credit sequence begins with a series of Hugo's own drawings of ruined castles (*Art et glam*), stormy seas (*Ma destinée*), towns in ruins (*Ville avec le pont de tumbledown*), and so on, merely serves to reinforce this reading. There are very few rich textures, only Adèle's silk dresses—even though her clothes, rather than bespeaking a woman at the peak of her sexuality, entomb her in their dark shades of brown, dark taupe, and burgundy red.

The shooting style harkens back to an earlier age of French cinema, recalling the pessimistic mode of 1930s poetic realism, with Truffaut's use of fades to shift from one scene to the next, of simple superimpositions to evoke the mind in a dream state, to say nothing of his use of the master of poetic realist music, Maurice Jaubert's "Préambule et Pastourelle" to score the film. The music is dark, especially the "Préambule," to which Truffaut repeatedly returns; the more jaunty "Pastourelle" hardly offers a respite, as it seems to act in ironic counterpoint to the actual goings on (for example, when Adèle is spying on Pinson having sex with his mistress). The structured use of repetition with opposition of certain episodes is very reminiscent of Marcel Carné and Jean Renoir's work of counterpoint in their 1930s films (for example, Adèle spying in on Pinson and his mistress in the bookshop is matched by the shot of her spying in on them having sex but is reversed in a later shot of Mr. Whistler spying *out* on Adèle as she faints). The bleakness of the film style is enhanced by the dominance of the single shot, often in medium close up—all of which accentuates Adèle's increasing sense of isolation. Dialogue is shot as a series of single shots with only the occasional two shot (for example, Adèle forcing Pinson to kiss her in the churchyard). The use of shot/countershot is completely absent, indicating a lack of connection for Adèle, both to people and a sense to reality. She it is who retranscribes reality into her own imaginings. Much as her own father before her, her obsession (moral error, to return to Foucault) is in the word. Surely, rather than decompensating through erotomania, her psychosis manifests itself as mythomania—hardly the ravings of a lunatic, it has to be said!

If, at best, Truffaut's film offers us an ambiguous rendition of Adèle H's disorder, such is not the case for Nuytten's Camille Claudel. In the first place, the temporal structure of the film is entirely appropriate to the tale, falling as it does into four major episodes as follows:

Adèle H., Camille Claudel, and Margot de Valois

Camille meets Rodin (1885) 30 min.	Camille and Rodin (1885–1898) 60 min.	Camille leaves Rodin (1898=>) 32 min.	Camille's breakdown (1905–1913) 44 min.
Film opens with Paul running to Camille's lodgings declaring the words "Camille has *disappeared*"; Camille the unruly daughter, devoted to her art is clawing out clay for her modeling; we learn of her mother's hatred; Camille becomes Rodin's assistant; presents him with her first sculpture in marble (a foot); distraught that Rodin says nothing about her sculpture, she "disappears."	This section opens with the news that Hugo is dead; this event overshadows Camille's gift to Paul of her sculpted foot; Camille returns to Rodin's studio, they become lovers; their work is inspired the one by the other; but Camille remains jealous of Rodin's common-law wife, Rose; Camille falls pregnant but does not tell Rodin; she asks him to marry her; Rodin prevaricates; she has an abortion; Rose attacks Camille; again, Camille "disappears."	Camille beseeches Rodin to choose her, but he won't; she leaves him declaring she will now work for herself; she "disappears" herself; she sets up her own studio, makes friends with poets and musicians (including Debussy); the agent Blot takes her on; she exhibits her work alongside Rodin's; meets Rodin, they almost resume their relationship until he sees her sculpture of *L'âge mûr*, and a terrible quarrel ensues.	Camille is becoming delusional; as if now the agent of "disappearing"/erasing her own self, she progressively strips herself of her possessions to cover debts; she goes to see her father who now applauds Paul's great talent; Blot continues to back her and puts on a major exhibition of her work in his gallery, she attends, but her brother Paul, seeing her unkempt state, leaves—a final destructive rejection; Camille then destroys the work in her studio; Paul has her declared insane and taken away to an asylum—this time Camille has *disappeared*.
Music: 9 min., 30 sec.	Music: 12 min., 10 sec.	Music: 9 min., 15 sec.	Music: 5 min., 15 sec.

We note from the above analysis the way in which Camille's story unravels along a series of disappearances—all of which (until the final disappearance, right at the end of the film) are of Camille's doing. That is, she is the subject of her own *disappearings*. In episode 1, she chooses to pursue her art at all times; when she is not taken seriously as an artist, but seen as a piece of skirt to be chased, she takes herself away from those who fail to understand her (her mother, Rodin's assistants, Rodin himself). In episode 2, despite her tremendous love for him, when faced with Rodin's inability to commit to her, she again disappears. Rodin's refusal to leave Rose leads Camille, in episode 3, to definitively leave him—knowing, only, that she must pursue her art, her own genius and not be swallowed up by him (or her love for him). In the fourth and final episode, this "disappearing" takes the form of self-erasure through four stages, until she is finally erased by others and made to disappear for good by her family. First, although perfectly lucid, penury is driving Camille to strip herself of what few possessions she has in order to continue with her work. Second, having severed all ties with Rodin, she becomes increasingly isolated and self-isolating, to the point of delusion. Lack of means drives her to drink, a third stage of disappearing. And, fourth, as a result of her brother's rejection of *her* and the general public's rejection of *her work* (at the gallery), she makes complete her own self-erasure by smashing up all her work in her studio and then taking it and burying it in the very clay of Paris from which she had emerged with such high aspirations at the beginning of episode 1, the time of her very first "disappearance." Finally, others commit the last rites of disappearing Camille by having her interned.

As the above makes clear, Nuytten's construction of Camille's persona is centered around a specific thematic: the issue of rejection and approbation in relation to family, love, and art. But the way in which he delivers this persona to us is primarily through the senses, in particular the haptic. Camille claws at the clay, she pulls at it, works at it, tires it so it will yield to her vision. She works with the hardest of sculpting matter: marble and onyx—we repeatedly see her chiseling away and polishing the pieces she makes. We observe her labor of genius and love. We witness her tactile understanding of the human body as she touches faces, strokes body lines, all of which serves her revolutionary artistry: namely, creating sculptures of the soul (as Paul puts it in his eulogy at the gallery opening). Yet we also behold her despair as, one by one, those who loved *her* and admired her *art*, abandon her—her body now becomes the site of that pain and suffering, in the image of the ragged, bodily derelict

Clotho sculpture she had created before her. Rodin rejects *her* and then her *sculpture* (*L'âge mûr*, in particular). Paul's cruel summing up of her life—"She achieved nothing, but I succeeded"—as he sends her off to be buried alive, merely confirms his own abject jealousy of her talent. Even her father, in her last meeting with him, expresses his pain at her failure, while declaiming the greatness of his son's poetry!

Nuytten's use of the musical score, composed for the film by Gabriel Yared, gives tonal texture to the haptic nature of the film. Drawing on the music of Mahler, Britten, and Brüchner for the feel of the score, Yared produced two themes primarily for strings with some timpani: one, the most complex and dominant (with a total time of 28 min., 50 sec.), for Camille and Rodin, the other for Camille (5 min., 20 sec.) ("Film Music Stories"). The first theme opens with the credits, and, within the film, there are several strands to it. First, dark rich tones, at times deep to the point of lugubrious (offered up by the cello)—and which on two occasions accompany Rodin at work, seeking and finding inspiration thanks to his relationship with Camille; but the tone is a warning (indeed, it reappears at the end of the film in dirge form). Second, tender, harmonious sweeps and swellings—which accompany Camille and Rodin's evolving love affair and mutual understanding of each other's creative genius. Third, high tones, at times atonal, rising to harsh painful climaxes (offered by a solo violin)—which resonate with Camille's moments of despair. Indeed, inherent within atonal music is a feeling of destabilizing rootlessness.

With the first theme, it is the density of sound that is striking. Yared used a full string orchestra with timpani and harp and a secondary chamber orchestra group to achieve this level of deep resonance ("Film Music Stories"). The effect on us is to feel the passion and the pain experienced by both Camille and Rodin. When Camille offers herself to Rodin for the first time by posing with her body, she lays her head on a/the block for him with her hair falling forward and her shoulders exposed as if a sculpture. This passionate gesture, which expresses Camille's bringing her art, her body, and love all together in one manifestation of commitment to Rodin, is matched by the melodious swelling of the music that is tender yet carries with it undertones of pain (worthy of Brüchner). A similar conjuncture between music and image occurs when Rodin is feeling Camille's face with his eyes shut, the better to understand her whole being, before then turning to his clay model of her to adjust his tactile readings of her face. In all this beauty and creativity, there is pain, the music tells us. When creativity and love are shared and equally committed to, as they mostly are in episode 2 (the longest episode, and the one with the most music, including a diegetic waltz suggesting harmony), artistic genius is almost bearable. But, as the occurrences within this musical score of harsh high tone climaxes (in their Mahleresque fashion) remind us, this theme also warns of the terrible dangers of mixing passion and art—a potion for extinction (a fear Mahler carried with him to his death).

The second theme is a far less elaborate scoring, more of a jaunty, youthful, skipping dance and is solely attached to Camille. The variations on the jaunty tune function almost as an interior journal of Camille's trajectory. We first encounter it in episode 1 where it occurs in three instances: the first, as she sets off with her clay and arrives at her studio (1 min., 30 sec.); the second, while she is lying with Paul on his bed and they talk of their love for each other (20 sec.); the third, when she is happily engaged at work in her studio shaping the bust of Giganti, as he reads from Hugo (30 sec.). The tempo is consonant with her own joy. In episode 2, the tune has all but faded away, appearing only the once (30 sec.) at a far slower pace and scored over her visit to the doctor (towards the end of this episode), where she discovers she is pregnant. This diminution of her joy (marked by the slower tempo) presages the beginning of her discord with Rodin (triggered by his refusal to leave Rose). The tune reemerges at the beginning of episode 3 (2 min., 30 sec.), first at a slow pace then at its earlier tempo of episode 1, as Camille sets out on her renewed ambitions for her own sculpture (working on *Le Baiser*) and explains her ideas to Paul. Thereafter, nothing. The theme is completely absent in the last episode. What is left in terms of music (5 min., 15 sec.) is the dirge-like funereal music embedded in the first theme—death and Clotho beckon as Camille, completely wrapped up in her ragged clothes, is dragged off to her living internment.

In Nuytten's film we are presented with a courageous free-spirited woman who has a sense of her own destiny where art is concerned. Moreover, the representation of Camille's mental disorder remains in its rightful place (at the end); and we are not made the prurient voyeur of her disintegration—in fact, in this last episode, the one who observes her is the young doctor's son, Robert, and his interest has been a fascination with both her and her art. Throughout the film, we are brought in touch with Camille's interiority in its numerous manifestations: emotional, aesthetic, and sensorial. The decor matches her trajectory, the luminous spaces only gradually giving way to the darker recesses of the final episode. Her story is viewed from within, as if at each turning we are confronted by one of her *sculptures intérieures* or by a facet thereof.

We come to understand the woman and her process as her wondrous art emerges out of the Parisian clay; the very clay from which the new Paris is also emerging, being completely rebuilt under Haussmann. How fitting that Nuytten should document Camille's modernity, her art nouveau, alongside the modernization of the City of Light.

The question of cinematic disorders shifts rather with Adjani's third film, *La reine Margot*.[1] While there is the adaptation disorder already mentioned in the first part of this chapter (which considerably perverts the portrayal of Margot), it is also the case that the film itself acts metonymically as a parable for the dreadful nature of all civil wars—surely one of the greatest disorders of all. This parable begins with the music itself and ends with the exsanguination of the body politic through a thirty years' War of Religion—on the one side, the intransigent drive for dynastic power of the Valois family, assured of their divine Catholic right to supremacy and sovereignty over France, and, on the other, the Protestants whose growing numbers represent a major threat to that supremacy (the one side seeking to eliminate the other). And this is where the music functions so meaningfully. It is not just this war that is referred to here, but surely the Bosnian-Herzogovinan war of 1992–95, a civil war between Orthodox Serbs, Catholic Croats, and Muslim Bosniaks (this latter suffering the most deaths). The composer of the score, Goran Bregovic, a Bosnian, draws his musical inspiration from Balkan, Middle Eastern, and Israeli folk traditions (Delon and Provini 127–29).[2] Thus, the opening a cappella is a Croatian folk song; the closing chant of the film, *Elo Hi*, is a Hebrew song written by Bregovic and the Israeli singer Ofra Hazan (who sings it) and her producer, the Israeli Bezalel Aloni; the wedding song ("Le matin") is sung by the Serbian Branka Vasiç and the choral music of the Saint Bartholomew's Day Massacre ("La nuit") by the Grand Choeur de Belgrade. In this regard, Bregovic's music makes the point that his music is without borders, partitions, exclusions, the very things that, conversely, the body politic imposes. His composition for this film is both a savage and ironic commentary on war, particularly civil war. In terms of savagery, the most violent part of the score is "La nuit" beginning with the inexorable chanting of the male chorus and the wailing in the background of the female voices; a single bell tolls; strings go pizzicato stretching to a strident ear-piercing atonal height; metallic sounds punctuate all of this, just as the swords plunge, slash and sever the Protestant bodies; this harsh battle-like music (where only one side is armed) finally draws to a close as a solo flute gasps for breath. As for irony, the opening a cappella (church-like chant), is a love song ("U te

Sam Albuja"; I fell in love with you), yet it is somber in tone and deeply masculine in rendition (two tenors, one baritone, and a bass). Composed of only three lines, it continues, "I will never want another girl, even if she was the Empress." Navarre and La Môle both succumb to Margot (a queen after all!)—the former is chosen for her, the latter she chooses. In having sex with the former she saves his life; conversely, in having congress with her loved one she signs his death sentence. The closing song ("Elo Hi") implores God to spare human suffering ("a bit of mercy my God, please give strength to everyone"). After what we have just witnessed, a king literally bleeding through the skin to his death, decapitated lovers, massacred Protestants, poisoned individuals (kings, ladies of the court, dogs)—little can be left but despair. Even the love theme to Margot and La Môle's affair ("Margot") played over their nude love-making scene is a gloomy lullaby and Margot's closing words to this scene echo this dreadful sorrow: "I'm now on the side of the oppressed, no longer that of the executioners."

Music here is used as metaphor, then, rather than as a phatic guide, and which links episodes through repetition (as do certain events) to give texture to this dense tapestry of a film, which decries the horrors of religious conflict and political strife. But it is also a music that suggests, through its nomadic palette, the potential of transhumance in the form of migration and change, the very thing the Valois dynasty rejects with its lust for blood and total carnage. This, then, is a first aspect of the film itself as a metonym of cinematic disorder. Consider now, briefly, the actual editing and pacing of the film. The rhythm of the film follows the overall sense of excess that rides through the narrative line. The film opens in a moment of conflict (between La Môle and Coconnas), it briefly dips into a slightly less intense, albeit still festering, mode to then begin rising through the wedding celebrations up to the moment when Margot rushes out to find a man to have sex with.

There is a quick dip in tempo that follows before the crescendo restarts for the Saint Bartholomew's Day Massacre (the longest sequence in the film at 10 min.). Overall, half of the sequences are at crescendo status the other half at a less feverish pitch. The sequences themselves are brief, averaging about four minutes per sequence (equally, the shots are rapid, averaging 5 sec.; Delon and Provini 89). It is as if the sequential shape of the film were that of a crenelated battlement on a fortress tower. This speed has for effect to disorientate characters within the film as much as us the spectator (where are we, why, and who are we with?)—just as one example, recall how Henri de Navarre's face appears constantly squeezed

Figure 2.2. Margot's nightly escapade to look for sex in *La reine Margot*.

with anxiety. But this speed also serves to expose the political madness in full throttle (smoke and mirrors, poison and imprecations, insinuation and denunciation, escape and entrapment)—Chéreau's disemboweling of the Medici political system, if you will.

The use of decor is also connected to this idea of disemboweling, of turning the inner body out. As was mentioned earlier, the labyrinthine nature of the Louvre, as characterized by Dumas, is missing from Chéreau's adaptation. In its place there are apertures and orifices. Apertures in the form of doors and windows through which bodies spy, slip, and disappear; orifices in the form of rooms within rooms suggesting hidden sexual spaces or again in the form of the cavernous canal tunnel beneath the Louvre, which is Margot's escape route but which is also the space of effluence for the Palace's waste (*voie d'échappement* in both instances in French). These apertures and orifices are markers of treachery, spaces of sexual encounter and human excretion, and as such serve as backdrop to Chéreau's full representation of the transgressive body for whom no bodily passage is too awesome and for whom, therefore, nothing is impossible—be it betrayal, rape, incest, evisceration, torture, or death.

Finally, there is the play of power relations—again a domain of excess and dysfunctionality. Catherine de Medici is represented as a huge black widow spider spinning her web often unseen (note how she hides in dark corners, looks down from balconies above, or out of windows down onto her victims). She is often silent, a glance telling all. Much as women in politics at that time had to find their way to power by being indirect, so too Catherine resorts to subterfuge, innuendo, and falsely repeating the words of others—we note, furthermore, that her terrible schemes are carried out by a third person, at a remove from her body therefore. She creates disorder at a distance. If Catherine uses language very little, such is not the case for her dissident daughter, Margot, who employs both language and her body in her endeavors to exert power. And in the first half of the film she is very effective. Through language, Margot staves off a number of threats to her husband; through her body, she protects the wounded La Môle from the Saint Bartholomew's Day Massacre. Also in the first half of the film, she asserts her sexuality both as a woman entitled to take sex as she desires it (her street encounter with La Môle) and as a knowing woman who must protect her husband (by consummating their marriage). Thus, she asserts a doubleness (masculine/feminine). Of course, this disorderly doubleness will not be allowed to prevail. So, in the second half of the film, the pendulum begins to sway the other way in terms of power relations. First, when she makes love with La Môle and he asserts that he will not be subject to her, we are confronted with a mild manifesto of equality, if you will, as they lie naked together. Furthermore, it is she who pleads with him never to leave her. More significantly, of course, it is in the scene where Margot is publicly raped by her two younger brothers, with Charles looking on, that she is completely disempowered. The masculine in its *true* form has reasserted itself!

And what a masculinity it is: sweating, fighting, murdering, hunting, preening, queer, multi-sexual, and bleeding. . . . It is particularly the bleeding that intrigues me in the light of the theme of this book—cinematic disorders. The exsanguination of Charles's body, literally bleeding through the skin (that liminal surface between the inner and outer world), is surely the clearest reference to the abject body that Kristeva speaks of. It is also, I would conjecture, the AIDS body (a body that tragically touches upon a number of personages involved with this film including the singer Ofra Hazan, who died of HIV complications in 2000, and the death of several of Chéreau's close friends).

In terms of the abject, it marks the moment when we are separated from our mother (when we are ejected from the womb covered in blood, excrement, etc.). From being within, we become outside, liminally located (the skin bears the marks of the mother's interiority). But the question becomes, Who is subject, who is object? Thus, in abjection, the fear is that the distinction between self and other breaks down. The abject then is the place where meaning collapses (Kristeva 2) and our reaction to such a threat of nonmeaning is one that does not respect borders, positions, rules (4). We know of Charles's complete dependency upon his mother and yet his simultaneous desire to separate from her. We observe him in this endeavor to separate as he persists in his own machinations, refusing to abide by rules, systems, or order (even in his beloved hunts he refuses to follow protocol). His conduct is truly disorderly, his volatility dangerous to be around. And yet as we know from his ending, he is no closer to asserting his own identity than he was at the beginning of this film (or indeed his birth).

In a sense, then, this film has as much to say about lack of identity, unruly systems, and disorder as does the abject. All three brothers, in that their crimes flirt with death as if it were their love object, are embodiments of the fragility of the law of the state—the very thing they are put on earth to protect and yet are unable to accomplish.

In conclusion, then, in many ways it is easy to see Chéreau's film as an indictment of contemporary politics, in particular Europe's failure to respond swiftly enough to the horrors of the Bosnian war; the inability of the French state to properly embrace or commit to two major grassroots political movements that spanned the length of François Mitterrand's two presidencies—namely, SOS Racisme and Anti-SIDA, both of which, as is well known, Isabelle Adjani fully engaged with. It is a film that exposes, literally, man's inhumanity to man—from the consequences of the simplest of utterances (Charles's invoking the death of the Protestants: "No one must be left, all of them"), through the use of poison to rid the body politic of unwanted bodies, to the climax of genocide (the massacre). This latter manifestation is surely the nadir of inhumanity: bodies are treated as refuse and the mass grave marks the total dematerialization of their beingness. Thus, of the three films we have considered, *La reine Margot* is undoubtedly the most polemical, with its mise-en-scène of the insanity of political disorder. As far as Nuytten's 1988 docufiction is concerned, while hardly polemical to the same degree, it could safely be said that his *Camille Claudel* readily represents the cultural value of this woman's genius and, as such, embodies the refreshing view of François Mitterrand's minister of culture, Jack Lang, who declared, "Economy and culture: it's the same fight"—after all, that is the point Camille consistently makes throughout the film. Sadly, however, Truffaut's film bears no witness to the contemporary climate of the mid-1970s, with its greater freedoms for women accorded under the presidency of Valéry Giscard d'Estaing (for example, the contraceptive pill, abortion on demand, and various laws on gender equality). His *Adèle H* focuses pruriently on a woman's breakdown in much the same way as a nineteenth-century romantic novel might wallow in a heroine's misery of lost love and her inevitable descent into madness. Intriguingly, these three films represent a screening of disorder, corporeally, in three distinct modalities: first, with *Adèle H*, from outside the body, second, with *Camille Claudel*, from within the body, and, finally, with *La reine Margot*, from the liminal space between the outer and inner corporealities, namely, the skin. From objectification via subjectivity to abjection—an excellent triad of embodied cinematic disorders.

And last but by no means least, of course, there is the star herself, Isabelle Adjani: the woman upon whom so much has been projected and written, as if, like the three characters she has embodied above, she too must bear the brunt of her difference and the myths propagated about her—a cinematic disorder of others' imaginings, it has to be said. A trained stage actor who does not fit the mold of traditional film stardom in that she is uninterested in the trappings of celebrity, Adjani is an actor who works from her own interiority (hence her predilection for complex roles); she prefers not to rehearse the sequence about to be shot, but to come at it fresh, and on her terms, which earns her the label of "difficult." She is a woman whose name signified nothing distinctive to her spectators until it became public knowledge that she was the daughter of immigrant parents: her mother a German, her father an Algerian—a revelation that seemed to open the floodgates to certain scurrilous elements of the press to speculate not only on her Frenchness but also on whether or not she was dying of AIDS. She is an actor whose infrequent presence on the silver screen seemed to provide license for the media to speculate on her health; an actor who has become typecast in some critics' imaginary as the incarnation of "passionate and rebellious heroines often close to madness" (Delon and Provini 190), seen as "an hysteric" whose specialism is "schizophrenic characters" (191). And yet she is a woman of principle, outspoken on civil rights—which earns her the opprobrium of, amongst others, the National Front Party. As the daughter of a Muslim father, she is circumspect about nudity on screen, refusing frontal nudity (indeed her nude scene in *La reine Margot* with La Môle is a great rarity; and this is why the shot of her pubis in the rape scene is so shocking). She has been a long-standing supporter of SOS Racisme; she showed herself unafraid, at the 1989 César televised awards, to declaim from Salman Rushdie's *Satanic Verses* in support of the author and against the fatwa proclaimed on his life. A woman in her own right, a citizen of great courage, and a committed actor, her words of riposte on TF1's *Journal de 20 Heures* in January 1987 against rumors of her imminent death from AIDS serve just as much to echo the sentiments of this chapter in relation to cinematic disorders: "If you will, what is so horrible for me today is to feel obliged to come here and declare: 'I am not ill,' as if I'm supposed to say: 'I am not guilty of any crime.' It is monstrous that, in this day and age, people treat illness as if it were a crime, particularly in relation to AIDS, and that one has to justify oneself" (Adjani, as cited in Choulant 104).

Notes

My thanks to Gabór Gergely for his helpful feedback and Sandra Cook for some enlightening discussions on *La reine Margot*.

1. For a very full analysis of this film, I refer you to the excellent study by Gaspard Delon and Sandra Provini—it covers virtually every aspect of the film from production through to reception. Also, Julianne Pidduck's study is rich in its insights, examining the film from a more Anglo-Saxon feminist point of view.

2. Bregovic's film score to *La reine Margot* can be accessed on YouTube.

Works Cited

Bertière, Simone. *Les reines de France au temps des Valois*. Vol. 2, Fallois, 1994.
Choulant, Dominique. *Isabelle Adjani, la magnifique*. Mustang, 2014.
Delbée, Anne. *Une Femme*. Fayard, 1998.
Delon, Gaspard, and Sandra Provini. *Chéreau: La reine Margot*. Atlande, 2015.
"Film Music Stories: Camille Claudel #1." *YouTube*, uploaded by Gabriel Yared, 27 Nov. 2014, https://www.youtube.com/watch?v=pTCii3y704w.
Foucault, Michel. *Madness and Civilization: A History of Insanity in the Age of Reason*. Translated by Richard Howard, Tavistock, 1965.
Gourdin, Henri. *Les Hugo*. Grasset, 2016.
Hayward, Susan. *French Costume Drama of the 1950s: Fashioning Politics in Film*. Intellect, 2010.
Holmes, Diana, and Robert Ingram. *François Truffaut*. Manchester UP, 1988.
Kerri Mahon, Elizabeth. *Scandalous Women: The Lives and Loves of History's Most Notorious Women*. Penguin, 2011.
Kristeva, Julia. *Powers of Horror: An Essay on Abjection*. Translated by Leon S. Roudiez, Columbia UP, 1982.

Lang, Jack. "Jack Lang: La culture et l'économie, c'est un même combat." *L'economiste.com*, 15 Sept. 2015, https://www.leconomiste.com/article/977258-jack-lang-la-culture-et-leconomie-cest-un-meme-combat.

Le Normand-Romain, Antoinette. *Camille Claudel et Rodin*. Hermann, 2014.

Meurice, Émile. "La folie d'amour d'Adèle H." Espace d'échanges du site IDRES sur la systémique, 2010, http://spip.systemique.eu/IMG/article_PDF/article_a702.pdf.

Paris, Reine-Marie. *Camille Claudel*. Gallimard, 1984.

Pidduck, Julianne. *La Reine Margot*. I. B. Tauris, 2005.

Pinet, Hélène, and Reine-Marie Paris. *Camille Claudel: Le génie est comme un miroir*. Gallimard, 2003.

3

Musical Madness on Hangover Square

MURRAY POMERANCE

A Flaming Creature

LATE IN THE NIGHT OF November 4, 1605, the Catholic dissident Guy Fawkes, joined by signature and pledge to Robert Catesby's band of Catholic conspirators and thus bound to the destruction of the House of Lords (and the concomitant assassination of James I), was arrested while protecting his treasure of dynamite. Tried with others, convicted, and sentenced to be drawn and quartered (i.e., partially hanged; then led semiconscious to a table where, nude, he would be castrated, disemboweled, and beheaded, in that order), he managed to leap from the scaffold and end his own life. By Parliament's January 1606 Observance of 5th November Act (repealed 1859), the intended revolution date was affixed as a national celebration and memorial, with fires, fireworks (after the mid-seventeenth century when, owing to the European fascination for chinoiserie, they were imported from China), shouting, and considerable merriment, and a general reconstitution through imaginative recountings of the lethal anti-royalist plot. In some locations, the party erupted into testy Protestant-Catholic squabbles. By the eighteenth and nineteenth centuries, bonfire parties were much in vogue in England on what had come by then to be known as Guy Fawkes Day, or Bonfire Night, with rough-constructed stuffed, impaled, and bemasked effigies of Fawkes set alight, then tossed to the top of the gaily flaming heaps.

It takes but little imagination to figure either the filmmaker John Brahm (1893–1982)—born in Austria, later escaped to Hollywood from Hitler's Germany—or the English-born screenwriter Barré Lyndon (Alfred Edgar; 1896–1972) culturally and aesthetically conversant with the tone and raucous imagery of Bonfire Night. Thus, the placement of a November 5 bonfire at the heart of their Twentieth Century Fox production *Hangover Square* (1945) might well seem easy and unsurprising. But Guy Fawkes bonfires do not appear in the source material for the film by Patrick Hamilton (1904–62). Born and raised in East Sussex, nearby Lewes—during the nineteenth and twentieth centuries a principle site of annual Guy Fawkes celebrations—Hamilton did not apotheosize the conception of the bonfire at the heart of his novel *Hangover Square: A Story of Darkest Earl's Court*. What appears in the film is thus an expansion, even an accretion, upon the potent original story to which Lyndon and Brahm are so faithful, bringing into the film's structure, and the viewer's consideration, the question of how the Guy Fawkes bonfire, and the idea of consummatory and ritual memorialization, might provide a pathway into appreciation of the story.

In the case of *Hangover Square*, November 5 is the date of a particular murder—one must say "particular" because this is a crime drama and there are to be found a great number of murders here. A desperate and angry composer of serious and passionate music, George Harvey Bone (Laird Cregar [1913–44]), having been borne beyond the limits of frustration and forbearance by the impertinent persistence of his lady friend Netta Longdon (Linda Darnell, replacing Marlene Dietrich, who abandoned the project) to have one of the themes he has been working out for an important concerto recrafted for her personal use in a nightclub routine aimed at the undiscerning masses, finds that he can tolerate her demands no more, nor, equally, her crass personality, and strangles her in his sitting room with the thick velvet cord of his draperies. The body he drops upon, then rolls up in, his Persian carpet. He hoists it onto his shoulders and marches out into the streets where, mirabile dictu, boisterous youths are shouting and racing to a Guy Fawkes bonfire. They have piled up consumables to a height of some twenty feet or so, a towering pyramid, and the flames have been lit. Bone ascends the ladder with Netta's camouflaged corpse still on his shoulder, and deposits his package, a crude effigy, at the pinnacle.

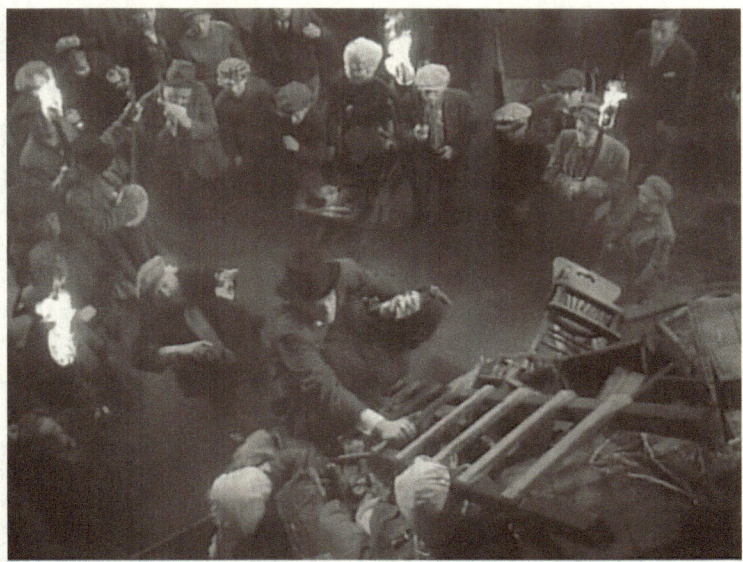

Figure 3.1. George (Laird Cregar) mounting the Guy Fawkes bonfire with Netta's (Linda Darnell) disguised body in *Hangover Square*.

The murder victim will certainly be reduced to ash, thus made unidentifiable, unlocatable, unknowable as a corpse. The murder is perfect, so much so that it rankled the Breen Office, which wrote June 29, 1944, demanding elimination of the strangling, "a crime that could very readily be imitated" (Breen to Joy); and again March 28, 1945, requiring that the "scene showing cord being put around Netta's neck, when being strangled by George" should be cut and that showing "George putting Netta's body on bonfire" be reduced. Reduced? One can imagine Brahm & Cie incinerating the footage until it was ash itself.

From one point of view, it would not be doing a disservice to this chilling film to say that Bone is, simply enough, a serial killer; that Netta is far from his first victim, although we do not meet them all; that, in fact, stirred into action—it would better suit him to say, thrust away from the musical meditations of his everyday life—by the unexpected sonic intrusions of noisemakers from early modernist society (cars with horns and brakes; even nearby horsecarts clattering on the paving stones outside his window in Hangover Square), he finds himself plummeting sharply into a black trance, a state of being foreign to his creative self, and thus becoming the pariah who (apparently) skulks off into the night to find some vaguely sacrificial (and always female) victim. The Bone killings entirely notwithstanding, it is the sounds that do it, both to Bone and to us, producers of *reduction*, barging as they do, quite sharply, into (and lowering to the gutter) the complacent creative euphoria out of which he delivers his startling and evocative melodies. Our Bone wants nothing but to sit at his piano, or to daydream of sitting there. He is, without doubt, a musical soul, from top to bottom. And indeed, the short-lived Laird Cregar who gave this performance was no less musical than Bone, having himself performed, live on camera, all the piano work in the film, especially the brilliant Bernard Herrmann concerto with which the story ends (this arrangement is virtually unheard-of in Hollywood representations of pianism, since most actors cannot play the piano at all and those who can do not fare well with difficult challenges, like the Herrmann music). "Cregar was thrilled that Lyndon had changed George Harvey Bone from the jobless loser of the novel to a genius composer," writes Gregory Mank. "The character star had been taking singing and piano lessons and hoped to showcase his talent; Fox even promised him he could perform some of his own compositions" (328). But, returning from a stock engagement, Mank continues, Cregar "read the shooting script of *Hangover Square* and absolutely refused to play it. 'First thing you know,' said Cregar, 'I'll be known as the Bette Davis of 20th Century-Fox'" (329). Very like Bone, Cregar was overweight, depressive, self-absorbed, morosely inward. Zanuck put him on an eight-week suspension, but, as reported Louella Parsons, "he apparently thought better of his revolt and is back on the lot."

Cregar's flippiness may cause any observer to wonder whether he was just a picky professional watching carefully to preserve his career from tarnish through incompetent performance, or just mad. And one may reasonably have the same problem deciphering Bone. The killing sprees occur entirely outside his consciousness, as though in dreams. And the relation between his violent impulse and his civilly restrained creativity is often attributed to the extremely creative, that is, those who inhabit a space at the very margins of cultured bourgeois discourse. *Hangover Square* participates in a long-lived Hollywood fictional constitution of the mad musician, the creative genius who cannot in his melodic transports remain sane; or the figure who trespasses across the boundaries of everyday routine by way of musical prodigy.

Less interesting, perhaps, than the twistings of the film's plot—the estimable Lyndon's credits include *The Greatest Show on Earth* (1952) and

The War of the Worlds (1953)—is this odd and challenging conjunction between musical genius and murderous impulse, the abject craziness of Bone; that to conceive a multiple killer it might make sense to compose a composer; or, to explore the inner life of a musical genius it might seem logical to have him secretly desiring other people's deaths. Since I write as a person whose youth was somewhat devoted to concert pianism, the fascination here is largely personal to the degree that Bone/Cregar's keyboard activity brings to mind my own; and I can attest not only that violence against the human body does not play a role in practicing at the keyboard, or in preparing to play a work like the Herrmann concerto, but also that, indeed, while concentrating on the myriad difficulties of fingering, phrasing, pedaling, and, in general, bringing a score to life, the human body as an object of interest entirely disappears. I know of absolutely no linkage between the musical and the criminal impulses—not to seem too much to be protesting innocence—nor does it seem deeply realistic to me, at all, that this somnambulistic murderer (Bone always returns from his escapades with no memory of them) might be taking a vicious fugue from melodious invention. That little whistling ditty offered by the horrific murderer in Lang's *M* (1931) aside, killers needn't be musical; needn't have tonal talents; and none of the many musicians I have met—I may count among them Rudolf Serkin, John Browning, Karel Ančerl, Leonard Bernstein, and Jessye Norman—have struck me as killers.

What, then, are we to think is happening in *Hangover Square*? What sort of creature is being born out of Bone's fleshy (!) music, that he himself does not and cannot recognize and that terrorizes the civil world? Indeed, looking at the film as a study in psychopathology, one can say it hardly matters that this composer/pianist's dark life is that of a killer, since he must have plenty of *cauchemars* that bring on his dissonant chords, his jerky strident rhythms, his power. Serial killing is dramatic—wonderful—for a script, a creepy mystery for viewers. But any really naughty activity could have done to make Hamilton's (and Brahms's) point at its simplest. Bone the bookseller; Bone the entymologist; Bone the clerk in the Office of Civil Surveying. Why and how do we imagine, inside him, that creative genius, most especially musical genius, breeds uncivilized, uncontrollable forces?

I think the pathway toward an answer here lies not with Cregar the performer: there are legion films in which sophisticated musical talents are configured as psychologically warped, not least Irving Rapper's *Deception* (1946), with its maniacally obsessed composer/conductor Hollenius (Claude

Rains); or Wiene's 1924 *The Hands of Orlac*, with Conrad Veidt as an archcriminal-cum-keyboard genius. It is neither Cregar himself nor the grimy London square in which he lives that pinions this construction, but some deeply held conviction in our profoundly anti-intellectual culture, played upon by this among a long history of filmmaking teams, that positions mental instability and musical creativity together in a diabolical duet. Let me suggest a few factors that might weigh on this problem.

Terminal Status Anxiety

It gives many outsiders pleasure to think of music as an affiliation with the ineffable gods of harmony and wind, of composition as both esoteric and divine. Both musical inspiration and musical invention are easily thought elevated, even ethereal pursuits, affected by incalculable, indiscernible forces. Yet one can also understand that, like carpentry, composition is work, and involves the materiality of craft as much as the spirit's touch. C. Wright Mills wrote sensitively of the craftsman's labor: "The craftsman's work is the mainspring of the only life he knows; he does not flee from work into a separate sphere of leisure; he brings to his non-working hours the values and qualities developed and employed in his working time. His idle conversation is shop talk. . . . The leisure William Morris called for was 'leisure to think about our work, that faithful daily companion'" (223).

The composer, to be explicit but also pragmatic, is always hearing music, always in the middle of composition. Mills's implication is that there is nothing outside the creative act, at least nothing of relevance to the craftsman. So it is that the craftsman Bone must be startled out of his musical consciousness by intrusive sound—this sound I take to be the standard byproduct of modern urban development, so that he is shown as a man, or at least a reflection of the kind of man, whose sensibilities developed before the technical clashes of urban civilization gained prominence. The craftsman, further, must continually hold himself open to the influences of life, must be not only sensitive but intentionally vulnerable. Bone, that is, cannot maintain his composition if he closes himself off to the kinds of intrusion that are corrupting him. "In order to give his work the freshness of creativity," Mills adds, "the craftsman must at times open himself up to those influences that only affect us when our attentions are relaxed. . . . Leisure may occur in such intermittent periods as are necessary for individuality in his work" (223). Leisure, that is to say, preoccupation. Might we think of killing as Bone's leisure? His working concentration is surely disrupted, devastated by urban progress. Mills quotes Henry James's essay on Balzac: we have lost "that unstrenuous, brooding sort of attention required to produce or appreciate works of art."

But the all-inclusiveness of the composer's life, the vast reach of the territory—symbolic and real—from which the musician takes inspiration are not without anxiety. The surrender of the creative psychology to musings and intimations, fundamental to musical composition, is difficult and painful to sustain when one feels the work demeaned, overlooked, and finally unheard, because unperformed. That is, if to be a creative musical artist one slaves at labor, and is to some extent rendered passive and powerless in that slaving, the completion one seeks is a polished work that has its platform. What can happen, then, when the musician-craftsman finds his "faithful daily companion," his artistic work, attacked by a bourgeoisie ill equipped to appreciate it in the context of the frame he would most wish for it? What happens when Netta Longdon hears Bone at the piano and uses her sexual guile (she has already seduced him) to demand that he hand over his melody, part of his work in progress, so that she can use (read, abuse) it as part of her (cheap) music hall performance?

The craftsman-composer's status as artist is continually to be fought for, after all, since he does not emerge from a social class, or in a cultural context, where that status is conferred automatically by virtue of his labor and then assured through a regular system of respect and honor. The labor of Bone's every moment at the keyboard is thus doubled. His attentions are riveted upon the ongoing heartbeat of his "companion," in this case the concerto; but his fears are directed against anyone who would interrupt or corrupt his musical work in any way. With strange noises, such as the city routinely produces and such as he is in no position to thwart or, with his sensitive hearing, avoid, the fears trigger a fugue state in which his personality morphs and his delicate sensibilities turn brutal. But with Netta, his girl, the object of his loving fascination, whatever can he do but accede? On the spot, he permits her. She seizes the tune, bastardizes it, makes it crudely popular. But this ruins his artistic prospect and instigates "the fear of failing and disgracing oneself in the eyes of others," a state of affairs that, as Alain de Botton reminds us, is "an inevitable consequence of harbouring ambitions, of favouring one set of outcomes over another and of having regard for individuals besides oneself" (292), all of which outcomes are inescapable if one's music is to be heard—heard seriously, heard in its *form*. Here is Stravinsky telling his pal Robert Craft about Diaghilev's first response to the beginning of *Le sacre du printemps*: "In spite of his surprise when I played him the beginning of the *Sacre* (*Les Augures Printanières*) at the piano, in spite of his at first ironic attitude to the long line of repeated chords, he quickly realized that the reason was something other than my inability to compose more diversified music; he realized at once the seriousness of my new musical speech, its importance and the advantage of capitalizing on it" (Stravinsky and Craft, *Conversations*). Netta being no Diaghilev, Bone can restrain himself no longer—since she has dirtied his purest love. She must die—die not only in fact but in myth, so that after he has garroted her and rolled her up in his Persian carpet, she is to be consumed by the (Guy Fawkes) fire that purifies.

No murderer, Bernard Herrmann was in other ways an elegant model for George Bone. He persisted in seeing himself—arrogantly, some of his detractors thought—as a serious composer, far above the demands of motion pictures. Of other filmic work than his own he complained that it was a resort to the "lowest common denominator"; he quit the academy because "there's no point to belonging to an organization in which one is judged by one's inferiors—not one's peers" (Thomas). He was on social terms with Gerald Finzi, Ralph Vaughan-Williams, and other "serious" composers. As his biographer Steven Smith writes, "Despite the many achievements—his film work with Orson Welles, Alfred Hitchcock, and others, his fifteen years as conductor of the CBS Symphony—Herrmann's life was an ongoing battle with demons: lack of recognition as a 'serious' composer, his having chosen the high-salary, invisible medium of film to work in; failure to see the performance of the composition he considered his most important; and his inability for twenty-five years to secure a conducting post" (3). His close friend, the writer Abraham Polonsky, testified to Herrmann's high aspirations: "I first heard Ives with him. I first heard Berg and *Wozzeck* with him. I went to the Met with him—I don't know how he got the tickets, but he did. We went to concerts of the League of Composers. And Benny knew everybody. . . . He could find his way into the most sacred places; he'd say, 'C'mon, we're going to so-and-so's house'—and while we were there we would meet seventeen famous people. But Benny was a musical climber, not a social climber" (18).

His continual insistence that "he was not a 'film composer' but a composer who worked in film" (2) is reflected in Bone's offended, high-toned, initial rejection of Netta's cooing imprecations to have his music for her act. But she has caught and caged his heart, and he has no voice to refuse her.

And when Bone's concerto crashes to its conclusion, Sir Henry Chapman (Alan Napier) and the retired Scotland Yard man Middleton (George Sanders), who traps the killer at the concert, are not standing in ovation but perched outside in the snow, pronouncing the final words upon the affair. "It is important," wrote the film's producer Robert Bassler to Brahm, "that the lines be read with sadness and resignation and weltschmerz." Bassler wanted to "imply the worth of Bone's music without actually using words like great and magnificent, which might be an overstatement, in view of the fact that we are dealing, as you pointed out, with Herrmann, not Beethoven." "Why didn't he try to get out?" Sir Henry asks about Bone. And Middleton replies, "It's better this way, sir."

Ear

A still more important consideration, however, is the composer's ear and its susceptibility to intrusion. Craft details life at Stravinsky's house in Los Angeles, including interruptions from telephones, "which can be expected to split through thoughts and feelings about thirty times a day, normally, and on eight resonant extensions," and

> other rackets: a piano-practising neighbour, very conscientious at scales; and another, equally dutiful with a bugle and set of "traps"; and birds, as dependably melodious at night as the Hi-Fi canaries at Forest Lawn; and ear-piercing smog-warning sirens (or are they Viet Cong warnings?); and helicopters, for whom the Stravinsky residence appears to be an important marker on an aerial freeway. As no one could be more sensitive to these auditory tortures than the composer—he still flinches at any noise a full second faster than anyone else—it is a marvel that he can work at all. (Stravinsky and Craft, *Dialogues* 17)

Sensitive to *auditory tortures*. Flinches at any noise. This could be a description of our Bone, except that Bone's flinching is considerably the more material, indeed choreographic, as he puts down his hands, lifts himself up, meanders away in a muscular trance.

Is not musicianship a hyperattunement to the acoustic dimension? The composer is not translating from his visual experience, after all, but has developed his sensibilities to a certain extremity, a vibrational responsiveness. One could say he hears the world: in *Saboteur* (1942),

Hitchcock has a hospitable blind hermit announce, after playing Delius quite beautifully on his piano, that he sees with his ears. Nuances of harmony and form are signal in composition, but there are no nuances more powerful, more influential, more catastrophic in potential outcome, than noises, the world that subtends—but is not—one's work. We need to recognize in appreciating *Hangover Square* that it is set in early modernity, a time of considerable machination and intensively increased social pressure as regards space, action, and privacy. Mechanical sounds have a notable tendency to permeate space, to transcend boundaries. Bone is unable to secrete himself in a wholly protected sonic environment, and even were he to succeed in doing so this environment would offer little by way of inspiration. He is a victim of his circumstances, and in his susceptibility to noise he is, as Craft suggested of Stravinsky's frequent experience, tortured.

The musician is thus especially prone to losing control of himself because he has given up control in the first place, resonating with the sounds of his world, being a receiver. If we add to his conundrum some rudimentary knowledge of historical circumstance, we can see that a man like Bone thinks, in his creative moments, of euphony, not cacophony. He has to have been influenced by Glazounov (who said Stravinsky had no ear!), by Prokofiev, by Strauss, perhaps by the very young Rachmaninoff. If Schoenberg's *Verklärte Nacht* appeared at the end of the nineteenth century, his twelve-tone method didn't arrive until the 1940s. The *Skandalkonzert* was in 1913—the film is set in 1910—but Bone is writing out of a much earlier ethos, while being, at the same time, conscious of his new, urbanized world and its sounds. The music he writes is thus, at the same time, desperately melodic and throbbingly rhythmic, a derivation from two ages, the romantic and the modern.

This painful dualism is evident as *Hangover Square* terminates. The finale is structured as a tour de force dramatization of Bone in concert. His musical chum Barbara (Faye Marlowe) is seated in the front row. Her father, Sir Henry, is conducting the orchestra, in the gigantic atrium of his own elegant home (presumably in Belgravia). This glittering soiree represents and constitutes the apogee of elegant urban culture, and Bone at the keyboard, performing his own magnum opus, is the London culturati's diamond in the rough. The police are after him, and will enter the premises while he is playing, finally forcing him to leap up from the keys—Barbara dutifully rushes to take his place, without losing a beat. As the concerto winds toward its cataclysmic conclusion, we hear in the music the kind of strained harmonies and definitively pronounced, even petrified chords that stand in for the now glaringly absent composer, *creator spiritus* and tormented body. The body is for him an extension of the eardrum, a fleshy *tympanum* sensitive to all invocations, all agonies, to every hope of harmony and regretful defeat. Soon he is back at the keyboard, and the pounding finale has arrived. He has meanwhile set the house afire, the flames are leaping, and the audience, including Barbara and her father, have fled outside. The orchestra members, too, rush away—an ingenious dramatic effect, as in Bone's (that is, Herrmann's) actual composition there is only a piano part at the very end. The last thing to be heard is a chain of complex, triple forte, extended and echoing, portentous, and disharmonious chords, *sostenuto e molto espressivo*. Only the piano, Bone's companion, "speaks" the final words of the film—musical words, not text—as the grand house, waiting for his final notes, goes up in flames. As the revised final shooting script of August 3, 1944 stipulated, "The last chord of all comes from beyond a screen of flame." Claudia Gorbman addresses the finality of the music when she writes, "Musical temporality wins out. *The music must finish*, no matter what; he has become enslaved to musical logic" (159).

If urban life in modernity is mechanical and repetitive; if the social press in aggravation is a lonely crowd; if (as was described with Stravinsky) interruption, not tranquility, is the order of the day; and if the musician is placed so as to hear, vibrate, and respond to this world, there can be little surprise in his movement toward extremity under adverse conditions. Is Bone psychopathologically deranged, then, in a final consideration? Is he mad, the archetype of the "mad musician" to which audiences by 1945 had so thoroughly become accommodated? Are his connections to reality broken, his faculties for social interaction dismembered? Or may we say, with some authority, that this "madman" is a craftsman victimized by his circumstances?

A Victim of Sound

The point, however, is that Bone *is* deemed mad, not only by the authorities but by his closest intimates and even the girl who loves him. Cinematographer Joseph LaShelle euphemized, "I took the rose-colored glasses of normalcy off the camera, and put on a pair that looked at the world with the warped and misproportioned vision of insanity" (*Hangover Square* pressbook). Further, so transparent is the diagnosis, and so clearly symptomatic the case, from the earliest larval stage, as we see in the film's beginning all the way through to the monstrous culminating development, that the audience, too, is committed to the belief in this sharply portrayed linkage between musical genius and madness. What, after all, can it be that so neatly and crisply effects this affirmation but the simple fact that the composer-performer Bone hears voices.

He is privy to clandestine voicings of melody, and his calling is to transcribe them so that, read by instrumentalists, they can be made audible—perhaps even pleasurable—to the multitudes. What he hears no one else can hear—not until much later, after he has done his transformative work. Who sings to him—if in truth this is what happens—sings to no one else: he calls her his muse. Netta's corruption lay in her desire to infiltrate that private relationship, trying to seduce the muse to her side. The point with composers, always, is that they hear the melody *before* they write it down, that by hearing they are forcibly displaced from social intercourse, thrown into Caliban's cave, where a thousand twangling instruments ring about their ears. Bone is not only a man with highly developed hearing, he is, in effect, an ear. His entire body composes that *tympanum* of which I made mention, the taut skin that vibrates with stimulation. He is more capable than the other characters in this film, or in his society, of being touched, affected, wounded, tickled. Capable so much more than others that his sensitivity is developed as a social problem. The concerto, as finally we hear it—the work is in a single movement, of roughly ten minutes' duration—not only testifies to Bone's having heard voices; it *is* the voices he heard, but long after he heard them. We must remind ourselves that he has been composing all through the film; that the finale is only a public rendition of the—until now—hidden score.

Shall we say the "madness" of the musician comes from the fact that he knows the score! The rest of us—surely all the other characters in *Hangover Square*—muddle through our existence from sentiment to sentiment, without a clearly organized formation of feeling such as Bone is able to accomplish as he writes. He vibrates and finally whines with sensation, a wholly improper reaction to circumstances that others think mundane. But if in his sensitivity he is uncommonly prone to musical inspiration, we must account him generally attuned to—indeed a victim of—sound. What the modern world has done to such creatures is an all-out attack, to reproduce the effect of which the filmmakers have augmented the sound level of the intrusive noises Bone hears, that drive him off to murder. He loses track of himself, forgets himself—which is to say, his musical impulse is replaced by something grimmer and without redeemable quality. Gregory Mank archly but uncomprehendingly writes that his "schizophrenic character switches from gentle genius to suave criminology aficionado" (328). For Bone, the murderous action is an uncontrolled sonic response, an unshaped music. I think it erroneous to read him as a double personality, a civilized musician harboring an inner violent soul, a madman, bent on killing; and to suspect that even in a more tranquil surrounding he would—quite insanely—behave the same way. The film works to show us how the forces of modernity act to destabilize and wrack a certain devotedly refined sensibility; as Alton Cook wrote in his review, "Mr. Cregar is presented as a musician driven into murderous trances by discordant sounds." Cregar himself "shed 100 pounds during production period of 'Hangover Square,'" his labor "evidenced especially in agonized close-ups of him as the brilliant but unbalanced composer" (Thirer). The film was shot in sequence in order that the weight loss could be undertaken and sustained by the performer, but he did not survive it. He died shortly after production wrapped, of a heart attack on December 9, 1944.

Works Cited

Bassler, Robert. Letter to John Brahm. 11 October 1944. John Brahm Collection, U of Southern California.
Breen, Joseph I. Letter to Col. Jason S. Joy, 20th Century-Fox. 29 June 1944. Production Code Administration Records, Margaret Herrick Library, Academy of Motion Picture Arts and Sciences, Beverly Hills.
———. Letter to Col. Jason S. Joy, 20th Century-Fox. 28 Mar. 1945. Production Code Administration Records, Margaret Herrick Library, Academy of Motion Picture Arts and Sciences, Beverly Hills.
Cook, Alton. "'Hangover Square' Has Nothing to Do with Lost Week Ends." *New York World-Telegram*, 7 February 1945.
De Botton, Alain. *Status Anxiety*. Vintage, 2005.
Gorbman, Claudia. *Unheard Melodies: Narrative Film Music*. Indiana UP, 1987.
Hangover Square pressbook, U of Southern California.
Herrmann, Bernard. Concerto for *Hangover Square*, piano reduction score. Davidson Library, U of California at Santa Barbara.
Mank, Gregory William. *Hollywood Cauldron: Thirteen Horror Films from the Genre's Golden Age*. McFarland, 1994.
Mills, C. Wright. *White Collar: The American Middle Classes*. 50th anniversary ed., Oxford UP, 2002.
Parsons, Louella. "Hollywood." *Chicago Herald American*, 11 Aug. 1944.

Smith, Steven C. *A Heart at Fire's Center: The Life and Music of Bernard Herrmann.* U of California P, 2002.
Stravinsky, Igor, and Robert Craft. *Conversations with Igor Stravinsky.* Faber and Faber, 1959.
———. *Dialogues.* U of California P, 1982.
Thirer, Irene. Review. *New York Post*, 8 February 1945.
Thomas, Kevin. "Film Composer Settles a Score." *Los Angeles Times*, 4 February 1968.

4

Screening Multiple Personality Disorder in the Age of Kinsey

Lizzie and *The Three Faces of Eve*

R. BARTON PALMER

Disease as Cultural Map

SHIRLEY JACKSON'S *THE BIRD'S NEST* (1954) introduced many in the fiction-reading public to what the medical establishment then termed multiple personality disorder (MPD). Since the publication of the second edition of the *Diagnostic and Statistical Manual of Mental Disorders* in 1968, this somewhat exotic condition, whose manifestations are rich with dramatic possibilities, has been officially designated as dissociative identity disorder, nomenclature that unfortunately omits any reference to the condition's most characteristic and striking manifestation: the coexistence and problematic interaction of distinct selves within the same individual (see American Psychiatric Association). As her biographer Ruth Franklin observes, in *The Bird's Nest*, Jackson was appealing to much that was *dans le vent*: "Postwar Americans generally showed an increased awareness of mental health issues," largely because of the thousands of returning veterans suffering with what was then called "battle fatigue," whose treatment was managed by the growing legions of the nation's psychiatrists (Franklin 332; see Hattenhauer for further details). It was perhaps inevitable that Jackson's novel would appeal to Hollywood. A film version, under the title *Lizzie*, directed by Hugo Haas and produced by Kirk Douglas's Bryna Films, was released in 1957. Somewhat remarkably, yet another film dealing with MPD, and interestingly connected to *Lizzie*, appeared the same year: *The Three Faces of Eve*, directed and produced by Nunnally Johnson, who also wrote the screenplay. More on *Eve* in the second part of this chapter.

In the early 1950s, MPD was known mostly to the medical and then still-developing psychiatric professions, as well as to many in the intelligentsia. To be sure, provided with a fictionalized pharmacological explanation, MPD of a sort figures as the theme of one of the nineteenth century's most popular novels, *The Strange Case of Dr. Jekyll and Mr. Hyde* (1886). And yet this tale was more or less ignored as an exploration of what happens when a single individual comes to harbor multiple selves in conflict. Instead, besides being seen by some as a slant treatment of the evils of drink, Robert Louis Stevenson's "case" mostly prompted moralizing readings that interpreted the unlikely pairing of the ostensibly good doctor with a homicidal, lascivious other as corresponding to the inner conflict that Paul describes in Romans 7:23. Certainly, Jekyll, who is no unbeliever, can, like the apostle, "see a different law in the members of my body, waging war against the law of my mind and making me a prisoner of the law of sin which is in my members" (New American Standard Bible). In conformity with Christian dogma, the habitus of Jekyll's indulgence in Hyde's unrestrained lust and violence ends with this self-destructive other's disruption of his erstwhile creator's only superficial virtue and easily abandoned respectability.

As commentators have not been slow to remark, in portraying this "fall" the novel engages with what was for Victorian England a complex class issue: the transgressive appeal to those in the ruling elite of a social landscape that promises a pulse-quickening, yet ultimately degrading escape from a life founded on propriety and restraint. A multiplicity of selves that are separate in matters of behavior and conscience enables a form of downlow living that is uniquely untroubled, even if morally reprehensible, until Hyde threatens to dominate, marking out as destructively hubristic this use of science to technologize for no good purpose the innate evilness of human nature. As Stephen Marcus has chronicled and anatomized, Victorian readers had a taste for such material, perhaps best exemplified by *My Secret Life*, signed mysteriously by "Walter." Walter offers an extended chronicle of his somewhat amazing sexual exploits, the indulgences of his "other" self, that are staged, like those of Hyde, in the netherworld of London's most disreputable districts (see Marcus for further details).

Unlike the moralizing *Jekyll and Hyde*, *The Bird's Nest* thoroughly psychologizes its case of MPD, with the narrative tracing the Freudian-based therapeutic approach of the tellingly named Victor Wright to what he identifies, with apparent correctness, as a mental illness rather than, as he first suspects, demonic possession. Wright guides his suffering patient, Elizabeth Richmond, toward wholeness by encouraging the best adjusted and most sociable of her four quarrelsome selves to dominate. While illustrating the power of science to identify and cure a disabling condition, Jackson's story is no simple endorsement of the Enlightenment technologizing of cures for existential discontent, whose root cause might well be, as the later Freud suspected, the social rules that restrict the free and pleasurable exercise of both will and appetite. In the novel, as in *Jekyll*, science, and the power to transform that it affords, is presented as morally problematic. With no little arrogance, and in clear violation of his Hippocratic oath, Wright stipulates that his patient is an "empty vessel"; he proclaims that his task is "enabling the *child* to rebuild" (emphasis mine), even as he recognizes that her current state of mental equilibrium might just be temporary (Jackson 249). More troubling, the doctor feels himself empowered to "select what is finest and most elevating from our own experience and bestow," a principle of human "management" that might have been drawn directly from Aldous Huxley's *Brave New World* (249). This scientific arrogance is banished from the film version; Haas's Wright, though his Christian name is still Victor, as in the novel, manifests no Frankensteinian ambitions.

In line with the neo-Freudianism of Frankfurt School psychiatrist Erich Fromm, then fast becoming one of America's most respected self-help advisors, Elizabeth experiences a sense of wholeness and an improved outlook on life. She proclaims to Wright, who solicits a closing comment on his efforts at her rehabilitation: "I am happy. . . . I know who I am" (Jackson 236). Nothing could be further from the self-destruction to which Jekyll's better half, recognizing the impossibility of otherwise banishing Hyde, is finally driven. And yet *The Bird's Nest* interestingly replays Stevenson's moralizing view of personality multiplicity, if only in a minor key. None of Elizabeth's repressed selves can truly be called evil, but they prevent her life from being anything but an internecine struggle between competing forces and agendas. Betsy, the troublemaker, is at best mischievous, eager, like a spoiled child, to get her own way at the expense of all the others. When she emerges and takes charge, she prevents Elizabeth from continuing her life as a rational adult, even as she enlists both Beth and Betsy in an effort to destroy whatever standing in the world that Elizabeth has managed to achieve. Only with Wright's assistance is this "empty vessel" filled with the makings of a personality that can take itself as a sure object of consciousness. Intervention reduces a troublesome multiplicity to a socially functional singularity that contests the notion of constant dispersal of selfness that Erving Goffman would in 1959 argue is the inevitable result of our interactions with others. Note that in the novel Elizabeth is happy because she has become the object of her own consciousness; the novel only hints at a continuing relationship with Wright.

The Bird's Nest incorporated interesting elements of the female gothic genre, and these were more strongly emphasized in the screenplay that Mel Dinelli prepared for *Lizzie* (on the female gothic, see Modleski). Centering on the defense of a woman's sanity that climaxes in the extirpation of disturbing, sometimes malevolent inner presences eager to take her over, the novel invites comparison with Daphne Du Maurier's bestseller *Rebecca* and Patrick Hamilton's stage hit, *Gaslight*. These properties both met with popular and critical success when adapted for the screen by, respectively, Alfred Hitchcock (1940) and George Cukor (1944). Jackson's story of an exotic mental disorder, and its successful treatment by an engaged and highly competent psychiatrist, offered a different take on themes already made popular by Hollywood and in the popular fiction that supported it, such as Olive Higgins Prouty's *Now, Voyager* (1941; film version, Irving Rapper, 1942). *Lizzie* was a film that, according to the trailer, offers what is ostensibly a fact-based dramatization of an actual mental disorder, one that makes the essential Freudian point about self: we are subject to powerful inner forces whose presence we only barely suspect, if at all.

In dramatizing the success of psychiatric treatment in ending a form of human misery that no other form of medical or spiritual intervention could remedy, *Lizzie* fits neatly into what Gabbard and Gabbard in *Psychiatry and the Cinema* describe as the brief golden age of Hollywood's fascination with the ostensibly remarkable power of psychiatry to combat and contain mental illness. This film also had a clear and forcefully presented cultural agenda. Dinelli, Haas, and Douglas pushed the story toward an exploration of compulsive female promiscuity, tangentially connected to MPD properly speaking. In the film, the disorder becomes an allegorical framework of sorts, a way of probing and representing the distinct and conflictual aspects of personality, seen, according to psychiatric theory, as etic, corresponding to some universal menu of variation, or emic, reflecting cultural experience, including values and patterns of behavior. *Lizzie* features unexpectedly graphic representations of an aggressive and single-minded interest in sex that is turned loose, as it were, by the process of the disorder from its "containment" within a woman who is shy and shows no interest in men. In a significant departure from the novel, Elizabeth is threatened by a self, who calls herself Lizzie and who proudly announces to her Aunt Morgen, in whose house she resides, that she is a "slut" after the woman comes home early to find her niece lustfully kissing and pawing one of her coworkers. This is only one of the several lovemaking (if that is the correct term) encounters that are staged between the pair. Such a dramatic confrontation, in which Morgen learns the truth of Elizabeth's recently unexplained behavior, must have seemed too sensational to be omitted from the trailer, even if prospective viewers had to read lips to figure out what Lizzie unexpectedly shouts out. It appears to be not only an accusation but also a confession.

Interestingly, the screenplay's fabrication of a sensationalized, eroticized, and evil multiple to give the plot an antagonist is very much in line with Jackson's dark vision (often sometimes mistakenly simplified as "gothic"). As Darryl Hattenhauer remarks of her fiction in general, her protagonists dispose of personalities that are always "liminal, protean, and processual," subject to the power of unsuspected forces that may emerge from within; in a larger sense, they are simply human reflexes of the "defamiliarization and estrangement" that haunts everyday living (26, 29). To be sure, the film presents as intriguing its revelation of uncontrollable multiplicity as a horror story in which outer and inner versions of the self struggle for control. According to its trailer, however, *Lizzie* also speaks to a titillating and more general fact of female nature: "How many girls admit to having more than one personality—or even wanting to?" Moreover, indeed it is true that the film spectacularizes the emergence of a transgressive dominatrix, who calls herself Lizzie. She has long been concealed, almost unbelievably, within the shy, unconfident, and decidedly unglamorous Elizabeth. The film's frank naughtiness is presented at first as liberating, which it is, if only in part, as will become evident. Similar themes dominate in *Eve*, even if they lack such bold development.

To be sure, the two MPD films of 1957 share a Stevensonian focus on sexual moralism. In particular, they spectacularize an assertive womanly desire that resonates with what James Jones observes was an American culture at the time that remained "anxious and ambivalent" about the issue, "placing little emphasis on women's erotic pleasure," though there were signs that this was changing (Jones 707; see Reumann 96–127 for a discussion of this period of cultural flux). Both films can be fairly characterized as "progressive" in according representational space to selves that are sexually transgressive. As explained below, this issue is soft-pedaled in *Eve*, in which female infidelity is handled in a light-hearted way. That film's success should be traced largely to Joanne Woodward's engaging and sympathetic performance as what critic Allison Graham terms a "noir siren" who, despite being a married woman with a child, carries on a "nightly masquerade in seedy bars" similar to Lizzie's forays in search of male company (47).

For Hollywood history, Jackson's novel is important because its adaptation three years later marked the first time that MPD was "performed" for the screen. *Lizzie* (Hugo Haas, 1957) dramatizes the experiences of an attractive, but socially awkward, young woman, Elizabeth (Eleanor Parker), whose hitherto more or less normal life is deeply troubled by the sudden emergence of this hostile "other" from within, of whose existence Elizabeth had previously been unaware. A series of notes threatening her destruction appear mysteriously on her office desk. At first, Elizabeth thinks she has made some enemy in her workplace, but is soon brought to the terrifying recognition that she is the note writer, even if the "she" in this instance is her complete opposite: aggressively self-confident, domineering, and sexually promiscuous. The conflict becomes disabling enough to require psychiatric treatment. A third personality who calls herself Beth emerges late in the story during a regression session conducted by Dr. Wright (Richard Boone). Under hypnosis, Elizabeth relives a childhood experience so traumatic that she retreated into the self that, though damaged, has been functional enough to allow her to lead a quite limited, if more or less normal, life. Beth, it turns out, is the original, better-adjusted personality she has repressed for many years. In fairly short order, she manages to banish both Lizzie and Elizabeth to the same subconscious psychic limbo where she was herself so long confined.

In the person of Lizzie, Elizabeth becomes her own deadly enemy, vulnerable to a kind of paranoid panic because, as is revealed, she is an inadequate, shock-induced version of what she would have been. The agon here dramatized is inner, a war waged with developing self-consciousness and recovering memory that restores an innate balance that had been lost many years before to trauma. Elizabeth's own safety and her mental wellness come to depend on the suppression of this destruction-minded other of whose existence she had no suspicion. Lizzie, as she confesses, can "see" Elizabeth and know her thoughts. Elizabeth does not dispose of the same epistemological advantage. She must rely on others to tell what "she" does under the spell of the other but later cannot recall. Significantly, Lizzie is not only homicidal (suicidal?), but also determined to violate cultural norms by leading a single-minded life of aggressive and heedless erotic abandon, conduct that would in short time destroy Elizabeth's position as a professional woman.

In the simplest Freudian terms, Lizzie is pure id, except that she can direct her instinctiveness with a certain amount of cunning. Devoid of moral compass, she is directed by no purpose beyond self-serving sexual indulgence and the undermining of Elizabeth, who, before she consults a psychiatrist does not even know that she is in a struggle for control over her very being. Yet, despite serving as a main character of sorts and being featured in the film's title, Lizzie is never more than a possible self, eventually prevented by the course of therapy from fully coming to life. By film's end, Lizzie has disappeared from view, and Beth has been installed as the master personality.

From a cultural perspective, it is interesting that this is more or less the same narrative and therapeutic result achieved in *Eve*. In both films, MPD figures as a form of dangerously transgressive multiplicity. The disease's unpredictable undecidability clearly threatens the social order, dependent on linked notions of "self" and "proper femininity." "Health," both individual and collective, demands a law-abiding singularity, a narrative goal achieved through the care administered by psychiatry, a relatively new branch of the medical profession then benefitting from "a growing conviction in American culture that psychiatrists were voices of reason, adjustment, and well-being" (Gabbard and Gabbard 75). To be sure, MPD asks a question difficult for this mental science to answer. Who are we truly, if other possible selves lurk within, ready to be called to the surface by either trauma or its recovered memory?

Ironically, Elizabeth's fears about her "future" eventually prove to be true. She is eventually revealed to be just as contingent as the later-appearing others, but in the range of personalities they offer as a group, she is as undesirable as Lizzie. She is merely one possible form this woman might assume, not the "person," solidly established and self-evidently unitary, who is in need of healing. That there is such an individual is the underlying assumption of the dialogue that has been at the center of Western medicine since its beginnings. MPD problematizes the physician-patient relationship; seeking treatment, Elizabeth winds up erased from view, replaced by another self, judged socially as more appropriate, that has only recently announced its presence.

More to the point, perhaps, the trio of selves constitutes an interesting gallery of cultural stereotypes. If Lizzie is the stereotypical bad girl whose assertiveness and single-minded pursuit of men embodies repressed desires, Elizabeth is the wallflower. She fears intimate relationships, but is cautious enough around others to seem more or less well adjusted, even if she is anhedonic, tentative, and awkward with everyone she encounters. It is thus not difficult to see why for years she has maintained her superiority over Lizzie, who will have no truck with social niceties. Yet Elizabeth is not good enough, the proof being that in the end she cannot resist the emergence of Lizzie, whose sexual energies she is unable to accommodate and ultimately repress. Displaying her street smarts, Lizzie scorns Elizabeth as a weak and unglamorized "square," a judgment with which the viewer might agree. In the therapeutic process, both Lizzie's disregard for social norms and Elizabeth's mousy refusal of adult sexuality are made disposable by the emergence of Beth, who becomes the winner in the contest of selves because she presents herself as the most conventional of the three, and is so endorsed by the obviously enamored Dr. Wright.

And yet for the most part the film belongs to Lizzie, who is the initial and most spectacular object of the thematization of the return of the repressed with its "indestructible" desires, the "derivatives of the unconscious," as Freud usefully puts it (for further discussion, see Le Guen). In scenes that are eerily reminiscent of the several film versions of *Dr. Jekyll and Mr. Hyde*, Haas's camera details how taking over Elizabeth means a physical transformation in which outer appearance signals an inner change as well. When Lizzie first emerges to prominence, she immediately applies heavy eye makeup and thick lipstick, does her hair in a sexy bun, dons a revealing blouse and tight skirt, then heads off to a local bar. This is a sequence that portrays the seamless ontology of MPD, as self blends into other self. It is also rich in cultural meanings.

Elizabeth's "disorder" manifests itself in a kind of monstrousness. The shy reclusive professional woman, unconcerned about her appearance, suddenly becomes obsessed with a superficial remaking that effectively marks her as not only "available" in its several senses but also on the prowl. In this new form, she exudes not sexiness, but sexual power. Her eyes gleaming with desire, Lizzie surveys the available men, demands that one dressed in a business suit buy her a drink (he quickly complies), but then abandons him when she spies a younger man who is also, with his dress (a tight white T-shirt with sleeves rolled up, showing his arm muscles), advertising his willingness to be a sexual object. Barely giving

Figure 4.1. Lizzie (Eleanor Parker), Elizabeth's other self, at a piano bar looking for men in *Lizzie*.

him a chance to agree, she drags the man off to a booth, enfoldng him in a passionate, yet also imprisoning embrace. The other customers in the bar are fascinated by the spectacle. They have no trouble in reading such an extended performance moment. That the wild-eyed floozy furnishes the film with its title and marketing icon indexes her power to displace the ostensible main character from the story and on screen. A clue to the filmmakers' desire to promote the story's sensationalism as much as its engagement with an intriguing personality disorder is that early on the project was, in a Mickey Spillane vein, called *Woman in Hell*.

That Beth is in the end the self who, now presented to the world, means that both Lizzie and Elizabeth are no longer present, even though their conflict otherwise dominates the film. However, Beth can also be seen as mediating between two extremes, retaining Lizzie's interest in well-poised and attractive self-presentation, while not rejecting Elizabeth's instincts for properly modest and friendly behavior. MPD, so *Lizzie* suggests, is a pathologically self-destructive multiplicity that, through proper therapeutic guidance, can be brought to a well-balanced singularity. In *Lizzie*, MPD involves not only an ordering of sanity-threatening disorder through the identification of inner psychological truth. Significantly, the therapeutic process also shapes a "personality" that reflects the consensus values of the middle-class world that the film evokes. Beth emerges as a young, professional, single woman similar to the others with whom she works at a city museum. At film's end, Beth fits better than Elizabeth ever did into the social order of her workplace. Her "inner Lizzie" may be put on the shelf of rejected cultural possibilities, but it seems that Beth's manner, grooming, and dress reflect much of Lizzie's desire to be appealing to the opposite sex.

A Slant Noirness

Director Haas (and producer Kirk Douglas for Bryna, who partnered on the project with Warner's) broke new ground in dramatizing an unfamiliar mental affliction, aligning it to a degree with the then-burgeoning postwar problem-film cycle (see Cagle). And yet, in both style and theme, *Lizzie* bears a closer affinity to entrants in another current Hollywood subtype, noir films that focus on female "duplicity," exploring a seemingly paradoxical good badness and, as does *Lizzie*, resolving it in favor of conventional social values. That women could be virtuous and transgressive at the same time is naturally no problem like alcoholism, racial prejudice, or anti-Semitism (principal subjects of the problem-film cycle), but rather a perennial cultural issue central to the long-established Western tradition of misogyny. Historian Howard Bloch notes that misogyny depends on two contradictory elements: the "estheticization of femininity" (especially in terms of simulation or glamorizing) that transforms women into objects of pleasure and worship; but also a "theologization" of this esthetic that condemns, as opposed to the life of the spirit, anything "pleasurable connected to materiality" (9).

In the barroom sequence, *Lizzie* presents a woman who fits this misogynistic stereotype, with purposeful self-glamorization connected to an unsanctioned, norm-bending pursuit of pleasure that involves the seduction of a man who finds himself unable to resist. In Western culture, the archetype of this story is the so-called temptation narrative featured in Genesis 2, which is restaged in many noir films, beginning most spectacularly with *Double Indemnity* (Billy Wilder, 1946). These films give continuing cultural life to the commonplace, established in early Christianity, that "meretricious allurement" is what marks women out as "the devil's gateway" (Bloch 41, 40). As far as film noir is concerned, however, Lizzie is a most unusual temptress, uninterested as she is in gaining power over men. Instead, her principal emotion is a deep anger directed at another woman, the dominant self that has kept her for years from expressing her sexual urges. This suggests that the film's theme is gender politics of a quite different kind. That Lizzie hates the virginal Elizabeth who has held her at bay seems a key point. In terms of the postwar cinema, an appealing badness is often said to be the hallmark of the stock character known as the femme fatale, whose ostensible virtue but moral instability or rebellion urgently requires male diagnosis and control (see Adler and Lecosse, for example). That women who strain against convention in one way or another can be understood as "fatal," of course, suggests that cultural criticism of film noir frequently finds itself caught in the trap of misogyny, with the concept of the femme fatale making it difficult to appreciate more complex portraits of womanly nonconformity and oppositionality, as Julie Grossman vigorously argues. One of her key insights is that "the ambitions and desires of women represented in film noir may express universal psychological factors, but they're surely deeply social as well" (3). Such is the case, I will argue, not only in *Lizzie*, but, as Allison Graham, among others, has usefully noted, also in *The Three Faces of Eve*, likewise released in 1957, which forms an interesting diptych with the Jackson adaptation.

Among postwar noirs that thematize female duplicity, *Lizzie* most closely resembles Robert Siodmak's *Dark Mirror* (1946), whose narrative focuses on the investigation of a murder that was committed by one of two identical sisters, Terry and Ruth (both played by Olivia de Havilland). However, which one is likely the ruthless killer of the doctor that Terry was dating? The out and about town young woman Terry? Or the quietly cerebral and unostentatious Ruth, who has been living in her sister's shadow? Several saw the woman who was with the victim that night, but their identification is useless in the circumstances since there is no obvious way for these witnesses to tell the two women apart physically. Ruth has a solid alibi for her whereabouts that evening, while Terry has convinced her sister to not tell the police that she was the twin whom others saw miles away from the scene of the crime. Terry persuades Ruth that she was at home, so she has no alibi to protect her from being accused of a crime she did not commit. Ruth, she pleads, must protect her with a seemingly insoluble ambiguity. No witness can be expected to tell the two apart. The prosecution of either sister must fail because of the need to exclude reasonable doubt.

With deeper probing needed, the investigation of the crime falls to a psychiatrist, Dr. Scott Elliott (Lew Ayres), an expert on twins who is romancing Ruth and is afraid for her safety. After completing profiles on the pair, he confidently (and correctly) identifies the malefactor as Terry, who is a sexually compulsive psychopath. The psychiatrist foresees that Terry will try to force Ruth to commit suicide and to relieve her from suspicion. Proof of her guilt, however, is still needed, which the detective obtains by tricking Terry into confessing. Ruth, of course, is simultaneously released from suspicion and from the bondage to her twin, who has turned out to be bent on her sister's destruction. At film's end, Ruth's previous proclamations of innocence have been vindicated. With her safety from an intimate source of evil and danger now assured, Ruth attains a respectable normality and can pursue her attraction to Dr. Elliott. This movement toward wholeness, dependent on the proper distribution of the labels "guilty" and "innocent," echoes the similar stabilization of the woman who in *Lizzie* can now be confidently addressed as Beth.

In *Dark Mirror*, psychiatry is mobilized not to engage in talk and regression therapy with a patient suffering from a disabling condition, though Dr. Elliott's interaction with the morally problematic twins does produce something like a therapeutic result for Ruth (who is shed of a disabling, destructive force in her life). Instead, collaborating with law enforcement, Dr. Elliott performs an act of cultural regulation, resolving an intolerable and threatening ambiguity. In *The Dark Mirror*, the personality of the woman under threat from forces over which she has no control is normalized. Like her counterpart in *Lizzie*, she has become proper, that is, conforming to middle-class standards of behavior and belief. The difference—which is "social" in the sense identified by Grossman—is that in *Lizzie* the proper woman is not one who must reject entirely the self-assertive sexuality that turns pathological in *The Dark Mirror*. In the spirit of a modernizing independence, Beth must instead learn how to contain, control, and enjoy its energies, a view of female nature that was emerging to prominence in America during the 1950s and is even more forcefully presented in Nunnally Johnson's *The Three Faces of Eve*.

What Is It about Eve?

In *Eve*, as in *Lizzie*, MPD compels an otherwise shy and reclusive young woman to act out in sexually aggressive ways that threaten to destroy her life. This behavior is sufficiently outré to threaten Eve with psychological breakdown and social ruin, just as it does with Elizabeth. The similarity between the films is no coincidence. Though rivals for a movie audience then eager for tales about psychiatry and mental illness, the two projects were interestingly connected as their productions proceeded more or less simultaneously. In fact, *Eve*'s release was held up for some weeks by Johnson, who in his role as producer was pressured by Bryna/Warner Brothers to do so. It seems that Johnson was not upset about providing an accommodation to fellow filmmakers, in part because he was eager to ascertain the appeal of MPD to audiences.

Lizzie effectively tested the thematic waters for *Eve*, though in an important respect the two films are quite dissimilar. *Eve* was adapted not from a novel, but from the "true case" recounted with great detail in a bestselling clinical history of the same name that had been written up by two Georgia psychiatrists. It seems that they were prompted by the critical and popular success of *Nest* to try their hands at such a story, since they had treated a woman suffering from the same disorder. Appropriately, the film was produced in the semidocumentary style, including some noir stylings, that had been pioneered by Louis de Rochemont a decade earlier. Public TV journalist Alistair Cook was deployed as both an onscreen and voice-over narrator, whose main functions were to establish the story's remarkable truthfulness and impart an air of authenticity (on the semidocumentary, see Palmer). That some sequences were shot in Savannah, Georgia, added authenticity to the production.

Despite these formal and stylistic differences, the two films offer stories that are remarkably similar in theme and plot line. This is not surprising, since *Eve* was inspired by Jackson's novel, which both Corbett Thigpen and Hervey Cleckley consulted when turning their case history into a story. Johnson had also read *Nest* and was intrigued by the possibility of making a film about MPD, but Bryna beat him to the punch in obtaining the screen rights to Jackson's novel. When Johnson learned that that two psychiatrists intended to publish an accessible account of a patient's experience that was strikingly similar to the travails suffered by Jackson's Elizabeth, he was intrigued. Sensing a second chance to bring MPD to the screen, the producer/director decided to purchase the screen rights after hurriedly reading their first draft, then aided the two doctors in putting the final touches on the docu-novel. Johnson even provided it with a very unclinical sounding title, whose catchiness was probably crucial to the phenomenal success it then achieved as both a trade book and a feature film (see Thigpen and Cleckley). *Lizzie* was a comparative failure at the box office; *Eve* went on to please audiences and critics alike. Bosley Crowther, reviewing the film in the *New York Times*, may have been right in describing the tale as "an exhibition of psychiatric hocus-pocus," but readers and viewers at the time found it absorbing.

The same sensational and culturally provocative elements in Haas's film version also figure in Johnson's *Eve*. With its erstwhile medical content drastically shortened, and its story of recovery thoroughly melodramatized, the film also shows a certain affinity with the good girl/bad girl noirs of the era, including most especially *The Dark Mirror* (a project, it bears remarking, that Nunnally Johnson produced and for which he wrote the screenplay). Unlike both *Lizzie* and *Mirror*, however, *Eve* features a substantially airbrushed version of the compulsive female promiscuity that is the principal quality of the powerful alternative selves who figure in these films. To be sure, all three of these productions conclude by effacing in the cause of health and happiness such unflattering portraits of womanliness. As the remainder of this essay will explore, this move toward the restoration of conventional sexual mores (and then regnant gender protocols) is crucial to the connection that these films establish to their particular cultural context. In that regard, the signal event was the publication of sex researcher Alfred Kinsey's second volume on American women in 1953, just prior to the release of *Nest*. Interestingly, the two MPD films share much in common with *The Chapman Report* (George Cukor, 1962), based on Irving Wallace's sensational, thinly disguised fictionalization (and pointed critique) of Kinsey's interviews and the conclusions he draws from them.

In focusing on young, attractive female sufferers to the exclusion of others, the two films follow the cultural line first traced out by physician Morton Prince's pioneering study of MPD, *The Dissociation of a Personality*, which was published in 1905. To judge from the fact that the book stayed in print through the 1950s, Prince's meditations on the condition and the amazing case history of a female sufferer he recounted with brio and style had attained a certain enduring popularity among the intelligentsia. *Dissociation*, in which the physician/author figures as obtrusive narrator and main character of sorts, provided much of the material (including courses of treatment and speculation on the condition's etiology) that figures in the literary sources of the two films. In fact, *Lizzie*'s Dr. Wright refers admiringly and by name to Prince's pioneering study, which is also praised for its perspicacity and even briefly summarized by the narrator in Shirley Jackson's *Nest*. Alistair Cook offers a version of Prince in *Eve*.

Dissociation appears to have been crucial in forging a close connection between the materials of patient history and the kind of engaging, even naughty, accounts of the culturally marginal that might be fashioned from them. What Prince wrote is more novelistic than "clinical" in the strict sense, though it does contain passages devoted to technical issues, while the book's general indebtedness to Stevenson's *Dr. Jekyll and Mr. Hyde* is striking. Unsurprisingly, the two films, like their written sources, reveal little that is new or especially intriguing about psychiatric theory or therapeutic regimes. In each case, the narrative is organized dramatically, turning on the deployment of hypnosis to uncover repressed memories of trauma, whose exploration limns a picture of how the personality multiplicity came to develop. Psychiatric intervention then eliminates the destructive conflict between personalities with opposed styles, values, and interests, a pattern followed in the literary sources of both *Lizzie* and *Eve*, as well as in their screen versions. To be sure, such simplistic depictions of the workings and results of psychoanalytic treatment had become a cliché in Hollywood films by the early 1950s.

Much like *Dissociation*, *Lizzie* and *Eve* are more invested in the complementary/contradictory performances of characters who are simultaneously singular and multiple, as they embody and act out enduring cultural concerns about the moral complexities of human nature. If, in the majority of Hollywood films, characters (actants as narratology has it) are an enabling function of narrative, in these two early MPD films story is constituted by the contested solidification of opposed elements into conventional selves, who are then able to acknowledge, in the Cartesian manner, that they exist. Narrative closure in these two narratives yields suffering patients who are now healed—or, to see it another way, two women, Elizabeth and Eve, who are assisted in becoming well-adjusted. "Adjustment" is a softer way of imagining how might be resolved the conflict between social norms and individual desire that is the subject of Freud's more tragically conceived view of the human condition presented in his *Civilization and Its Discontents* (see Fromm, *The Heart of Man* and *The Nature of Man*).

In these two 1950s MPD films, story thus yields character instead of being propelled by it. Another way of putting this is to say that the quasi-independent selves function as a collective protocharacter, whose melding into a distinct identity through the suppression of less than ideal elements soon reveals itself as the narrative goal. Interestingly, this manner of representing MPD makes possible an aesthetic similar to that which at the time dominated in the burgeoning international art cinema. The art films of the period were largely character studies in which incident served an only minimal plot, while theme was not often emphasized. In the MPD films, the contradictory self (aesthetically speaking, the Forsterian round character) emerges through a formal structure not dissimilar to the personification allegory that is a prominent feature of medieval and early modern works. That tradition is also invested in portraying the not easily harmonized elements of the individual self (e.g., the *Roman de la rose*, *Piers Plowman*, *The Pilgrim's Progress*). Like personification allegory, MPD thus provides a culturally inflected map of individual personality that is ideally suited not only to the representation and dramatization of cultural antinomies, but also to limning the parameters of the "normal" (aka the socially desirable) orientation of self. This ideal self can be shown emerging in the wake of significant internal conflict, as assisted, in a manner suiting post-Enlightenment scientism, by trained professionals.

Appropriately, as mentioned earlier, both films concern themselves with identifying and repressing those supposedly "feminine" styles that at the time had been recently and "scientifically," not to say scandalously, brought into cultural focus with the publication of Alfred Kinsey's report on women's sexual behavior and nature. MPD could well have been portrayed on the screen with more of a psychological focus tout court. After all, the clinical presentation of the disorder confirms, if from a different direction, Freud's fundamental understanding of the connection between mental surface and depth, as well as the way in which different areas of mental energy relate, especially conflictually, to one another. Surely, this is story material rich with dramatic and thematic possibilities. A sensationalizing focus on female promiscuity and its recuperation is not required.

Eve and *Lizzie*, however, focus on the contingent selves who are utterly dominated by a desire for promiscuous flirtation and, at times, casual sex with strangers. These "women" exist in a kind of subjunctive mood. They are not viable as freestanding individuals, barring a takeover of the characters who contain them. The sexually transgressive selves portrayed in the film are present, but subject to an unpredictable (and as it turns out permanent) disappearance from the stage of life. Furthermore, if their actions are undeniably real, and not without consequence, what they do is the result of a disabling disorder that makes them unwilled and, in large part, contre-coeur. Never fully actualized, such selves endure at films' end only as desires and energies that are (perhaps forever but maybe not) tamed beneath quite different and more conventionally acceptable surfaces. The psychomachia in which they compete for dominance does not conclude in their favor, at least for the moment.

Eve focuses on the ways in which the present self, Eve White (Joanne Woodward), who is, as it were, "out" and "in charge," finds herself oppressed, repressed, and thoroughly miserable in living a conventional life as a woman and mother, married to an evidently responsible but uneducated working class man, Ralph (David Wayne). Eve Black articulately voices her discontents with such a life. Not only is she, like Lizzie, an avowed mortal enemy of the weak but conventional self then currently in charge. She is also scornful and dismissive of Ralph's evident unsophistication. Significantly, it was in 1957 that Betty Friedan oversaw the survey of her college classmates that collectively expressed similar complaints about the experience of married women, and would come to constitute the founding document of second stage feminism when published as *The Feminine Mystique* in 1963. If the docu-novel details the early stages of Eve's treatment once symptoms of inner conflict and incoherence announce their presence, Johnson's film speeds through these troubling episodes, foregrounding instead the emergence of the charming, voluble, but unabashedly transgressive self who names herself "Eve Black" and immediately announces her desire to undermine her "host." Tellingly, this other self emerges only after Eve shows shockingly clear signs of her dissatisfaction by trying to strangle her young daughter. In the film, the force of Eve Black's attempt to destroy her counterpart and the child "she" bore is downplayed, receiving much more attention in the docu-novel.

The publicly adulterous behavior of Eve Black in time drives away Eve's husband. The film makes light of her nocturnal excursions in search of male company by suggesting, however unlikely it might be, that she never sleeps with any of these men, an aspect of her misbehavior about which the book is more circumspectly silent. Ralph's departure leaves

Figure 4.2. Eve Black (Joanne Woodward) ready for a night on the town in *The Three Faces of Eve*.

Eve a single mother with little, it seems, in the way of prospects for putting her life back together. In a limited and temporary sense, true to the spirit of the Production Code, the narrative punishes Eve for her rejection of conventional moral values. On a psychological level, the story drives toward the integration of Eve's selves. Yet in aid of showing how she comes "well-adjusted," the film provides Eve with a new social normality that allows her to escape what is presented as the dead end of lower class life. From a cultural point of view, Eve's "multiplicity" offers her a gloomy choice between the severely limited freedoms of a stay-at-home wife and mother, catering to the whims of an oppressive husband, and the illusory glamour of brief forays to honky-tonks. The highlight of these tavern evenings is that she gets the occasional chance to sing with the band and sashay around provocatively.

The film deftly recuperates what might otherwise be seen as a destructive, if merited, consequence of this "involuntary" rebellion against propriety. While loyal and in most ways supportive, Ralph is also possessive and determined to keep Eve subordinate; in the film's first scenes Eve is intimidated by his authoritarian manner. Faced with certain knowledge of her misbehavior, Ralph strikes her after, no longer dominated by her darker self, she denies having sneaked out. His anger is justifiable, but his physical abuse is clearly brutal (and unsurprising to Eve, indicating that she is accustomed to being battered). Ralph's unlamented departure from the scene is crucial to the process of healing and the accompanying upward social mobility that the film constructs as a happy ending. In the course of her treatment, which has proceeded for some years, a third personality emerges who identifies herself as Jane.

In terms of speech, manner, and intelligence, both Eves, along with Ralph, are poor whites. Ralph and Eve White show anxiety and uncertainty in their encounters with the doctors treating her condition, while Eve Black manages these meetings more smoothly, but only by playing the unabashed flirt and violating social norms at every turn. Jane, however, speaks educated English, with just a trace of a Southern accent. Her manner is assured and confident; she is neither flirty nor withdrawn, but easily relates to her doctors as their social equal, obeying the same middle-class rules of social interaction. The psychiatrists quickly agree that "Jane" is the personality whose dominance would insure the continuing health and happiness of their patient. As is revealed, Jane is the self who would have been dominant had a traumatic childhood event not forced her into psychic storage. In both films, hypnosis uncovers the true personality, revealing the other selves as the product of mental disorder.

Just as in *Lizzie*, Eve Black challenges the dominance of a self that has repressed too thoroughly her desire for independence and assertive sexuality, but these transgressive "women" are in each case erased by the therapeutic process that "produces" Jane. Jane's recovery is completed by Jane's marriage to a middle-class man who clearly seems her social equal and treats her respectfully. As Allison Graham puts it, "Jane" takes her place in a "reconstituted, modernized Southern white family," who inhabit the "brightly-lit world of 1950s domesticity" (52). The story recycles key elements of the classic bildungsroman, with the emphasis on the healing of mental/emotional/moral stability substituted for education generally speaking. In her attractive young husband, Jane has discovered a sanctioned outlet for her sexual desire, as she enters into the so-called "companionate marriage" then being promoted within a burgeoning therapeutic culture (see Coontz 229–62; Reumann 1–53).

Recognized by many viewers as "serious," *Eve* proved the more appealing of the two films to critics. Then unknown Joanne Woodward won the Academy Award for Best Actress with her adroitly managed portrayal. Both films present MPD as a treatable mental condition, stigmatizing as undesirable an indifference to "attractiveness" (and the respectful male attention it might earn) but also a presentation of self that is designed to signal a willingness, even a compulsion to engage in sex regardless of the "rules" meant to regulate it.

The MPD films of 1957 are surely part of the postwar cycle of Hollywood releases that offer heroic portraits of the power of psychiatry to heal even the most difficult of mental difficulties, including in this disorder the lack of a stable, central personality. And yet these films also speak to what many in America at the time thought was a crisis in public morals, though there was considerable acrimonious disagreement about what exactly was the threat to the national culture. In 1953, the same year that readers encountered Jackson's *The Bird's Nest*, the publication of Alfred Kinsey's *Sexual Behavior in the Human Female*, based on extensive interviews, became a cultural event of unexpected magnitude and significance, underlining an aspect of the continuing national conflict between traditional views of human nature and purpose, and more modern ones, which were then on continuing ascendance (see Jones 701–37; Reumann 86–117). Kinsey's research offered documentation of women's sexual interests and behavior, as well as Kinsey's views on the subject, including his then controversial opinion about the nature of the female orgasm and the regular failure of traditional intercourse to produce it. The publication of Kinsey's work on women, in the words of Jonathan

Gathorne-Hardy, prompted "violent eruptions of public and then press disapproval and disgust" (395). Margaret Mead blamed Kinsey for "the sudden removal of a previously guaranteed reticence," and supposedly provoking a legitimation of previously taboo sexual expression that would greatly harm American culture. For many in American culture, the researcher, pulling away the curtain on female eroticism, posed a clear and present danger to traditional views of gender, marriage, and the family (quoted in Gathorne-Hardy 397).

Kinsey's fellow citizens could simply "accept neither the language nor the activities," which included compulsive indulgence (then termed nymphomania), masturbation, and extramarital liaisons (395). The publication of a lightly fictionalized account of Kinsey's canvasing practices, Irving Wallace's *The Chapman Report* (1960), suggested that the furor was, at one level, about the need to reset what was deemed normal sexuality for women. In Wallace's reimagining of Kinsey's investigations, the interviewers become disenchanted with the mission, even as they take on the task of counseling women who become troubled after turning their sexual histories into confessional narratives, as the code of reticence that had previously guaranteed that sex was not discussed is swept away in the name of scientific truth. Because of production difficulties, and the intervention of the Legion of Decency, the film, unlike the novel and unlike Kinsey's two books, evinces doubts about the enterprise itself, in the spirit of allowing sleeping dogs to snooze on.

In line with what critics such as Mead had feared, Cukor's film version provides what is meant to be a horrifying dramatization of the destructive effects of unbridled interest in what would a decade later become known as zipless coupling. The miserable, guilt-ridden alcoholic (Claire Bloom) who simply cannot resist men, no matter the circumstance, winds up murdered. And the two married women pursuing affairs (Shelley Winters and Glynis Johns) learn difficult lessons about their failure to observe conventional moral rules. Interestingly, however, *The Chapman Report* also argues for the necessity of restoring some kind of balance in the face of the growing view that women had a right to sexual pleasure. Cukor's film focuses on the relationship between the chief interviewer Paul Radford (Efrem Zimbalist, Jr.) and one of his subjects, Kathleen Barclay (Jane Fonda), who suffers from a profound fear of sexual intimacy. Radford gently coaxes her into what the film defines as a satisfying receptivity, producing something like a happy ending for her character, and emphasizing, as do both *Lizzie* and *Eve*, that to be well-adjusted requires not only the refusal of self-destructive sexual indulgence and a childlike refusal of relationships with men, including marriage and children.

As a narrative scheme, the anatomy of MPD allows the inner truths of female nature to be exposed to view, functioning much as the Kinsey interview. The true subject of *Lizzie* and *Eve*, we might say, consists in what adjustment should be made to these truths and how that adjustment might be achieved with the inevitable assistance of male experts. Reumann is speaking of *The Chapman Report*, when she writes the following, but this comment is equally apt for the two films discussed in this chapter: "A new and therapeutic social order has triumphed in which both sexuality and science are kept in their place: proper sex is marital, emotionally fulfilling, and springs from love; while proper science is rigorous and avoids sensationalism" (123).

Works Cited

Adler, Laura and Élisa Lécosse, eds. *Dangerous Women: The Perils of Muses and Femmes Fatales*. Paris: Flammarion, 2014.

American Psychiatric Association DSM. *Diagnostic and Statistical Manual of Mental Disorders, Fifth Edition: DSM-V-TR®*. Washington DC: American Psychiatric Publishing, 2013.

Bloch, R. Howard. *Medieval Misogyny and the Invention of Western Romantic Love*. U of Chicago P, 1991.

Cagle, Chris. *Sociology on Film: Postwar Hollywood's Prestige Commodity*. Rutgers UP, 2017.

Coontz, Stephanie. *Marriage, a History: How Love Conquered Marriage*. Penguin, 2005.

Crowther, Bosley. Review of *The Three Faces of Eve*. New York Times, 27 Sept. 1957, https://www.nytimes.com/1957/09/27/archives/screen-3-faces-of-eve-personalities-study-opens-at-victoria-the.html.

Franklin, Ruth. *Shirley Jackson: A Rather Haunted Life*. Liveright, 2016.

Fromm, Erich. *The Heart of Man: Its Genius for Good and Evil*. New York: Harper & Row, 1965.

—— and Ramon Xirau, eds. *The Nature of Man*. New York: MacMillan, 1968.

Gabbard, Glen O., and Krin Gabbard, *Psychiatry and the Cinema*. 2nd ed., American Psychiatric Press, 1999.

Gathorne-Hardy, Jonathan. *Kinsey: The Measure of All Things*. Indiana UP, 2004.

Goffman, Erving. *The Presentation of Self in Everyday Life*. Doubleday, 1959.

Graham, Allison. *Framing the South: Hollywood, Television, and Race during the Civil Rights Struggle*. Johns Hopkins UP, 2001.

Grossman, Julie. *Rethinking the Femme Fatale in Film Noir: Ready for Her Close-Up*. Palgrave Macmillan, 2009.

Hattenhauer, Darryl. *Shirley Jackson's American Gothic*. State U of New York P, 2003.

Jackson, Shirley. *The Bird's Nest*. Penguin, 1954.

Jones, James H. *Alfred C. Kinsey: A Life*. W. W. Norton, 1997.
Le Guen, Claude. *Le refoulement*. Presses univérsitaires de France, 1992.
Marcus, Steven. *The Other Victorians: A Study of Sexuality and Pornography in Mid-Nineteenth-Century England*. Routledge, 2017.
Modleski, Tania. *Loving with a Vengeance: Mass-Produced Fantasies for Women*. 2nd ed., Routledge, 2009.
Palmer, R. Barton. *Shot On Location: Postwar American Cinema and the Exploration of Real Place*. Rutgers UP, 2017.
Prince, Morton. *The Dissociation of a Personality: A Biographical Study in Abnormal Psychology*. Meridian, 1957.
Putnam, Frank W. *Diagnosis and Treatment of Multiple Personality Disorder*. Guilford Press, 1989.
Reumann, Miriam G. *American Sexual Character: Sex, Gender, and National Identity in the Kinsey Reports*. U of California P, 2005.
Thigpen, Corbett H., and Hervey M. Cleckley. *The Three Faces of Eve*. McGraw-Hill, 1957.

5

The Cine-Telescopic Psyche

1950s Serial Killers and Sexual Psychopathology in *The Sniper* and *While the City Sleeps*

ROBERT MIKLITSCH

MENTAL DISORDERS AND, IN particular, sexual psychopathology, as *The Cabinet of Dr. Caligari* (1919) indexes, can be traced back to the origins of cinema itself. However, one could argue that, at least with respect to motion pictures, the figure of the serial killer achieves a certain visibility in the 1950s with the advent of new mass media such as television. One could also argue that the trope of the serial killer is not only historically tied to questions of gender—to, that is, the sexual aggressivity associated with both "abnormal" and hegemonic masculinity[1]—but to technologies of violence. Two films that explore the relation between cinema and psychosis, technology and psychopathology, are Edward Dmytryk's *The Sniper* (1952) and Fritz Lang's *While the City Sleeps* (1956).

While the City Sleeps is one in a series of American pictures directed by Lang in the 1950s, including *The Blue Gardenia* (1953) and *Beyond a Reasonable Doubt* (1956), that examines the role of the mass media and telecommunications in contemporary society. Numerous critics have noted that *While the City Sleeps* is less about its ostensible, sensational subject matter, a "lipstick killer" on the loose, than Kyne Enterprises, a media conglomerate (television, newspapers, and wire and photo services) that is a synonym for Lang of the increasingly panoptical, totalizing impulses of modernity. In fact, *While the City Sleeps* is arguably structured by a deconstructive relation between normality and mental illness in which "there is no separation between the disturbed depths of society . . . and the acceptable modes of living within that society" (Lucas 311).

In both *The Sniper* and *While the City Sleeps*, the serial killer targets women, compelled by a repetition compulsion that is primarily motivated by an unresolved relationship with his mother. But if both films posit—at least at the level of individual psychology—the same cause (comic books are also, inter alia, a contributing factor in *While the City Sleeps*), *The Sniper* dramatically shifts the social and diagnostic focus of Lang's picture. *The Sniper* is "perhaps the first film to seriously deal with a serial killer on a clinical level" and, as such, acts as a "bridge from the film noirs of the 1940s to the case-study mentality of the 1950s crime portraits" (Rubin 43; Cettl 420). Moreover, unlike *While the City Sleeps*, which does not broach any sort of solution to the problem of psychopathology, *The Sniper* constitutes a trenchant "indictment" of contemporary society's "failure to deal with mental problems" (Macek 261).

In what follows, I begin by offering a synoptic reading of *While the City Sleeps*. I then present a more detailed "close reading" of *The Sniper*, since the extant literature on Dmytryk's film is not nearly as extensive as it is on Lang's. In the coda, I reflect on the similarities and differences between the two films. More importantly, I argue that the real significance of *The Sniper* has less to do with its liberal "message" about mental illness, important as it is (see Dmytryk 112–13), than the way in which the film cinematically performs it. To do otherwise, it seems to me, is to reduce the medium to the message. Hence my concluding remarks on what I call the "cine-telescopic psyche."

While the City Sleeps:
The "Maniacal Mind" and the Mass Media

While the City Sleeps opens, precredits, with a killing: in the course of making a drugstore delivery, Robert Manners (John Barrymore, Jr.) sees the shadow of a woman dressing as he hands a package to a janitor, George "Pop" Pilski (Vladimir Sokoloff), who's been working on the plumbing in her apartment. Once Pop leaves, Manners returns to the apartment under false pretenses and, when the woman's back is turned—the sound of bath water can be heard running in the background—the film cuts away to a close-up of his black-gloved hand pressing the "button lock." Manners departs and the camera tracks behind the woman as she goes into the bathroom and kneels down beside a bathtub. Hearing the door open, she turns and the camera zooms into her face for a tight close-up as she throws up her hand in self-defense and screams. (The woman's scream-opened mouth and the ambient sound of bathwater running in the background anticipate the shower sequence in *Psycho* [1960].)

The camera movement mimics, as Tom Gunning notes, the killer's violence and thereby literalizes the link "between sight and violence, image and death" (438). In this manner, the opening scene of *While the City Sleeps* connects the medium and Manners's disorder, cinema and sexual psychopathology. Lang's film introduces, moreover, a dialectic between cinema and the mass media when the camera dissolves from a message scrawled in lipstick on the wall of the dead woman's apartment—"Ask Mother"—to New York City at night where a neon sign, an encircled "K," is distinctly visible on the side of a skyscraper. (The capital letter references both Lang's *M* and Welles's *Citizen Kane* [1941].)

Postcredits, Amos Kyne (Robert Warwick), the patriarch of Kyne, Inc., is propped up in a hospital bed in his office monitoring a series of teletype machines. After reading about the homicide, he calls in the heads of the various departments at Kyne: Mark Loving (George Sanders), news service; John Day Griffith (Thomas Mitchell), managing editor of the *New York Sentinel*; Harry Kritzer (James Craig), "Kyne Pix"; and Edward Mobley (Dana Andrews), columnist, television correspondent, and Pulitzer Prize–winning reporter. The exchange between Kyne and Griffith establishes the "tabloid" tenor of Kyne's company:

KYNE: How many women in the United States use lipstick?

GRIFFITH: How many women are there?

KYNE: I want every one of them scared silly every time she puts any on. Call this baby the "Lipstick Killer."

That Kyne wants to exploit the public's dread and, it is also implied, fascination with "true crime" stories in order to make a "killing" on the murder is particularly noteworthy given the parlous condition of his health.

Kyne has kept Mobley back and is airing his disappointment about his dissolute, playboy son and the future of the company when Ed switches on the television set located at the foot of the bed and the Kyne logo reappears, this time complete with fanfare. However, when Ed turns around, Kyne has passed away, and it's as if TV has killed him (Gunning 446). Although the film's dominant narrative emerges when Walter Kyne, Jr. (Vincent Price) dangles the title of "executive director" of Kyne, Inc., for whomever identifies the "lipstick killer," the most arresting subplot in the context of psychopathology revolves around the triangular relation between Mobley, his girlfriend, Nancy Liggett (Sally Forrest), and Manners.

For example, as Mobley is kissing Nancy on the threshold to her apartment, the camera pans to a close-up of his hand pressing open the button lock. After they say goodnight to each other, he is descending the stairs when he pauses and the camera cuts to a low-angle shot of Nancy's legs. In the reverse shot, Mobley's head is wedged between the bars of the banister as if he's in jail:

MOBLEY: Want to roll up your stockings?

NANCY: There's a lot your mother should have told you.

MOBLEY: I didn't ask my mother.

The fact that Mobley here repeats Manner's "clue" ("Ask Mother") is just one indication that he should be read as a double or doppelgänger of the killer (Kaplan 57).

Since Mobley once worked a crime beat, it is also no surprise that it is the reporter rather than a police officer or psychiatrist who assumes the role of the profiler in Lang's film. After Mobley sits in on an interrogation of the janitor and later glances at some of the crime-scene photos, what he sarcastically refers to as "pin-ups," he tells Lt. Burt Kaufman (Howard Duff) to "look for a young guy" and that the murder was "premeditated by a psycho and not his first." "Do you know how much stuff is written and published for the instruction of potential law breakers?" The lieutenant, who worked together with Mobley in the past, responds, "Take the so-called comic books sold to kids of all ages in drugstores."

I will return to the issue of "so-called comic books" in the conclusion, but Mobley picks up where Kaufman leaves off and, musing on the killer's message ("he's a Mama's boy unless I'm mistaken"), argues that the clues left at the crime scene are an "impertinence" intended to mock the efforts of law enforcement. Suddenly, the phone rings: there's been another homicide. Cut to the scene of the crime where there's a chalk outline of the dead woman's body and the clue this time is a magazine called *Strangler*, whose cover features a gruesome drawing of a screaming woman and a man's hand closed tight around her neck.

On the heels of this, the second homicide, Mobley and Kaufman, having decided to team up again, agree to bait the killer on television. The cut from a broadcast on the TV in Loving's office to a wide-angle, deep-focus shot of a cameraman in the foreground and, in the background, Mobley sitting behind a desk decorated with a Kyne icon lays bare the televisual apparatus and reiterates the relation between television and "crime culture," the mass media and the "pulps": "My reason for giving importance to this particular story is my hope that the killer may be listening to me. For I believe that in his progress to the chair or to the insane asylum that he has reached a way station where his sick and warped ego demands to be fed with the milk of self-importance. And so . . . I'm going to say a few things to the killer face to face." Mobley begins to tick off a litany of "items," two of which have a visible impact on Manners, who's watching the broadcast in his pajamas in the bedroom of his mother's home. First, when Mobley states that the killer "reads the so-called comic books," Manners drops the ten-cent comic book rolled up in his hand, and we see that it's titled *The Strangler*. Second, after Mobley accuses the killer of being a "Mama's boy"—"The normal feeling of love that you should have toward your mother has been twisted into hatred for her and all of her sex"—Manners's mother (Mae Marsh) knocks at his door. Gunning rightly emphasizes Lang's depiction of television as a "means of surveillance" but, in this scene, it is almost as if TV has the power to summon Manners's mother (436).

In the brief scene that follows, we learn in the course of Manners's outburst that his father abandoned his mother and him, that he's adopted, and that he was brought up "exactly like a little girl." Manners's psychopathology is all but spelled out here, a classic psychoanalytic scenario with, true to the evolution of psychiatry in the 1950s, a behaviorist spin.[2] Organic issues aside, Manners's environmental "triggers" include a double dose of abandonment, first by his biological parents, then by his adoptive father, while the psychoanalytic angle is evident in the volatile combination of an absent father and an "overprotective mother" (Kaplan 55). The consequence, in Manners's case, is a distinct feminization, one that foreshadows Norman Bates (Anthony Perkins) in *Psycho* and that's refracted in Lang's film in the cuckolded character of Walter Kyne.

The volatility of Manners' complex manifests itself when, having worked himself into a violent rage, he puts his hands first on his mother's shoulders, then her hair. (He's standing, she's sitting in the chair he just vacated, and the angle is high.) Manners is about to strangle her when she unwittingly manages to deter him by declaring, "Oh, I have such a good boy." Mrs. Manners, the "good-bad mother," then leaves to get his breakfast, at which point he switches on the TV just in time to hear Mobley conclude his broadcast on a "personal" note by announcing his engagement to Nancy.

Meanwhile, Mobley's waiting at a restaurant with Griffith and Lt. Kaufman for Nancy to arrive so he can tell her about the "next step" in his plan, which is to use her—"a nice girl with a button lock on the door"—to lure the killer into acting again. When Griffith comments, "That's the kind of guy you're gonna marry," Nancy retorts, "I *like* the kind of guy I'm gonna marry!" and immediately assents to the plan. Mobley, relieved, shows her the announcement in the paper—"*Congratulations* Edward Mobley TO WED Nancy Liggett"—which appears on the front page of the *Sentinel* right below a headline story about the "lipstick killer." The match cut from Nancy opening the newspaper to read the notice to Manners on the street doing the exact same thing confirms Mobley's assumptions about the killer's "maniacal mind"—"He'll get mad at me and anybody I like. . . . Sooner or later he'll come out after the bait." The cut also suggests, of course, that Mobley is not above putting his fiancée's life in jeopardy to find the "lipstick killer."

Cut to Kritzer's apartment where Manners interrupts Harry in a passionate clinch with Kyne's wife, Dorothy (Rhonda Fleming), with a delivery of a bottle of Scotch. While Kritzer goes for the money to pay him, Manners sees Dorothy reflected in a mirror as she lifts her skirt and puts one foot on a couch to adjust her stocking. (Manners's voyeurism recalls the staircase scene where Mobley stops on the stairwell to gaze at Nancy's legs.) Although Manners is forced to leave when Kritzer returns before he can push open the button lock, as he starts down the stairs he sees a bouquet of flowers and a note ("To Dearest Nancy—who deserves a better fate—than Ed Mobley") outside Nancy's apartment, which is located right across the hall from Dorothy's. Nancy's not home, but when we next see Manners, he is sprawled out on his bed, filling in the features of a newspaper drawing titled "Fill In This Face"

Figure 5.1. Suspect gazing at a "Fill-In-the-Face" newspaper drawing he's filled in, in *While the City Sleeps*.

with an idealized, even romanticized version of himself (Gunning 439). (Compared to Lang's earlier films, this self-portrait reads like a debased rendition of the artist-as-criminal trope: to wit, Manners is no Mabuse.)

Later, Ed and Nancy meet up again with Kaufman, who informs them that the police have learned that Manners committed two previous murders and that he began as a burglar: "He steals only ladies' things from lone, unprotected girls. This guy is a real nut on dames." Since Nancy has in the meantime learned, along with everyone else at Kyne, Inc., that Mobley spent a night out with Loving associate Mildred Donner (Ida Lupino), she remarks with not a little edge to her voice, "And this description begins to fit Mobley," a comment that explicitly thematizes the mirror relation between Manners and Mobley. Ed, undeterred, proceeds to outline the "next move" in his plan to catch the killer—"Put Nancy's picture in the paper or use her on a telecast"—when she storms out. The straight cut to Manners standing outside and partially hidden behind the window of a book shop suggests that Nancy's life is in imminent danger. Mobley, however, starts brainstorming with Lt. Kaufman about the killer:

> MOBLEY: His crimes have become more and more frequent, more violent, bolder. He's got to have a new element in them now. . . .

KAUFMAN: What do you mean?

MOBLEY: . . . something daring. Every murder he committed has always been at night?

KAUFMAN: Yes.

MOBLEY: Then maybe the next one will be in cold daylight. . . .

KAUFMAN: You think . . .

MOBLEY: Yeah, that figures. The final insolence—broad daylight.

If Mobley's "unique understanding of the murderer" appears to come from recognizing his own similarity to Manners (Kaplan 58–59), this uncanny perspicacity is also what makes him suddenly, and belatedly, realize the peril that Nancy may be in at the moment.

The plainclothes cop assigned to protect Nancy has just seen her home when Manners, sporting black gloves, approaches her apartment and, finding the door locked, presses the buzzer. Nancy calls out, "Who is it?" After Manners pretends to be Mobley (yet another—in this case, inverted—twist on the profiler-killer theme), Nancy is about to open the door when she thinks better of it. Manners, furious because thwarted, violently tries to break down the door until he hears the elevator. It is Dorothy. However, before she can get safely inside Kritzer's apartment, Manners forces his way in and attacks her. Manners has the element of force and surprise in his favor (see the high, overhead shot of Dorothy pinned under him as he tries to strangle her), but she fights him off and runs to Nancy's apartment. Manners flees. Mobley, though, chases him to a subway station (cf. Lang's *Man Hunt* [1941]) and then into a darkened tunnel where the two exchange blows. Manners manages to escape again, climbing a steel staircase to a manhole and pushing it open, only to be dragged out and arrested by the police.

There are any number of things that can be said about the above sequences, but I would only note two. First, the narrative displacement of the killer's attention from Nancy, the "good girl," to Dorothy, the femme fatale (Kaplan 58–59), parallels Mobley's last-minute transformation from cynical enabler to "knight in shining armor." Second, the reprise of noir semantics in the chase sequence, which recollects the "thriller" elements evoked in the introductory frames of the film ("a high-angle, typical *noir* shot of a street glistening with rain"),³ prises open the preceding morally ambiguous, metaphorically intimate space between Mobley and Manners even as it radically reduces the physical proximity between the two characters.

The extended coda, a comic one in which everyone gets their comeuppance except Mildred, who has been hired as a columnist, and Mobley, who is honeymooning in Florida with Nancy when he's named "executive director," points up the satirical as opposed to criminal or "serial killer" thrust of Lang's film. In the final analysis (interminable as it must remain), the character of Robert Manners in *While the City Sleeps* is a vehicle for Lang's critique of television as the most recent, and perhaps insidious, stage in the ambiguous project of modernity.

The Sniper: Crime and Punishment

> High among police problems is that of the sex criminal, responsible last year alone for offenses which victimized 31,175 women. Adequate and understanding laws do not exist. Law enforcement is helpless. Here, in terms of one case, is the story of a man whose enemy was womankind.
>
> —Foreword, *While the City Sleeps*

The opening credit sequence of *The Sniper* establishes the sexually oriented mindset of the protagonist, Eddie Miller, sensitively played by Arthur Franz. (My recourse to the term "protagonist" rather than its antonym, "antagonist," is intentional. The audience, as I will elaborate in more detail below, is encouraged to sympathize, even empathize, with Eddie, although this interpellation may not be immediately apparent.) The camera laterally pans to the left from a bed on which the pages of a newspaper are scattered to a dresser. A hand inserts a key into the lock and the top drawer is pulled out to reveal a long-range rifle. The title appears on the screen in bold capital letters: THE SNIPER.

You don't have to be a Freudian psychoanalyst to discern the subtext of the above scene, one that's underscored when Eddie takes a rag out of the same drawer. As he's taking the rifle apart to inspect and clean it, he periodically gets up from his chair to look out the window. The object of his gaze becomes apparent when the camera cuts to a heterosexual couple⁴ who are climbing the steep staircase of an apartment building that's located across the way from his window. The straight, reverse cut to a telescopic shot from Eddie's point of view—a circle bisected by the crosshairs of the sight—crystallizes the film's formal and thematic concerns. We do not know exactly *why* Eddie is doing what he's doing (the remainder of the film will explore this, the issue of motivation), but the earlier masturbatory imagery suggests an intimate connection between violence and sexuality as well as between frustration and aggression where the latter, aggressive drive is a form of fantasy.

The fantasmatic scenario is accented at the beginning of *The Sniper* when, in a tight close-up, Eddie pulls the trigger and, despite the fact that we just saw him removing a bullet from the dresser, there's only a clicking sound. While one could argue that the introductory scene of Dmytryk's film exploits the desire of at least some part of the audience to hear the rifle fire and see what the bullet does to the unsuspecting victim, the film initially frustrates this desire. Eddie himself turns away from the field of vision, his face twisted with remorse. At this point in the narrative, which can only be characterized as in medias res (since, to reiterate, we do not know what has brought Eddie to this moment in time), he is still able to exert a certain degree of self-control.

The straight cut from inside to outside, from the intense interiority of Eddie's cramped apartment to the exterior of a movie theater past which, hands in pockets, Eddie walks—the movie that's playing is *Raiders of Tomahawk Creek* (1952)—introduces additional links, in this case between the mass media and violence. The reference to *Raiders of Tomahawk Creek* is especially resonant given the regenerative role of violence in the western (see Slotkin). The irony, of course, is that if California represents the western movement, the "frontiersman" has migrated inside, both literally and figuratively.

When Eddie does venture outside for a walk (presumably to exorcize his demons), what he sees does not so much pacify as excite his already inflamed imagination, his fears *and* fantasies. First, a boy and his mother are standing in front of the display window of a fashion shop; when the boy complains, twice, that he wants to go home, his mother slaps him. Cut to Eddie reflexively touching his cheek, as if he's just been hit. Later, walking alone in a park (the camera tracks in reverse and periodically cuts away to point-of-view shots to disclose the objects of Eddie's gaze), a couple is walking with their arms around each other's waist and another couple is passionately kissing on a bench.

Eddie's clearly perturbed, but his reaction, at least from the perspective of a putative "serial killer" film, is surprising. When he inadvertently bumps into an older couple, the man dresses him down; however, after a bell rings and a traffic light changes to "STOP," Eddie, instead of reacting, enters a drugstore where he uses a pay phone to call for help. Still, the deep-focus composition suggests that even as Eddie is seeking medical counsel, he's imprisoned in a culture of romance from which single, "maladjusted" people like him are categorically excluded. While he stands in the foreground trying to contact the doctor who treated him when he was incarcerated, a male "soda jerk" and a young woman are bickering like lovers in the background. Eddie desperately endeavors to convey the urgency of his request to the operator, insisting that "it's a matter of life or . . ." (the ellipsis is telling), but he's unable, as the now happily conversing couple puts it as he walks out the door, to "catch [his] party."

Angry, Eddie returns to his apartment where he heads straight for the dresser only to pull up suddenly when he realizes that he previously locked the drawer and threw the key on the apartment floor. The close-up of his hand reaching for the key and then his fingers slowly closing into a fist captures the conflict between Eddie's desire to act on his emotions and his simultaneous desire to muster the necessary will-power to arrest this impulse. The scene concludes on an extraordinary, and extraordinarily expressive, note: after Eddie smashes his hand against the sink, he switches on an electric stove. As the burner begins to radiate with heat, the camera cuts to a low-angle shot of Eddie looking at his hand as if it is separate from his body, the burner reflected like a sun on the ceiling above him. The camera stays on Eddie as he puts his hand on the now hot burner and holds it there, the shadow of his hand blotting the sun-like shadow.

The subsequent sequence, set in the emergency room of a hospital, underlines the futility of Eddie's cry for help and complicates the import of the "drugstore" scene. Both the intern and doctor agree that Eddie's second-degree burn is "self-inflicted." Yet despite the fact that Eddie volunteers that he was in the "psycho ward" in prison for hitting a girl and doesn't "feel right," they release him. Although the intern recommends sending him "upstairs," the doctor reminds him that he's already sent up "five loonies" in the last two weeks and cynically responds, "They'll only keep him around for three days, wrap him up in a cold sheet, and give him back to the Indians." When an ambulance, its siren wailing, arrives at the entrance (there's been a car accident), Eddie becomes an afterthought, his incredulous question to the intern about his hand—"Don't you think that this is a funny way to get hurt?"—left hanging fire.

Given the foreword, the discourse of femininity is, it is clear, central to the libidinal economy of *The Sniper*. Thus, as the intern is bandaging Eddie's hand, he recommends that in the future Eddie should leave the cooking to women: "Yeah, friend, a man's got no business fooling around with stoves—it's strictly women's business." This advice is unsolicited, but the fact that it comes from a male authority figure effectively feminizes Eddie, an inflection that foregrounds both Eddie's precarious sense of masculinity and the rigid gender codes operative in the United States in the 1950s.

Consider, in this context, his female supervisor at Alpine Cleaners and Dryers where he is employed. The very first time that we see Eddie there, the camera is set at the back of a truck and the composition is extremely restricted. While Eddie is checking the individual slips on the dry-cleaned clothes hanging inside the truck, the supervisor is standing outside on the dock:

SUPERVISOR: Aren't you away yet, Miller?

MILLER: I will be in a minute. It's not easy with this hand.

SUPERVISOR: Sure you can drive?

MILLER: Don't worry. I can drive.

SUPERVISOR: I don't worry. The company worries. Just remember if you have an accident, you're responsible.

It is obvious that, for whatever reason, Eddie's supervisor doesn't have any sympathy for him, or for his injured hand. As such, she's the very embodiment of the maternal superego: strict, caustic, cool.

The remainder of the film, which can be said to unravel from the above, loaded scene, is composed of "triggers," Eddie's actions, and the public response to these acts. The occasion for the first act of violence occurs in the aftermath of a delivery Eddie makes to Jean Darr (Marie Windsor), an attractive brunette who performs as a singer-pianist at a nightclub on Union Street and who, unlike his supervisor, is unusually nice to him. After Eddie lays her clothes on her bed and helps her take down a suitcase from a closet, he agrees to do a favor for her—she needs a "rush job" on the brandy-stained, figure-flattering white dress that she's wearing—and she tells him to get a beer from the fridge while she changes. The scene is suggestive not simply because it emphasizes the difference between how the supervisor and Darr treat him but because of the sexual frisson between Darr and Eddie in the bedroom. This said, the casting of Windsor, whose persona was associated at the time with the femme fatale, intimates that she is not nearly as nice as she seems. Accordingly, when her doorbell buzzes—it's her trumpet-playing boyfriend—she asks Eddie to finish his beer on the back porch as if he were a mere "servant" (Santos 124). Eddie's injury, which he claimed was a result of being spiked while playing baseball ("I didn't know you were a ballplayer—man of many talents," Jean purrs), here realizes its metaphorical charge as a sign of castration.

The significance of Eddie's expulsion is not merely thematic but, precisely, *cinematic*, since it is the first time in the film that we get a panoramic view of San Francisco from Calhoun Terrace in Telegraph Hill to the Golden Gate Bridge in the background. In fact, the wide-angle, location photography spectacularly on display in this shot distinguishes *The Sniper* and prefigures *Vertigo* (1958) (see Kehr). And as in Hitchcock's film, landscape or space in *The Sniper* is an index of a character's psyche. In Dmytryk's film, Eddie's response to Jean's slight will be to assume a position of godlike dominance from which he can survey and punish the women who, at least in his mind, have hurt him.

Cut to a close-up of a briefcase, the camera panning from Eddie's feet past his bandaged hand to his determined face. When Eddie turns his head, a light goes off in the apartment across the roof from where he is standing. The following sequence, in which Eddie shadows Jean as she walks to her job, descending the Montgomery Steps as she goes, also prefigures *Vertigo*—with the proviso that Eddie resembles Scottie Ferguson (James Stewart) *after* he has discovered that he has been duped by Madeleine Elster (Kim Novak). Once Jean arrives at her destination, Eddie steals up to the roof opposite the club (note the pointed slats of the white picket fence) where, as he waits for her to leave for the night, he caresses the stock of his rifle. The gunshot when it comes is sudden: one moment Darr has stopped, poised in front of a glass-encased picture—"JEAN DAAR AT THE PIANO"—and the next moment her head is crashing into the case, the glass shattering like the beer bottle that Eddie, humiliated, broke at the end of the previous sequence. The fact that Darr's image is doubled in the publicity photo right before she is shot bespeaks her symbolic status (Santos 214)—that, in other words, Eddie is not so much murdering a particular person as a proxy for, as the foreword puts it, "womankind."

If *The Sniper* in this scene broaches the issue of female objectification (see, for example, *The Cover Girl Killer* [1959]), its critical purchase cannot be reduced to the "male gaze."[5] I am referring here to the scene

Figure 5.2. Sniper Eddie Miller (Arthur Franz) takes aim on the object of his hatred in *The Sniper*.

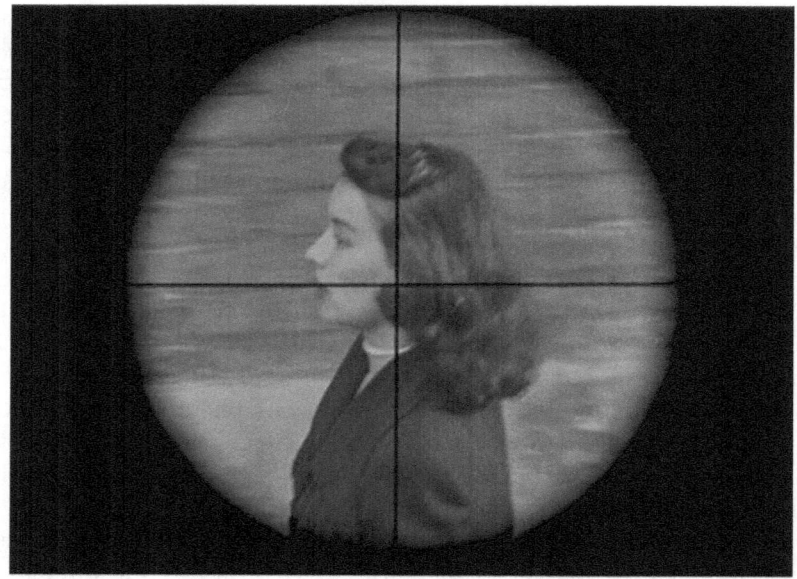

Figure 5.3. Eddie's target.

where Lt. Kafka is sitting at a desk in Darr's apartment and speaking to a "ballistics" expert on the phone while outside, beyond the frame of the window, a row of spectators is visible. This metaspectatorial shot comments on Eddie's fetishistic and, ultimately, murderously sadistic gaze (this is the male gaze in all its virulence); however, it also comments on the audience's own fascination with everything criminal. In other words, in *The Sniper* even more so than in, say, Hitchcock's *Rear Window* (1954), the viewer is complicit in a voyeuristic culture of violence, a distinctly American one of which Eddie himself is cause and symptom.

In *The Sniper* this culture possesses a determinate historical dimension, since Kafka relays to Sgt. Ferris (Gerald Mohr) that the casing comes from the sort of weapon, a M1 carbine, that is routinely issued in the Army. Although we can assume from Eddie's record, which we are privy to at one point, that he never served in the army, his character nevertheless reads as a "maladjusted veteran," a figure that was a staple of the 1940s "tough guy" thriller (see Krutnik 65–72). From this cultural-historical perspective, *The Sniper* can, in turn, be interpreted as a *post*war crime film in which the violence that was projected during the Second World War outward onto an external, "foreign" enemy has now been turned inward, internalized, interiorized—but not, crucially, domesticated.

While the issue of domesticity in Dmytryk's film may appear oblique, it is in fact material, since, as the "stove" scene and the intern's withering remark about women's work illustrate, the discourse of American masculinity was seriously in play circa 1952. This problematic resurfaces in *The Sniper* when Eddie returns to his apartment and removes Darr's dry-cleaned, now stainless white dress from the dresser where he has hidden it. Since he is fully cognizant of its incriminating character, he first rips it up, then proceeds to the basement where he burns it in the furnace. The look on his face as the dress goes up in flames—his pleasure is tangible[6]—is the compensatory inverse of the pain he experienced burning his hand. However, as in the opening scene of the film, the pleasure passes and Eddie turns away in pain. The "shock" cut to the landlady's cat, which has been watching him the whole time, exposes Eddie in a moment of jouissance, after which he suffers the full force of the gaze of the other and its punitive aftereffect, guilt. Consequently, as soon as he returns to his room, he removes an empty ammunition carton from the dresser and writes on the cardboard flap, "TO THE POLICE STOP ME—FIND ME AND STOP ME—I'M GOING TO DO IT AGAIN."

Cut to a woman, May Nelson (Marlo Dwyer), who previously approached Eddie at a bar and gave him her address only to reject him when he claimed to be an engineer ("I build things"). Now she's drunkenly making her way home to her apartment on Green Street, stumbling down a steep street at night. The fact that the film never reverts to a counter or reverse shot, as in the initial killing—all the audience sees is the bullet penetrating the glass pane of a window and striking the back of Nelson's head—intimates that Eddie's self-control has dwindled to the point where he is almost entirely subject to his demons.

The police response to the note, which Eddie has deposited in a public mail box, is literally farcical. The lineup of potential suspects—"rapists, defilers, Peeping Toms, etc."—is presented as a show for the policemen in the audience, and the interrogating officer acts as if he's an emcee at a comedy roast. Later, at a restaurant in Chinatown, police psychiatrist Dr. James Kent (Richard Kiley) tells Lt. Kafka that he "won't get [the sniper] by running show-ups like the one I saw." Instead, he tenders a speculative profile of the killer, observing that he's "somebody who's been getting tough with women from the beginning."

When Kafka queries him about the motive, Kent concedes that "it could be a thousand reasons," then ventures:

> Maybe some woman did something mean to him when he was a kid. He may not even remember what it was, but [pointing to his head with chopsticks] something in here remembers. Perhaps it was his mother, usually it is in these cases. Whoever it was . . . he's killing her over and over again. [Throwing his chopsticks down] I better stick to a fork. He's killing her over and over again. He's been doing it in his mind for years. Now that he's doing it for real, he's gonna keep right on doing it . . . as long as he doesn't get caught, as long as his cartridges last.

Kent's surmise about a "mean" mother as the unconscious cause of the sniper's behavior recollects the early, "movie theater" scene where Eddie sees a mother slapping her son; it also prefigures Mobley's psychoanalytically inflected profile of Manners in *While the City Sleeps*. More to the point, perhaps, Kent's own rhetorical emphasis—"He's killing her over and over again"—performatively mimes the sniper's repetition compulsion.

Cut to Eddie watching a TV in the window of an appliance shop—a baseball game initially catches his ear—where a society woman, Mrs. Fitzpatrick (Lilian Bond), is being interviewed about the "motif" for a charity ball that is being sponsored by the Women's Civic League.

(Mrs. Fitzpatrick, having invoked "American history"—"no costume after 1900"—assures the female interviewer that "Indians" are welcome—"After all, Indians are part of our history, too."[7]) This televisual scene recalls the initial, "theatrical" killing of Jean Darr; the difference is that since Eddie hasn't had any personal interaction with Mrs. Fitzpatrick—it is totally mediated—she functions even less like a real person and more like a surrogate for women in general, as evidenced by Mrs. Fitzpatrick's association with the Women's Civic League. Moreover, Mrs. Fitzpatrick's class and social status—her home is the Spreckels Mansion in Pacific Heights—means that her death, which occurs off-screen, will receive enormous media attention and therefore reverberate in the public sphere in a way that a drunk like Mary Nelson's does not. Bluntly, bromides about American democracy aside, not all deaths are equal.

The conference in the mayor's office at city hall, with the mayor, chief of police, and inspector sitting on one side and on the other the representatives of the public sphere, delineates the tension between the city's governing body and the body politic, which, according to newspaper publisher Liddell (Carl Benton Reid), "is alarmed and frightened." Although the chief of police accuses Liddell's newspaper of slanting the news and exploiting hysteria, councilman Harper (Harlan Warde) accuses the police of inefficiency and incompetence. When the chief responds that they are "short for patrolmen" and mentions a recent request for a budget increase, another councilman, Mr. Wise (John Brown), counters that "taxes are high enough as it is," and Liddell adds that "we're getting very little value for the taxes we do pay." Liddell then exclaims—this is his peroration—"We want this man caught, and caught quick, and punished, punished, punished!" As the last imperative indicates, this is a critical scene, adumbrating as it does the conflict between the police and the press as well as the seemingly insuperable problems that a serial killer presented for law enforcement in the early 1950s.

Equally importantly, the scene provides a context *and* pretext for Kent to articulate the "social problem"—mental illness—that subtends the genre, the "serial killer" film, of which *The Sniper* is a species:

> KENT: There are hundreds of thousands of sex offenders walking American streets at this moment who could be the sniper. . . . When this man is caught, you'll find he has a record dating back to when he was a kid. If his first act had led to treatment instead of jail, three women wouldn't be lying dead today.

HARPER: The fact remains three women are lying dead today.

LIDDELL: And the killer is still loose.

KENT: Yes, loose because of us and a killer because of us. . . . This time we can do something. You all have weight and power not only in the city but the state. Put your weight behind getting a new law passed. Let every socially dangerous sex offender as soon as he is caught for his first offense be committed to a mental institution. There he can be cured or put away indefinitely.

Kent's speculations about the sniper's past echoes the previous scene at the police station where Kafka and Ferris are examining police records and one in particular catches the lieutenant's eye. It is Eddie's, although Kafka doesn't realize it at the time. Studying the sheet, Kafka tells Ferris that Miller's first conviction was for "cracking a girl's skull with a baseball bat" and that he recently served an "eighteen-month sentence" for another assault against a woman.

The last piece of information retrospectively explains the beginning of the film when Eddie calls the state prison to talk to the doctor who treated him there. The implication is that Kent's recommendations about "early detection and treatment" are sound (Santos 127), since if Eddie had, in fact, been able to contact his doctor, perhaps none of the killings would have occurred. Writing about Dmytryk's film, Martin Rubin states that the "conjectures of the psychiatrist, although not discounted, are left unconfirmed," but a careful reading of *The Sniper* suggests that Kent's "conjectures" about the sniper's record are, as it were, dead on, as is his argument for hospitalization as opposed to incarceration. While it is true that Eddie was remanded to a state prison rather than committed to a mental hospital, as Kent would have preferred, Eddie's phone call suggests that the treatment he received at Huntsberg was therapeutic. Finally, the narrative's retroactive confirmation of Kent's "conjectures" testifies to the probity of his closing brief for new and better legislation.

All of this said, the film dramatizes the sort of push-back that progressive ideas like Kent's face. Wise wonders where the money will come from for mental institutions, which criticism inevitably redounds to the issue of taxes and governing. The scene ends on a dispiriting note when Liddell refers to Kent's "ideas" as "psychiatric mumbo-jumbo" and issues a not-so-subtle threat about the fate of the current administration if it is not able to find the sniper sooner rather than later.

The cut to a woman on a roof taking down her laundry and, standing right behind her, a police officer is succeeded by a pan, cued by an off-screen whistle, to another policeman stationed on an adjacent roof and pointing to something in the distance. In the reverse, long shot, a man is crossing a roof on Montgomery Street and, in a binocular shot from the POV of the first policeman, he is carrying a rifle. Although the binocular shot suggests that law enforcement is zeroing in on the sniper, once the officers, having scrambled across rooftops, apprehend the man, he turns out to be an adolescent boy (Danny Mummert). Later, at police headquarters, Kafka is forced to release the suspect because, as he points out, the hammer on the rifle doesn't work and there is no firing pin. As the suspect is being led away, he turns around and assails Kafka, "I know where there's plenty of guns, plenty of bullets, too. You think there's only one guy in this town who doesn't like people. . . ." Before he can finish his rant, however, Kafka slaps him, the boy breaks down, and the lieutenant, remembering Kent's advice, tells the arresting officer to take him to the "psycho ward" at the city hospital.

The boy's outburst, not unlike Manners' in *While the City Sleeps*, highlights the anomie and alienation of metropolitan life in midcentury America, in which citizens do not see themselves as integral parts of a vital public sphere so much as individual monads unified only in their disassociation from the socius. If Kafka's considered reaction to the adolescent "copy cat" hints that, in the future, things may be better, in the present the "maniac," as Liddell says, is still "loose." The straight cut to Alpine Cleaners and Dryers reprises the first scene set there and, like it, suggests a cause-and-effect relation. The supervisor orders Eddie to change the "filthy" bandage on his hand: "I don't want to see it . . . on Monday." She won't; caught up like a shroud in the branches of a tree, the bandage marks instead the killing of yet another woman—this time while walking with her boyfriend in Buena Vista Park, on Sunday, in broad daylight. (The fact that Eddie acts during the day, as Manners does near the end of *While the City Sleeps*, evinces his increasing sense of desperation.)

The dissolve to an amusement-park banner with a target in the center—"SHOOT LIVE AMMUNITION"—is the pointed segue to one of the most provocative sequences in *The Sniper*. After Eddie sees a sailor and girl kissing on a Ferris wheel, he decides to try his luck at a shooting gallery: he shoots and hits a target, then, seeing the couple kissing again, tries to turn the rifle on them until the chain catches and the proprietor rebukes him. Turning back to the shooting gallery, Eddie hits nine straight targets before throwing the gun down in disgust. The next amusement, a "dunking game" where a woman perched on a ledge is dropped into a water tank if the player can hit the circular target with a baseball, constitutes an even more condensed instance of Eddie's "triggers." The blonde taunts Eddie—"He looks like a pitcher, an empty pitcher!" (a jibe that unwittingly hits home)—and despite the fact that Eddie misses the target the first time, he proceeds to hit it three times in a row, repeatedly dunking the woman. Then, before she can climb back onto the perch, he throws the remaining balls at the cage with such fury that the woman screams in terror. The reappearance of the baseball motif at this point in the film—one of the bystanders quips, "Offhand, I can think of three baseball clubs that can use this guy"—recalls Eddie's first conviction for assault ("cracking a girl with a baseball bat") and signals that he is rapidly regressing in the service not of the ego but the id.

The police have, meanwhile, finally begun to make some progress on what the inspector has referred to as a "motiveless" crime. The "dunk tank" woman issues a complaint and Kafka, reading a teletype, comments that "some dame says that a guy has been throwing baseballs at her—funny because that's her job" until he remembers Eddie's original conviction for assault. At the same time, Ferris takes a telephone call and learns that Eddie was treated at an emergency room for his burned hand. The final lead—the one that breaks the case wide open—occurs when the Alpine checker, riding a trolley car, hears the man sitting next to her talking about the sniper's bandage and immediately gets off to call the police.

Yet even as law enforcement is closing in on Eddie, the film is opening up, returning to the panoramic location photography first employed in the "back porch" scene. Cut to a close-up of Eddie removing a bullet from his briefcase, then to a high, overhead angle as he surveys the street below, where a woman with brunette hair is walking by herself. Cut again, this time to the telescopic point of view, which tracks the woman until another woman calls out to the first woman and the brunette turns, smiling. In the second, wider reverse-shot, Eddie's looking down at the street, holding the rifle in the left foreground, while in the right background, a painter is using a pulley to scale a smokestack that towers against the sky like an obelisk. Although Eddie doesn't shoot, turning away at the last moment, the painter sees him and, pointing, screams, "Hey, the sniper! Hey, over there, the sniper!" When nobody seems to hear or listen, the painter throws his bucket onto the asphalt below, the white paint exploding onto the sidewalk like an abstract expressionist painting. Eddie, enraged at the painter for pinpointing him when he hasn't done anything ("Why did you have to do that? I didn't kill her"), shoots the man, the lifeless body sliding back down the smokestack and disappearing from the frame. Off-screen, a woman screams and Eddie flees.

The next, equally spectacular sequence elaborates on the verticality of the previous one, cutting from low, steep angles (as when Eddie climbs down a series of fire-escape ladders) to extremely wide-open ones (as when he races across the loading dock of a deserted warehouse) to a long, high perspective (as when Eddie climbs a zigzagging wooden staircase toward the camera—which is fixed at the top—pausing, breathless, next to a sign that reads "PRIVATE NO TRESPASSING"). If the restricted framing momentarily traps Eddie and, in the process, counterpoints the exhilarating freedom of movement exhibited in the previous "escape" part of the sequence, the sign itself can be read as an elliptical allusion to the celebrated opening of *Citizen Kane*: Eddie is not a monumental figure like Kane, but, like Welles's "everyman," he's a prototypical American, and just as Kane ends up isolated and alone, so does Eddie.

Eddie's elderly landlady, the only truly benign feminine presence in the film, has just been listening to the radio—"[We] request that any citizen who knows of any man who has had a burned right hand to report him to the police"—when he suddenly appears and she sees his scarred, bandage-free hand. Terrified, she puts her hands over her mouth, and it's as if Eddie is a monster (which, in some sense, he is). The hand, which appears in close-up in a shallow-focus composition and turned away from the woman, is the final expressionist touch in a film rich in expressionist passages and sound-images or, to use a "loaded" word, "shots."

Compared to the two preceding sequences but true to the film's antiexploitational ethos, the conclusion to *The Sniper* is decidedly anticlimactic. As Eddie sits on his bed assembling his rifle, Kafka and Ferris belatedly arrive, siren blaring, at Filbert Street in Telegraph Hill. The police have already cordoned off the area, and onlookers are pressing up against the barricade. A girl says, "We wanna see what's going on," and another, older woman says, "I hope they kill him." A camera atop a KPIX truck is filming the action and people are hanging out of windows, so much so that Inspector Anderson (Frank Faylen) remarks that "some solid citizens are gonna get their brains blown out if they don't pull their heads in." While the inspector waits for the sound truck to arrive so that he can communicate with Eddie, Kafka and Ferris steal around to the back of the boarding house where they ascend the stairs to the second floor.

"Miller, you coming out?" Kafka, who's standing to one side of the door, calls out, "This is the police, Miller, come out with your hands up."

When Eddie doesn't respond, one of the accompanying officers fires at the doorknob and the door swings back. Ferris pushes it open and the camera pans from the door past a stained-glass window to the bed where Eddie is sitting, holding onto the rifle for dear life. In the final, startling shot of the film, the camera zooms in closer and closer until it stops on a tight shot of the barrel pointing to the heavens and Eddie's impassive face as a single, streaming tear glistens in the light.

Coda: The Cine-Telescopic Psyche

Both *While the City Sleeps* and *The Sniper* can be described as case histories. The character of Robert Manners in Lang's film is based on William George Heirens, a seventeen-year-old student at the University of Chicago, who was arrested on June 26, 1946, in the process of burglarizing an apartment (see Kennedy, Hoffman, and Haines 318–25). (Although Manners strangles his victims, Heirens stabbed his first two and dismembered the third, a child.) Heirens famously left a message written in red lipstick on the living-room wall of one of the three victims: "For heavens [sic] / sake catch me / before I kill more / I cannot control myself."[8]

As for *The Sniper*, Edna and Edward Anhalt, whose Academy Award-winning story was the original source material for Dmytryk's film, claimed that they based the character of Eddie Miller "on the composite personalities of men who were convicted of violent crimes against women" (Macek 260), a case-historical approach that is mirrored in the prologue to the film. (In his speech in the mayor's office, Kent also alludes to the case of Albert Fish, the "Cannibal Killer," who reputedly molested one hundred women and murdered as many as fifteen [see Flowers and Flowers 25].) The prescience of the Anhalts's portrait of a serial sniper was confirmed when, on April 16, 1952, in the time between when they sold their story to Columbia and the release of *The Sniper*, Evan Charles Thomas, the "phantom sniper," was arrested and confessed to killing one woman and wounding seven others (see "L.A. 'Phantom Sniper' ").

An original story penned by the Anhalts was also the source for Elia Kazan's *Panic in the Streets* (1950), the "epidemiological" theme of which reappears in *The Sniper* in the guise of "mental illness as a contagious disease" or psychosis as a "plague" (Santos 125). The metaphor of a plague is especially resonant in terms of *The Sniper*, since it was the first major film that Dmytryk made after serving time as one of the Hollywood Ten and his second appearance before the House Committee on Un-American Activities (HUAC), when he "named names." Although the casting of Aldolphe Menjou, a "rabid witch hunter" (in the words of the *Daily Worker*), became a lightning rod in the wake of Dmytryk's recantation, it is not too much to suggest, I think, that the pathos of Miller's character can be attributed in part to the director's experience of having been imprisoned and "blacklisted."

One cannot perhaps emphasize these larger sociocultural currents enough, inasmuch as *While the City Sleeps* and *The Sniper* were both made during a tumultuous period in American history. Lang himself had expatriated from the Third Reich with the "association of being *undeutsch*" hanging over his head (Gunning 342), and the HUAC "mass hearings" from 1951 to 1954 no doubt played a part in the director's decision to return to Germany after making *Beyond a Reasonable Doubt*. Therefore, while Dmytryk's "Hollywood" career was starting up again circa 1952, Lang's was nearing an end. One irony is that whereas *The Sniper* was made at Columbia but recollects the classic expressionist and social problem pictures that Dmytryk made at RKO such as, respectively, *Murder, My Sweet* (1944) and *Crossfire* (1947), Lang's *While the City Sleeps*, which succeeded the Columbia-released *The Big Heat* (1953), was made at RKO, which, in yet another irony, became the production studio for *I Love Lucy*.

In light of the fall of the "house of noir," a number of critics have noted the impoverished set design of *While the City Sleeps* as an indication of its lower budget, but the most obvious tip-off may well be—with the exception of the subway "chase" sequence—the almost complete absence of location shooting. Simply put, *While the City Sleeps* is a "studio" picture and, accordingly, Lang's style in the film is epitomized by the use of mise-en-scène—for example, television sets—and, in terms of camerawork, interior point-of-view and forward-tracking zoom shots. By contrast, if *The Sniper* was, typical of Stanley Kramer's productions at the time, more "short budget" than not, Bernard Guffey's cinematography is characterized by extensive location photography as well as exterior POV and wide-angle shots. As Martin Rubin rehearses, "Magnified shadows; flickering firelight; amusement-park rides; an atmospheric soundtrack of sirens, foghorns, and trolley bells; and priapic towers and chimneys all serve to convey Eddie's . . . changing moods" (44). The vertiginous spaces of *The Sniper* register, in addition, the roller-coaster ride that is Eddie's psychic life: when he looks into himself, he looks into an abyss,[9] a chasm that, as in the celebrated dolly zoom in *Vertigo*, simultaneously attracts and repels him.

But perhaps the most obvious difference between *While the City Sleeps* and *The Sniper* is their respective depictions of the serial killer.

On one hand, Eddie Miller in Dmytryk's film looks (when, for example, he is working at Alpine Cleaners and Dryers) like what he is, a deliveryman, but when he's not working and carrying a briefcase, he looks like a businessman. On the other hand, when we first see Robert Manners, he is wearing a black cap and leather jacket à la Johnny, Marlon Brando's character in *The Wild One* (1953). Although in the wake of, inter alia, Anger's *Scorpio Rising* (1964), Manners's, if not Johnny's, "costume" reads as camp, in 1956 it would have been seen as a signifier of the emergent, rebellious youth culture. This incipient culture was associated, in turn, with juvenile delinquency—see, for instance, *Rebel without a Cause* (1955) and *Blackboard Jungle* (1955)—as well as, in particular, comic books. For instance, Fredric Wertham argued in *The Seduction of the Innocent* (1954) and in his testimony before the Senate Subcommittee on Juvenile Delinquency on April 21, 1954, that *the* "common denominator" in juvenile delinquency was the sort of comic books produced by Eclipse Comics (EC).[10]

One consequence of the above conflation of costuming and "comic book" causation in Lang's film is a stereotypical portrait of the serial killer in which Manners functions as a stock or stick figure for the rampant hysteria about juvenile delinquency. Given this, it may be more fruitful to ask, What is the difference between a serial killer who uses his hands and one who uses a long-distance rifle? Robert K. Ressler has observed that, historically speaking, strangulation—together with knives and suffocation—is the most common "weapon of choice" for serial killers, since they "want the personal satisfaction of causing death right at hand" (Ressler and Shachtman 48). In this sense, strangulation—even more so than a knife—satisfies the displaced desire for (sexual) intimacy. However, if strangeness or estrangement is a component of what Mark Seltzer calls "stranger-intimacy," telescopic rifles can be said to be the modern prosthesis par excellence since the telescopic sight is at once a form of self-extension as well as a prime example of the "primary mediation" between body and machine (6, 69).

The etymology of the word "telescope"—*tele* ("at a distance") and *scopium* ("to look at")—is instructive here. With respect to space, the telescopic rifle, via optical magnification, simultaneously preserves and collapses the distance between subject/shooter and object/victim so that the serial killer can enjoy intimacy from afar. At the same time (and I'm thinking of the temporal sense of "tele"), the telescopic sight can be said to be far-seeing, as in foresight or prescience. To wit, even as serial killers are engaged in the criminal act, they are necessarily rack-focused on the future inasmuch as the aggressive drive, like the sexual one, can never be satisfied. Hence the significance of repetition compulsion in the conceptualization of serial killing as what British policemen used to call "crimes in series" and what Ressler, referencing "Saturday" serial movies like the Phantom, terms "serial adventures."[11]

The latter cinematic notion, which was responsible for the change in terminology from "stranger killing" to "serial killing" (Ressler and Shachtman 29), points to the dialectic between "killer" and *Kultur* in *While the City Sleeps* and *The Sniper*. Although both Lang's and Dmytryk's film mark the traumatic emergence, at least for cinema, of the new medium of television, *The Sniper* not only anticipates the "sniper" picture—from *Targets* (1968) and *Dirty Harry* (1971) to, most recently, *American Sniper* (2014)—but accentuates the way in which the cine-telescopic apparatus structures the psyche, and vice versa. As the related, contemporary phenomenon of mass killings attests, the scope of this apparatus, whether understood as "normal" or "psycho," social or cultural—is, to say the least, enormous and has direct implications for the present moment, one where the public sphere appears increasingly pathological (Seltzer 6).

Notes

1. This is not, of course, to discount the existence of female serial killers. For an overview, see Eric W. Hickey (253–76).

2. On the popularity of psychoanalysis and the "resurgence of behaviorism" in the 1950s, see Michael Fleming and Roger Manvell (102). See also Bart Beaty (18–47).

3. Gunning appears to have momentarily forgotten the conclusion to *While the City Sleeps*, since he asserts that, after the "nocturnal" opening, "there is nothing *noir* in the look of this film" (436) and that Mobley "never has to undergo the discomfort that Casey Mayo [Richard Conte] experiences [in *The Blue Gardenia*] when he encounters . . . a flesh and blood embodiment of his unknown murderess" (447).

4. I mark the sexuality of the couple here, but unless otherwise noted, all further references to couples in the film will imply that they are heterosexual.

5. I am referring to Laura Mulvey's "Visual Pleasure and Narrative Cinema" (6–18). The literature on Mulvey's classic essay is enormous; my only point is that the gaze is not always "male" and can be collective.

6. See Peter Kürten, the "Vampire of Düsseldorf," who once told a psychiatrist, "I get pleasure from the glow of the fire. It gave me so much pleasure that I got sexual satisfaction" (Ressler and Shachtman, *I Have Lived in the Monster* 50).

7. The emphasis on "Indians" in this exchange not only echoes the reference to *Raiders at Tomahawk Creek* and the emergency-room doctor's remark in the

"hospital" scene but intimates that there is a connection between the treatment of the mentally ill and Native Americans.

    8. For a photograph of the scene, see Robert K. Ressler and Tom Shachtman, *Whoever Fights Monsters* (New York: St. Martin's, 1992), p. 80B.

    9. I am echoing here the subtitle of Ressler and Shachtman's *I Have Lived in the Monster*, that is, *A Report from the Abyss*.

    10. For an excellent revisionist reading of Wertham with respect to the latter's critique of comic books, see Beaty.

    11. See Ressler and Shachtman, who observe: "[Serial killers] are obsessed with a fantasy, and they have . . . nonfulfilled experiences that become part of the fantasy and push them on toward the next killing" (*Whoever Fights Monsters* 30).

Filmography

American Sniper. Clint Eastwood, 2014.
Beyond a Reasonable Doubt. Fritz Lang, 1956.
The Big Heat. Fritz Lang, 1953.
Blackboard Jungle. Richard Brooks, 1955.
The Cabinet of Dr. Caligari. Robert Wiene, 1919.
Citizen Kane. Orson Welles, 1941.
Cover Girl Killer. Terry Bishop, 1959.
Crossfire. Edward Dmytryk, 1947.
Dirty Harry. Don Siegel. 1971.
M. Fritz Lang, 1931.
Man Hunt. Fritz Lang, 1941.
Murder, My Sweet. Edward Dmytryk, 1944.
Panic in the Streets. Elia Kazan, 1950.
Psycho. Alfred Hitchcock, 1960.
Raiders of Tomahawk Creek. Fred F. Sears, 1950.
Rear Window. Alfred Hitchcock, 1954.
Scorpio Rising. Kenneth Anger, 1964
The Sniper. Edward Dmytryk, 1952.
Targets. Peter Bogdanovich, 1968.
Vertigo. Alfred Hitchcock, 1958.
While the City Sleeps. Fritz Lang, 1956.
The Wild One. László Benedek, 1953.

Works Cited

Beaty, Bart. "From Freud to Social Psychiatry." *Fredric Wertham and the Critique of Mass Culture*. UP of Mississippi, 2005, pp. 18–47.

Cettl, Robert. *Serial Killer Cinema*. McFarland, 2003.
"Edward Dmytryk." *Science Fiction and Fantasy Film Flashbacks*, edited by Tom Weaver, McFarland, 1998.
Fleming, Michael, and Roger Manvell. *Images of Madness: The Portrayal of Insanity in the Feature Film*. Fairleigh Dickinson UP, 1985.
Flowers, R. Barri, and H. Lorraine Flowers. *Murders in the United States: Crimes, Killers and Victims of the Twentieth Century*. McFarland, 2004.
Gunning, Tom. *The Films of Fritz Lang: Allegories of Vision and Modernity*. British Film Institute, 2000.
Hickey, Eric W. "The Female Serial Murderer." *Serial Murderers and Their Victims*. Wadsworth, 2010.
Kaplan, E. Ann. "Patterns of Violence toward Women in Fritz Lang's *While the City Sleeps*." *Wide Angle*, vol. 3, 1980, pp. 55–60.
Kehr, Dave. "The Sniper (Edward Dmytryk, 1952)." http://www.davekehr.com/wp-content/uploads/2008/05/the-sniper.jpg. Accessed 13 May 2008.
Kennedy, Foster, Harry Hoffman, and William H. Haines. "A Study of William Heirens." *Serial Murder: Modern Scientific Perspectives*, edited by Elliott Leyton, Ashgate, 2000, pp. 318–25.
Krutnik, Frank. *In a Lonely Street: Film Noir, Genre, Masculinity*. Routledge, 1991.
"L.A. 'Phantom Sniper' Confesses." *Madera Tribune*, 17 April 1952, https://cdnc.ucr.edu/cgi-bin/cdnc?a=d&d=MT19520417.2.8.
Lucas, Blake. "While the City Sleeps." *Film Noir: An Encyclopedic Reference to the American Style*, edited by Alain Silver and Elizabeth Ward, Overlook, 1992, pp. 310–11.
Macek, Carl. "The Sniper." *Film Noir: An Encyclopedic Reference to the American Style*, edited by Alain Silver and Elizabeth Ward, Overlook, 1992, pp. 260–61.
Rubin, Martin. "The Grayness of Darkness: *The Honeymoon Killers* and Its Impact on Psychokiller Cinema." *Mythologies of Violence in Postmodern Media*, edited by Christopher Sharrett, Wayne State UP, 1999, pp. 41–64.
Mulvey, Laura. "Visual Pleasure and Narrative Cinema." *Screen*, vol. 16, no. 3, 1975, pp. 6–18.
Ressler, Robert K., and Tom Shachtman. *I Have Lived in the Monster: A Report from the Abyss*. St. Martin's, 1997.
Santos, Marlisa. *The Dark Mirror: Psychiatry and Film Noir*. Rowman and Littlefield, 2010.
Seltzer, Mark. *Serial Killers: Death and Life in America's Wound Culture*. Routledge, 1998.
Slotkin, Richard. *Regeneration through Violence: The Mythology of the American Frontier*. Wesleyan UP, 1973.

6

Pathologies of Pedagogy in Midcentury Melodrama

The Miracle Worker and *A Child Is Waiting*

JENNIFER L. JENKINS

IN THE EARLY 1960S BOTH Washington and Hollywood took a long, hard look at how people with intellectual, physical, and sensory impairments were being educated and integrated into US society. Coincident with the Kennedy and Johnson administrations' progressive inclusivity legislation, *The Miracle Worker* (1962) and *A Child is Waiting* (1963) examine deafblindness and mental retardation as they affect family relations and social views of parenting. Arthur Penn's much-hailed biopic about Helen Keller and John Cassavetes's fictional social problem film about intellectually disabled children at a residential school both pair the experimental educational theories of their narratives with experimental film aesthetics. Despite being produced within the Hollywood studio system—albeit by the more progressive United Artists—each film reveals aesthetic techniques that were as experimental in their time, as was the pedagogy applied by Annie Sullivan (Anne Bancroft) and Dr. Clark (Burt Lancaster) in their respective educational settings.

Just as Sullivan rejects the notion that Helen is ineducable and searches for the key to unlock the mind inside the deafblind child, so

Dr. Clark rejects the accepted practice of warehousing the intellectually disabled, and challenges each child to rise to his or her potential. This commitment to individualism and denial of homogeneity among a strikingly diverse population of special needs students reflects some of John Dewey's more progressive pedagogical thinking. While Dewey wanted to change the educational environment to thwart passivity, progressive education for "retarded" children similarly sought to engage the child in creative, linguistic, musical, movement, and expressive activities. A parallel reading of these two films reveals the ways in which standard family melodrama tropes bend and break when the subject matter is disability. In keeping with midcentury developmental theories, both films position the mother as the problem: either too protective or utterly rejecting, and neither depicted sympathetically. Penn's film rejects sentimentality as firmly as did Annie Sullivan, yet his story does offer a redemption narrative for Helen once her isolation is breached. Abby Mann's remarkable screenplay for *A Child* shifts the redemption plot from the focal child, Reuben Widdicombe (Bruce Ritchie) to the apparently ineducable music teacher (Judy Garland). In each case, the teacher character must learn to reach the child on her or his own terms and in language she or he can access. Thus, the full range of audio and visual cinematic techniques comes into play to convey the child's view of the world and the teacher's response to it, challenging accepted Hollywood film language conventions. Penn deftly uses a black and white aesthetic to convey the visual boundaries of both Annie's and Helen's worlds, and pulls from his actors performances drawn from silent film acting styles. Cassavetes deploys his experimental filmmaker's toolkit to offer children's POV shots, reversing high angle associations with power and low angle shots with helplessness. With the camera in among the children, Cassavetes uses a remarkable number of close-ups on people who had hitherto been kept off-screen and out of the public eye. Penn's and Cassavetes's films, viewed in the immediate context of the Kennedy-Johnson administrations' groundbreaking and cotemporaneous Mental Retardation Facilities and Community Mental Health Construction Act (1963), reveal how progressive educational philosophy translates to the midcentury cinematic melodrama.

Pragmatist John Dewey's progressive educational reforms marked a sea change in US pedagogy. Coming as they did at the height of the Gilded Age, itself fueled by industrialism that largely depended upon child labor, Dewey's ideas challenged the very capitalist fabric of America. Educating children from early childhood onward would serve the greater good of society; collaborative, creative educational models based on integration across cultural, class, and ability levels would create a more empathic citizenry. It would take the Depression for child labor laws to be implemented along with compulsory education legislation, but Dewey's theories of integrative, communitarian child education, proposed as early as 1896, ultimately prevailed. In the decade following *Brown v. The Board of Education of Topeka, Kansas* (1954) and despite pushback against integration and continual resistance to secular curricula across the South, US schools became more diverse and more inclusive than ever before. Educational histories of the postwar period tend to focus on racial desegregation, but this was a significant period for disability rights as well.

Among its social programs, the Kennedy administration (1961–63) placed emphasis on mental retardation as a civil rights issue. Kennedy's agenda was widely believed to be rooted in his experience with his sister Rose Marie, or "Rosemary," whose intellectual disabilities were a guarded family secret.[1] The Kennedy family subscribed to the cultural view of the time, that cognitive and sensory disabilities were shameful and not to be seen publically. Indeed, Kennedy's 1961 Panel on Mental Retardation focused on "prevention" and quality of life: "Our goal should be to prevent retardation. Failing this, we must provide for the retarded the same opportunity for social development that is the birthright of every American child" ("Statement by the President"). The resulting amendments to the Social Security Act reflected the prevailing assumption that intellectual disability was rooted in maternal neglect, whether pre- or postnatal. The goal of the "Maternal and Child Health and Mental Retardation Planning Amendments of 1963" was "[t]o amend the Social Security Act to assist States and communities in preventing and combating mental retardation through expansion and improvement of the maternal and child health and crippled children's programs, through provision of prenatal, maternity, and infant care for individuals with *conditions associated with childbearing* which may lead to mental retardation, and through planning for comprehensive action to combat mental retardation, and for other purposes" (Public Law 88-156). Mother-blaming was widespread in the educational and medical literature of the time. Developmental and medical practitioners alike attributed retardation to a wide range of maternal misdeeds, from prostitution to perceived coldness to inability to breastfeed to multigenerational poverty. Concomitant with cause-and-cure agendas was a limited notion of personhood for people with cognitive and sensory impairments. It is worth noting that not until 1974 did an executive action, signed by Richard Nixon, "assure the retarded full status as citizens under the law" (Office).

These well-meant progressive steps in the second half of the twentieth century occurred in a social context not far removed from medieval views of mental and physical difference. Susan Schweik's study of the US criminalization of display and commodification of people with a wide range of disabilities reveals public abhorrence of difference on aesthetic grounds. So-called "ugly laws," adopted as early as 1867 and finally put to rest only by the Americans with Disabilities Act (1987), imposed penalties for the mere appearance in public of visibly disabled people. While rightly criminalizing the captive exhibition of physically and intellectually impaired persons, the laws also were applied to Civil War veteran amputees, "cripples" attempting to make a living as newspaper and fruit sellers, polio survivors, the merely poor, and mentally disabled people walking on the street with family members (Schweik 1–20). The emphasis on removing the "ugly" from public view codifies the association of difference with unsightliness, a view expressed by Helen Keller's half-brother James: "Half-sister, and half-mentally defective, she can't even keep herself clean. It's not pleasant to see her about all the time" (Gibson, screenplay revision, scene 13, 9). Such sentiments, while true to the Sullivan-Keller story of 1887, were still prevalent and openly, unapologetically voiced in the early 1960s when *The Miracle Worker* was produced on television, stage, and screen.

The etiologies of childhood cognitive disability were a hot topic in clinical and social literature at midcentury. Science of the day could identify causes for scarlet fever and meningitis (possible causes of Helen Keller's impairments) and also believed it could define the cause of autism.[2] Rather than genetics, as we now know, midcentury psychiatrists blamed poor, inexperienced, and unloving mothers for their autistic children's failure to thrive. In each of these films, parents are posited as contributors to, if not direct causes of, their children's issues.

Cinema as an art form is defined by the dynamic relation between form and content, aesthetic and narrative. It is the disalignment of these binaries that also most often disturbs people confronted with disabilities, particularly cognitive ones. Dysmorphic physical features in persons with Down syndrome and cerebral palsy, and behavioral variants in deafblind persons discomfit the public because they indicate a lack of continuity between form and content, body and mind. These are the anomalies that ugly laws were meant to address through an out-of-sight, out-of-mind strategy. In cinema, genre conventions exist to define the reflexive relationship between content and form, the story and how it is told. Westerns offer extreme longshots of landscape to indicate the alienation of the individual in a hostile environment, and cross-cut editing to simulate the tension between antagonists in a Main Street shootout. Romantic comedies play in soft palettes and well-lighted locations, leading and following the act 3 rainstorm that provides pathetic fallacy for the breakup, prelude to the makeup, and spectacle of union. Disability films, following the conventions of the melodrama, locate in homes, whether family or institutional, and use interior settings to indicate the claustrophobia of human relationships. Films that focus specifically on the sensory or cognitively impaired child often intensify that stifling domestic atmosphere with audiovisual experiments meant to represent the child's world as experienced through sensory or intellectual difference. This shift in the form-content dynamic draws attention to perceptual differences and is often a well-intentioned attempt to "speak" for the child. The dys- or misalignment of form and content, body and mind, presents a parallel binary between the disabled child and the cinematic medium. Just as "special" education sought to align the body and mind of the atypical child to sociocultural standards of normality, so midcentury cinematic representations appealed to genre tropes to contain the aesthetic variations that expressed the child's POV.

The Miracle Worker

The Miracle Worker was produced three times in five years: for television on *Playhouse 90* (1957), on the Broadway stage (1959), and as a feature film (1962)—all directed by Arthur Penn as he moved through different performance media. As Nat Segaloff admiringly notes, "It is also the only instance in which the same director guided the same material through three different mediums, adjusting his vision to accommodate each of them and ultimately achieving success in all" (92). *Variety*, reviewing the film in May 1962, caviled a bit about the adaptation of "the legit [onstage] version" to film, but nonetheless dared audiences not to see it: "The magnitude of its appeal may be leveled somewhat by a curious reluctance on the part of many people to expose themselves to such a grim, emotionally devastating experience. *The Miracle Worker* takes a lot out of a viewer, and there are those who shy away from anything that appears to demand total involvement, even if it is an ennobling and uplifting event" (Tube 6). There are hints of the sentiments that fueled the ugly laws here: *Variety* challenges viewers not to be squeamish or shallow in their approach to the subject matter of disability. The reward, of course, will be uplift and redemption both onscreen and for the enlightened audience who choose to attend.

Penn and his creative team, including producer Fred Coe, who had steered the production from *Playhouse 90* onward, were highly cognizant of the need to use the cinematic medium to its fullest capacity in the transition from stage to big screen. *Playhouse 90* engaged televisual aesthetics to the extent possible in a live broadcast, but provided no blueprint for audiovisual construction of the story as a cinematic narrative shot without a proscenium. Coming directly from the stage, the director and actors had gained twenty months' experience with representing deafblind constraints to theater audiences. Unable to convey visual impairment in the theater beyond use of lighting, the stage production had turned to audio devices to indicate both time shifts and the ocular disease that marked Annie Sullivan's childhood. Cinema, as a fully integrated audiovisual medium, offered a full array of aesthetic options for representing sensory impairment.

The teleplay, stage play, and film of *The Miracle Worker* all open with a moment of crisis: the revelation that the child is not perfect. In the film, this early scene is shot at cradle level, purportedly from the infant's eye view. Kate Keller's (Inga Swenson) realization that her daughter can neither see nor hear is troped as a moment of Gothic horror, with canted camera angle, chiaroscuro lighting, and a maternal reaction that anticipates the scene in Roman Polanksi's *Rosemary's Baby* (1968) when Rosemary screams, "What have you done to its eyes?" Both Keller parents scream and clap and wave a light near the child's eyes, to no avail. Despite the low-angle camera, the point of view is *not* the child's, as that would be pure blackness and silence.

The earliest representations of sensory inhibition in the film involve Annie Sullivan's flashbacks to her impoverished childhood. As she travels from Boston to Tuscumbia, Alabama, Annie's anxieties and uncertainties provide the backstory of her visual impairment and how she achieved an education. Penn explains how the theatrical staging of flashbacks moved from audio to audiovisual with the transition to cinema:

> "Where we had voices on the stage out of Annie's past," [Penn] describes, "now I wanted something visually equivalent. It was done by a very complicated process. We blew the image up to the point where the emulsion broke down to where you could just barely discern a figure. We had to blow it up thirty-two times so, in order to shoot a close-up, we used a very wide lens from all the way across the studio and cut a dot in a matte

in front of our viewfinder, and that dot is what we used. We knew that it would eventually fill the screen when we blew it up to that point." (Segaloff 94)

Pushing the technical and chemical limits of film, Penn offers the audience an experience of visual impairment early in the narrative, before Annie and Helen ever meet. Thus Penn is schooling us in empathy for both characters by providing a disorienting sensory overload. (The distortion is accurate for Annie, who was sighted and recognized its disappearance, but perhaps only metaphoric for Helen, who was never sighted—a distinction that bears thinking about.) The sensory dimension of the film's impact even extended to the invitations to the premiere. Embossed white-on-white lettering on stiff Bristol stock "conveys the feeling of braille, hence relates to the film's theme of a young girl taught to overcome the crushing handicap of blindness." A glossy black and white image from the central dinner scene is inside ("Out of Darkness" 40). The focus of Gibson's script is not, of course, braille but sign language, although both are coded systems based on symbolic representations of letters. Both of these examples attempt to approximate blindness for sighted audiences as a model of empathy.

As conceived by Gibson and Penn, the story of Annie Sullivan and Helen Keller focuses both literally and metaphorically on finding the key to unlock Helen's language brain. Keys as objects become onscreen instruments of power: Helen locks Annie in her upstairs room and hides the key; Annie locks the Keller family out of the dining room to achieve some discipline and order at mealtime; Annie moves Helen to the garden house to shut out the family's coddling influence. Finger-spelling offers the key to Helen's sensory impairments; thus it becomes the key to empowerment. This objective correlative provides the narrative with an underlying tone of optimism, taking the view that cognitive and sensory disability can be "unlocked" by the right teacher and methodology. This perspective subscribes to the curative agenda promoted in midcentury legislation, and in Keller's case was correct. Indeed, in the last act of the play and film Helen retrieves her mother's keys and gives them to Annie, in a symbolic and real acknowledgment that Annie has access to her.

Interestingly, William Gibson's story about Annie Sullivan and Helen Keller began as a ballet (Segaloff 84). The choreographed nature of the interactions between the two principals reflects that primal and kinetic relationship. They reel through interior and exterior space, connected by a doll, a spoon, a water pitcher, and spelling hands. Sullivan's determination to provide a linguistic correlate for each and every noun in their interactions makes the hand to hand contact (and combat) a linkage as critical as God's to Adam in the Sistine ceiling. In each version, the story hits three key pedagogical moments: the dining room scene; the water-pump scene; and Helen's reconciliation with Annie after finding language. The first two scenes answer each other in setting and struggle, although the second reverses the first with the catharsis of understanding. The reconciliation scene serves as a denouement, with the naming of Annie as "teacher" through Helen's hand-spelling. Each of these scenes in this Aristotelian sequence emphasizes the transformative role of the pedagogue in the story. From the beginning, playwright William Gibson insisted on Sullivan as the protagonist, pointedly remarking that the title was not "*The Miracle Workee*" (Segaloff 87). The Academy of Motion Picture Arts and Sciences agreed: Anne Bancroft was nominated for and won the Oscar for Best Actress, while Patty Duke's astonishing and equally honored performance was remanded to the Best Supporting Actress category.

The dining room scene inaugurates this relationship. In a nine minute, twenty-two second sequence comprised of seventy-eight shots, Penn's camera follows Sullivan and Keller as they struggle over sitting in a chair and eating with a spoon. The sequence is shot on a three-quarter set, with the camera at the fourth wall, and deft use of pan and match-on-action edits to keep the principals in frame. Most importantly, the film aesthetic diverges from traditional soundstage camera work in an attempt to convey the chaotic environment created by Helen's frustrated inability to communicate and her parents' indulgence of her feral behavior. Both Helen's perspective and Annie's are artfully conveyed by what *Variety* perceptively termed "visual storytelling."[3] Given that this nine-minute filmic sequence (written as eight but often running to ten minutes onstage) contains no dialogue, the visual focus on the principals and the need for the camera to be in among the action are critical. Each character garners full close-ups, reaction shots, POV shots, and moments of visible interiority in equal measure: Helen's lack of audiovisual perception does not hinder Penn from conveying her full presence and cognition in this sequence.

The shooting script labels this sequence as scenes 122–40, without scene delineation. Simple descriptions of action follow, as in Gibson's play script. Clearly the camera angle and editing decisions were left to the creative team. What is clear even on the page is the way in which this sequence is absolutely dedicated to tutelage rather than exploration. The lesson is a simple one: sit in a chair, eat with a spoon. Sullivan's repetitive insistence illustrates the kind of rote learning that was popular in the US from hornbook days forward. Annie knows that Helen is smart enough not to need such repetition, but the exercise will continue until Helen accedes to learning at all. Just as Helen learns the limits of acceptable behavior and Annie's patience, so viewing audiences—who might be inclined to share the Kellers' helpless acceptance of Helen's tyranny—learn that empathy without understanding is merely condescension. Watching all this take place on the distanced tableau of a proscenium stage is one thing; cinema presents a close-up experience of this lesson, with nowhere else to look.

The dining room sequence is almost entirely composed of two-shots, many at medium range, in order to capture Helen's frenetic actions and Annie's repetitive and determined responses. A sound bridge of Helen's feet kicking the floor leads into the sequence, which begins with the camera at floor level. The camera dollies back and tilts up to include in frame Annie at the table eating her meal as Helen wears herself out by kicking and pounding in the lower foreground. A short take of Annie eating while watching Helen out of the corner of her eye establishes an across-the-table, head-and-shoulders shot that will constitute the "normative" shot in the sequence. Any normality of action is subverted when Helen yanks Annie's chair away, an action seen only in its effects from the tabletop point of view. And so it begins: the dance of dinner.

Far more than a teaching exercise, this sequence is a battle of wills choreographed on the domestic space of a dining room. The lesson is intimately tied to place, since Helen will not be released from the locked room until she sits in a chair, eats with a spoon, and folds her napkin. Basic familial routine trumps higher learning at this point: adhering to the social contract is the foundation for all other lessons. Just as hand-spelling without comprehension is a first step, so learning to behave is prelude to learning everything else. This is a collaborative—if not cooperative—activity: neither of the two principals is alone in frame for more than a few seconds. When Helen is centered in medium close-up, Annie moves into frame to engage in the next movement of the dance. If Annie is the focus, Helen sneaks in with a pinch or lunges away from her reach. Almost like a silent film, much of the action is tracked by a fixed camera pan rather than a dolly shot, keeping viewers out of range of flailing arms and legs as the action rounds the table and races from one door to the other. At two points during the sequence, the camera appears to be (although probably was not) handheld, following first Helen and then Annie as they move sequentially around the dining table in a pas de deux. The two principals feint clockwise and counterclockwise around the table, crawl over and under it, cast out from and back into a chair on the far side of the table, pinch, slap and slap back, windmill, and wrestle together over the spoon, even sending Annie into a somersault at one point. The scene's effectiveness as cinema owes a good deal to skillful editing by Aram Avakian, whose patterns of match-on action, moderate jump cuts, and intercutting between the principals in nondialogue reaction sequences are nearly invisible. Avakian's intuitive editing simulates the stage audience's sightlines while providing the cinematic intimacy that is unattainable in live theater.

As noted, this scene promotes a pedagogy of repetition without critical thinking, although Helen clearly evinces the ability to outmaneuver her teacher. Annie Sullivan's method tied words to things. For Helen, critical thinking would follow once the association of language with objects was established. Indeed, the climactic pump scene not only captures Helen's moment of comprehension, but establishes the connection between (remembered) spoken language ("waa-waa"), the thing itself, and its symbolic representation in sign language. Helen accesses not only language but writing in that critical thinking moment.[4]

Penn and Gibson stage the pump scene as a dance, as well. As in the earlier sequence, this duet begins in anger and ends in learning rather than capitulation. The contrast of interior and exterior setting, before knowing and after, in the two scenes also speaks to the balletic construction of the source narrative. Back in the dining room after two weeks removed from the family, Helen quickly reverts to her accepted and protected feral habits. All that she has learned in the garden cottage is threatened by the family's low expectations for her behavior. This domestic battleground shows all the signs of an early defeat: Helen will not sit, will not use utensils, and resists Annie's corrections. After Helen soaks her with a pitcherful of water, Annie drags the regressing child to the outdoor pump to refill the pitcher. As she hauls Helen from the house, she rebukes the family: "I treat her like a seeing child because I *ask* her to see, I *expect* her to see, don't undo what I do!" Teacher and student move away from the house in a tracking pan left, toward the pump. The take continues unbroken as Annie pumps the handle, the water pours over Helen's hand, and Annie spells w-a-t-e-r into her other hand. A cutaway 90-degree shot of Sullivan shows her startled reaction to Helen holding tight to her spelling fingers. The shot cuts back to the tableau with the pump as Helen throws aside the pitcher, the dawn of recognition on her face. Three quick close ups on Helen's face, her

Pathologies of Pedagogy in Midcentury Melodrama 139

Figure 6.1. Breakthrough moment with W-A-T-E-R for Helen Keller (Patty Duke) with her teacher, Annie Sullivan (Anne Bancroft), in *The Miracle Worker*.

hand over the end of the pump, and Sullivan's reaction shot lead to the medium shot with the two principals on either side of the pump. As Helen slowly and painfully sounds out "waa-waa," Annie leans in on the pump handle, almost as though she is priming the association. And, of course, she is, and has been for the long weeks of their association. From that first epiphany, Helen spins about, finding other things to name and know: ground, pump, tree, step, mother.

Annie follows closely, spelling and saying (for the audience, since Helen cannot hear) the name of each. Teacher and pupil progress together through the yard in a series of chassés among nouns, waltzing into language. Dewey was clear that this kind of epiphany or discovery is essential to the growth of the thinking being: "An individual is not original merely when he gives to the world some discovery that has never been made before. Every time he really makes a discovery, even if thousands of persons have made similar ones before, he is an original. The value of discovery in the mental life of an individual is the contribution it makes to a creatively active mind; it does not depend upon no one's ever having thought of the same idea before" (*Later Works* 5:128). But the money shot of the whole film comes in a moment of stasis: Helen breaks from her parents' embrace and learns that t-e-a-c-h-e-r is Annie's noun.

Word and thing are joined in a semiotic synthesis. This is the catharsis moment for the plot and for viewers. (Theater and film reviewers alike reported few dry eyes among audiences.) It also provides a cosy takeaway: audiences can feel good about this narrative of uplift, and the historicity of the film doesn't challenge the status quo in terms of cultural value of teachers. Early on Sullivan says that she has nothing to lose in taking on the deafblind child, because she has no home and no money. Helen's "redemption" will prove to be her own, as well.

The irredeemable or ineducable parent is a standard figure in the midcentury disability film. In Gibson's narrative, the father rejects the child and is willing to have her institutionalized rather than have his dinner disrupted or his patriarchal authority challenged. His peremptory question to Sullivan—"Do you even *like* the child?"—receives the appropriate answer—"Do you?" The stern and unloving parent is also a common melodrama villain, and Keller (Victor Jory) fits the bill on several counts: he is an unreconstructed Southerner in 1887; he is a pompous and self-righteous autocrat in the family; and he blames his young second wife not only for their daughter's disabilities, but also for her inability to "control" the child. Similarly, he opposes all of Sullivan's methods and attempts to impose his will upon her, frequently reminding her that she is a Northerner, a girl, and a servant in his household. Only once Helen is housebroken and her intellect unlocked is Keller willing to own the child.[5] His final pulling of Helen away from "Teacher" into a rather creepy embrace as he carries her into the house suggests a change of heart, but it is telling that Helen ends the film rocking in Sullivan's lap.

The Miracle Worker is a story of cure: a child brought out of a near-feral state to language and learning by a talented and persistent teacher. Helen Keller was imprisoned by her impairments, but she was certainly not intellectually limited. Most films about deaf and blind students present just such a redemption narrative: the child conquers the disability and achieves some "normality." This storyline raises the issue of whether homogeneity is the goal of education, and serious, related questions about disability and personhood. As with racial uplift films—another subset of the midcentury melodrama that positions selfhood as disability—many films that focus on sensory impairments promote normative assimilation.[6] If "normality" is the goal, what happens to the essential individual when the unsightly or unseemly behaviors and traits have been tamed or modified? The redemption narrative also, I would argue, is easy on cinema-goers, who need not examine their own prejudices because they can feel good about their pity by approving social uplift from the safe distance of a theater or cinema seat. Whatever the overt or even unintended effect of cure and redemption films, they present a narrative that is simply not available to actual autism-spectrum and cognitively impaired children, their teachers, and their families.

A Child Is Waiting

Screenwriter Abby Mann reported that in his postwar writing class at New York University he met a woman who worked with retarded children. At her invitation, he visited their school and met their parents, and he came away with an idea for a social justice drama. Mann reported being quite moved by the children: "Kids who were trying their best. They had as much feelings as any of us; they had to ascend to whatever they could do" (Mann, interview 05:50).

A Child Is Waiting moved from prestige television to cinema under the guiding hand of its author, Abby Mann, at roughly the same time as did William Gibson's Sullivan-Keller story. Mann originally wrote the teleplay in 1957 for CBS's *Studio One*;[7] he later adapted the one-hour script into a 1963 feature film for United Artists. The subject matter—institutional education of autism spectrum and intellectually disabled children—was set in contemporary times and offered none of the historical distance of the Sullivan-Keller biopic.

Director Stanley Kramer, fresh off *Judgment at Nuremberg*, was originally attached to the project. When *Nuremberg* proved a success, Kramer found himself overcommitted, and hired John Cassavetes to direct. Having directed only two studio films, Cassavetes agreed to bring this challenging material to the screen. The two men had highly divergent views of the film content and thus its genre: Kramer saw the film as a love story set in a residential school for retarded children, while Cassavetes, following Mann, saw the story as a social issue film focused on the abilities and agency of the children. Ultimately, Kramer—who maintained some degree of control over the project—recut the film from Cassavetes's starker, unvarnished rough cut. True to Hollywood form, the promotion campaign followed Kramer's version: the film poster shows Judy Garland and Burt Lancaster positioned together in a heart-shaped pencil drawing, while the lobby cards also showcase couple Stephen Hill and Gena Rowlands as Ted and Sophie Widdicombe. Despite the film's title, the only publicity image depicting a child at all is one of Stephen Hill and the girl playing Jenny, the Widdicombes' second and "normal" child. This condescending sentimentality, also evident in Kramer's recut of Cassavetes's footage, led the young director to demand his name be removed from the film and, by his own account, to sock Kramer in the jaw (Cassavetes 122). Such was the degree to which this content inspired strong feelings and genre alliances.

The film begins with a dolly-in to a car, and around through the open door to a boy (Bruce Ritchie) sitting in the back seat of a large sedan. He is composed, sitting with his hands folded, observing. A shadow falls across him as a female voice says, "Hello, Reuben," and a large woman steps into frame, leaning into the car. As she tries to cajole him from the car, the scene cuts to a man standing on the porch of a neoclassical building, joined by a second man, Dr. Clark (Burt Lancaster). The boy remains impassive, and the scene shifts back to the porch, as the camera cranes in to track Dr. Clark as he descends the steps and leans into the car. At this intrusion, the impassive boy leans away. The next shot comes from over his shoulder, showing the degree to which Dr. Clark dominates the space physically. The doctor turns away and retrieves a pedal car with a loud bell and Klaxon, enticing Reuben out of the automobile with a toy that is often more appealing to younger children. As Reuben tries out the pedal car, his father (Steven Hill) sneaks down the steps and speeds away with the car door still open. Reuben leaps round to witness the abandonment, screaming "Daddy, Mommy" as Dr. Clark struggles to restrain him. The credit sequence begins.

As with *The Miracle Worker*, this film begins with a moment of recognition and a primal scream. In this case, the anagnorisis is the child's, the chaos of abandonment expressed in the distorted extreme close-up and guttural cries on the soundtrack. Given the columned, porched building and the baby-on-the-doorstep trope, this film narrative could easily turn gothic. Also as with *The Miracle Worker*, however, once the teacher enters the story the nascent gothic elements diffuse into mere melodrama.

After the credit sequence, shot over children's drawings—clearly a Stanley Kramer addition—with drums and rattles for score, the action opens with a dissolve though a dark cloud shape in a child's drawing onto a woman sitting in the back seat of a vehicle. As she comes into focus, we see her thinking and raising an eyebrow apprehensively. From a bird's-eye shot of her taxi pulling up the drive, we cut to a shot of the cab stopping just where Mr. Widdicombe's car had been. The woman exits the cab readily, and enters the neoclassical building. This sequence and the one that precedes it show two individuals coming to the institution for different reasons and with different degrees of agency. Jean

Hanson (Judy Garland) enters the building just as the class bell rings and doorways open along a vanishing point hallway. She goes from being alone in center frame to being surrounded by children in a matter of seconds. Shot from the stairwell landing down the hallway, this scene introduces Cassavetes's intimate and unapologetic presentation of the developmentally delayed children in the story. The children, played by students from the Pacific State Hospital for the Retarded in Pomona, California, garner so much screen time that Stanley Kramer had a hard time recutting the footage into the sentimental pity film he intended. As premier Cassavetes scholar and apologist Raymond Carney notes, Cassavetes's "affection . . . for the children . . . is so deep and sincere that for the first half hour of the film, it actually deflects our attention away from the plot and the supposedly more important adult characters around them" (78). In fact, children are on-screen on average every six minutes throughout the film's hundred minute duration.

Cassavetes's honest approach grants the children personhood without compromise or condescension. Given that intellectually disabled people had not been seen in a studio-funded feature film since perhaps Tod Browning's *Freaks* (1932), this matter-of-fact presentation is notable for its offhandedness. While the focus on the kids was a popular choice

Figure 6.2. First-day polite nerves of Jean Hansen (Judy Garland) as she enters a classroom of mentally challenged children in *A Child Is Waiting*.

with the otherwise hypercritical Abby Mann (Fine 141–42) and many of the crew, the principal actors, backed by Stanley Kramer, were less enthused—and not just because they weren't center frame in every shot. It is important to remember that in 1963 American mainstream culture was not above what Susan Schweik calls "exoticized enfreakment," that is, the objectification of disabled people into things (223). Schweik mentions in passing that such objectification constructs impaired subjects as screens onto which the culture may project all manner of anxieties, fears, and hatreds, asking (but not answering), "'What does it mean to become a screen?'" Schweik's focus is the overlay of disability and race in fiction, but her premise is a provocative one for examining the representation of disability, particularly cognitive disability, in cinema. It is important to note that her metaphor is *screen* rather than *mirror*: the culture is not interested in seeing itself in the projection, only in finding a place to locate, frame, and offset its anxieties and dread.[8] Indeed, 1963 was also the year that Diane Arbus shifted to a large format camera and literally made disability the screen, fully enfreaking her disabled subjects in the photographic medium. Thus when we turn to representations of education for this population, the issue is already fraught: Why should "they" be seen at all, and why should "they" be educated? Cassavetes's insistence on showing the students in classes, making, learning, and finding joy is a powerful answer, then and now. Like Abby Mann, Cassavetes spent time with retarded children and their parents, and was moved by their inherent dignity: "I found the kids funny and human and sad. But mainly funny—and real. . . . I wanted to show that they were human and warm—not 'cases' but kids. . . . My film said that retarded children could be anywhere, any time, and that *the problem is that we're a bunch of dopes, that it's our problem more than the kids.*' The point of the original picture we made was that there was no fault, that there was nothing wrong with these children except that their mentality was lower" (Cassavetes 123; emphasis added). Indeed, his approach is one that Todd Lekan identifies with social justice efforts on behalf of the disabled population: "Frequently, the 'handicap' is the result of past discriminatory practices, which has resulted in social environments that exclude individuals with various kinds of impairments. Justice requires that we repair the environments, not the people" (216). No less a cultural force than Bosley Crowther in the *New York Times* commended the film's impact, despite attributing it to Kramer: "Some painful but compelling instruction on how to adjust emotionally to the sometimes calamitous problem of the mentally retarded child is conveyed with courageous candor and dramatic-simplicity in Stanley Kramer's new film, 'A Child Is Waiting.'"

The two backseat scenes establish a parallel between Jean and Reuben before they ever meet. Although their reasons for being at Crawthorn are different, each is an outcast and a reject. Reuben has been labeled "defective" by the medical establishment and thus rejected by his parents, while Jean has failed to make good on her Julliard training as a pianist and thus is also in some way classed as defective. Jean and Reuben are paired, just as Annie Sullivan and Helen Keller are, by their disabilities. This affinity gives each teacher some insight and some motivation. *A Child* works hard to show that Jean's lack of training and excess of empathy—positioning her as the opposite of Annie Sullivan in terms of method—do Reuben little good and potentially much harm.

Oddly, Jean Hanson's emotionalism leads her to voice a defense of Reuben in terms that sound quite Deweyan. She argues for Reuben's right to resist Dr. Clark's methods, to be his own person rather than succumbing to the school's rigorous rules and discipline. Dr. Clark argues that structure is the only security the children will have, while Hanson tries to make the case for the greater good of individuality. It is Dr. Clark who actually echoes Sullivan in rebuking Jean for making Reuben a special friend, accusing her of lowering expectations: "You want to coddle them, you want to take the falls for them, you want to suckle them at your breast, you want to give them your love. Well, your love is not enough. They need more than that, more than that.... I'd rather fail this way, fighting for one inch of [Reuben's] dignity than to have him denatured by your love for him." To illustrate the consequences of such denaturing, Dr. Clark takes Jean to the state asylum, which houses men who were "like Reuben" but kept at home until adulthood. The criminally insane, the emotionally disturbed, and the cognitively impaired are all placed together in an underfunded facility that offers no education, no stimulation, simply warehousing.[9] This solution is diametrically opposite to Dewey's view of education, which is embedded in Dr. Clark's statement above. Dewey shaped his educational theory as an ethical approach to fellow beings, firmly rooted in neo-Enlightenment principles of democracy: "The democratic faith in human equality is belief that every human being, independent of the quantity or range of his personal endowment, has the right to equal opportunity with every other person for development of whatever gifts he has" ("Creative Democracy" 227–28). For Dewey and his avatar Dr. Clark, a just society depends upon and demands equal protection and cultivation of individual gifts, not incarceration due to difference—and not condescension disguised as sympathy.

Visiting day at the Crawthorn School presents a panorama of social attitudes toward intellectual disability across races and classes. As the multicultural students gather in their best clothes, a boy named Junius calls out the make and model of each arriving car. Various students and families meet up: the late-adolescent Abe and his embarrassed upper-middle class parents, who try to tip one of the teachers; African-American Junius and his mother and six brothers, who tease and joke with him, the most relaxed and loving family depicted; Eric, grinning from ear to ear with his older brother, an army sergeant in dress uniform. These students have visitors, but many others, like Reuben, spend their Wednesday afternoons waiting for visitors who never arrive. Cassavetes again gives ample screen time to the children, showing the joy of reunion, the confusion at parents' stilted reactions, and the disappointment of rejection. The children take center frame, while uncomfortable parents remain in shadows and inside their cars, able to flee at will. The distance between the children's accomplishments and their parents' expectations is vast, and the parents are shown to be unforgiving of or oblivious to small achievements, such as Abe's handmade basket for his mother. Visiting day ends with a mother saying to Dr. Clark, "If we could just get Willie to learn his catechism, I'd feel so much better."

After the disappointments of visiting day, Jean convinces a colleague to let her read Reuben's case history. This information occurs in flashback, with an (uncredited) authoritarian midcentury male voiceover. Reuben's parents, Ted and Sophie Widdicombe, are revealed to be college-educated urbanites who live in a stylish garden apartment and confront the boy's developmental delays with increasing anxiety and fractiousness. They are shot in medium close-up, but from a slightly low angle, as if to indicate Reuben's point of view. While he is not an onscreen witness to their conversations about him, the POV aesthetic suggests that he may be aware of the dispositions being made. The purportedly scientific or at least clinical recitation of Reuben's growth and development overlays the Widdicombes' incremental closing off of emotion and empathy for their son. The voiceover fades as Ted takes the lead in seeing specialists for Reuben, while Sophie puts her energy into Reuben's younger sister, Jenny. Rather than vignetting the visual image, Cassavetes uses a slight echo effect in the audio track of Ted and Sophie's dialog to indicate events in the past. When Ted comes home with the news that "he's defective," the voiceover returns to report that three other doctors confirmed the diagnosis of mental retardation. After a dizzying and potentially lethal mountain driving sequence that cuts between head-on and tail-on car shots, Ted places Reuben in Crawthorn State Training School. The voiceover reports that the Widdicombes divorced a month later, and Sophie remarried and took custody of Jenny. This retrospective sequence ends with Reuben in the back seat of the sedan, just where the film began. Cassavetes offers this familiar image without commentary or sentiment, although Kramer's choice of musical score employs strings to play up the melodrama of Reuben's institutional commitment. We do not get a shot of Jean closing the file, nor her reaction to the embedded narrative. Instead, the focus remains on the Widdicombe family as the locus of this now-medical melodrama. Both parents are shown to be emotionally unavailable and unable to reach Reuben, although Ted does arrange for his care. The rejecting parents in Mann's screenplay of *A Child is Waiting* reflect some of the cultural theories of autism of the time. Led by Bruno Bettelheim, many clinicians viewed the cause of infant autism as "refrigerator mothers" and maternal failure to bond (Weusten 55–59). Parental rejection of disabled children was common and accepted in the day, when parents were advised to have another child and forget the institutionalized one. Cassavetes's footage is decidedly not sympathetic to these parents, showing how they have failed the children rather than the reverse.

The annual school picnic shows the kids being kids and enjoying their day of free play. Kramer's obvious recut of Cassavetes's footage attempts to shape this sequence into a budding romance between Jean Hansen and Dr. Clark, yet, again, Cassavetes's shot selection (and apparent lack of coverage) foregrounds the easy, familiar if not familial relationships between staff and students at Crawthorn. The sequence simply cannot be recut into a workplace romance. By this point in the film, distinct characters and personalities have emerged among the children, none of whom was a child actor except for Bruce Ritchie. They ad-lib within the scenes, and keep the professional actors on their toes in terms of listening and responding. What comes across in this picnic sequence is the immense capacity for joy among the children, and their empathy for each other. This is precisely the goal of Dewey's integrative theory of education: that children learn at school how to be members of a community.

Exactly midway through the film, Dr. Clark gets the opportunity to educate visiting elected officials (and us) in the realities of public support for training schools. The legislators ask for "tangible results" for a "normal life" comparable to those at schools for the deaf and blind; Dr. Clark counters with figures: five hundred children on a waiting list, $2,700 a year in state funds for each student—negligible when compared to allocations for roads, public monuments, and recreational facilities. As Dr. Clark builds to a full Lancastrian tirade, he pronounces the children's condition a sickness that can happen to anyone: "It happened to a sister of the President of the United States!"

When Reuben's mother arrives in response to a letter from Jean, she justifies her detachment as being "best" for Reuben. Sitting and coldly smoking in a severe suit and elbow-length black leather gloves, Gena Rowlands's demeanor and coldness as Sophie hints ever-so-slightly at the images of Nazi medicine that had filled the headlines of the 1950s. She absolutely refuses to see Reuben, and runs from the school to a waiting car when Jenny spots her brother through a window. This final solution elicits a second primal scream from Reuben, shown in medium close-up with a wide-open mouth and anguished eyes. Cassavetes denies Sophie a sympathetic answering shot, fading to a darkened dormitory where Reuben has exhausted himself with grief.

Later that evening Reuben, bereft of both his mother and Jean, runs away. His brief odyssey reveals more to the audience than to him about the challenges he would face in life outside the institution. This crisis of the lost child brings the narrative back into the realm of domestic melodrama, as Sophie takes to her bed with worry? guilt? grief? She seizes the center of attention, even drawing Ted back into the emotional theater of her midcentury bedroom, with tasteful chinoiserie furnishings, stenciled seagrass wallpaper, and a modernist mother and (female) child painting on the wall. Her perfect new life with lawyer husband and cute "normal" daughter has been breached. As the suffering mother, Sophie steps center stage to occupy the melodramatic position of victim, eschewing any role in Reuben's disappearance. From her raised, dais-like bed, she tells Ted to go see him because *he* doesn't care about the boy, then in the same breath admonishes Ted for not caring about the boy. He answers by saying that he wishes Reuben were dead; Ted confesses that he thought to run the car off the highway on the way to Crawthorn. But, he concedes, he will do what needs to be done in terms of private care. At least he was willing to die with, if not for, his son. This sequence varies between medium long shots and shot-reverse shots, following patterns of domestic melodrama that place familial discord in intimate settings. Sophie here is less mater dolorosa than devouring mother.

When school official Goodman (Paul Stewart) visits Ted Widdicome on a build site, the two men compare notes on parenting children with cognitive disabilities. Cassavetes positions the camera slightly low and off-kilter as Ted meets Goodman's advice with hostility. Framed by a half-built modernist space, the two men discuss the meaning and quality of life for their children. Goodman explains that when his own daughter Rose, who is now 28, was born he viewed it as a "tragedy." He notes that he had a child "you can't even take out in the street without people staring," invoking again the specter of ugly laws. "But Rose doesn't know she's a tragedy, so the tragedy must be in ourselves," concludes Goodman. As Goodman leaves Ted to think about that, a sound bridge takes us into the school's Thanksgiving play, with a multiracial array of Down's children in pilgrim costumes seated around a table. The boys are very taken with their pilgrim hats and deliver their few lines with conviction, prompting and reminding each other to look at the audience. Again they garner close-ups, and their fun is palpable. As the camera moves from child to child, we see children whom we have come to know as individuals during the preceding ninety minutes. Ted arrives just in time to hear Reuben recite a poem, and reacts with stunned disbelief, viewing his son in a whole new light. Thus the moment of redemption or transformation in this film comes through language, as in *The Miracle Worker*. In something of a reversal of Helen Keller's situation, Reuben has an active vocabulary, and needs only to harness it to ideas. His recitation proves the connection of language to ideas for himself, for Dr. Clark, and for Ted. Shot in extreme close-up, Reuben's expression remains impassive as he works diligently through the poem. Even through his Thanksgiving Indian makeup his concentration is evident. The rousing applause when he concludes brings no reaction from him at all. Only when he searches out and finds his father in the crowd does he react by rushing into a hug, his face hidden in Ted's coat. The choice of extreme close-up in the poem sequence commands close audience attention: we cannot look away from his searching eyes as Reuben sounds out his lines of verse.

The final scene takes us back to the beginning, as another set of parents arrives with a boy who will not exit the car. Dr. Clark asks Jean to see to the child, repeating the opening scene of a staff member leaning into the back seat of a sedan. This time, however, the camera is positioned on the child's side of the car, looking past Earl at his eye level through the window to Jean and Earl's parents approaching the car. As Jean leans in, she does not dominate the frame, but shares it with Earl. They talk about whether or not he would like to come in. "I say no," says Earl. Jean doesn't press, but tells him about the school, and then asks again, "Will you come with me now? Come on." She cajoles him with an endearment, and as Earl scoots across the seat to leave the car he says, "Darling?" Jean laughingly admits that he's a bit old, at eleven, to be called "darling," as she leads him into the school.

Disability as a form of objectification turns people into things, as ugly laws and Diane Arbus illustrate. Susan Schweik suggests that "we might reframe the question of *The Monster*—"What does it mean to have no face?"—as "What does it mean to become a screen?" (223). This reformulation is useful in thinking about the representation of disability in these films: What does it mean to have no sight, hearing, agility, higher cognition? In such films, the children become screens for their parents and teachers' responses to them. Cinema places that screen on-screen, achieving a kind of reflexive mirroring that can be uncomfortable but is still distanced by the medium.

Because they subscribe to the generic tropes of melodrama, such disability education films often present redemption narratives, with either a representative student or the instructor facing challenges and overcoming them in a weepy but uplifting ending—and an Academy Award nomination. Given US culture's ambivalent view of both disability and teacher compensation, such cloying resolutions are patronizing at best. These two films established the tropes of redemptive disability cinema, a genre that enjoyed a resurgence around the time of the writing and passage of the Americans with Disabilities Act (1990), with *Children of a Lesser God* (1986), *Rain Man* (1988), *My Left Foot* (1989), *Rudy* (1993), *The Other Sister* (1999), and *i am sam* (2001), to name a few. This is precisely the kind of heroism that Dewey found to be utterly beside the point of educating each student to his and her abilities.

Notes

1. Despite her ability to read and write and her active social presence during Joseph P. Kennedy's term as US Ambassador to the Court of St. James, Rosemary's slowness and teenage sexual rebellion led her father to subject her to a lobotomy, a failed procedure which left her with mental and physical impairments that required institutional care for the rest of her life. Her father never saw her again after the lobotomy (Perry *passim*).

2. For example, Abram Blau, Psychiatrist in Charge, Child Psychiatry, at Mt. Sinai Hospital in New York, reported at the 1961 World Congress of Psychiatry in Montreal, "I define childhood schizophrenia as a developmental disturbance in the growth and integration of the psyche. . . . The primary pathology arises from developmental arrest, retardation, or distortion affecting basic patterns of thinking, language, and behavior" (225). The conflation of schizophrenia with "developmental arrest [or] retardation" was the kind of thinking that led to widespread use of lobotomy as a "therapeutic" measure in the 1950s and 1960s.

3. "Where the picture really excels, outside of its inherent story values, is in the realm of photographic technique. It is here that director Penn and cameraman Ernest Caparros have teamed to create *artful, indelible strokes of visual storytelling and mood-molding*. The measured dissolves, focal shifts and lighting and filtering effects that have been conceived and achieved enrich the production considerably" (Tube 6; emphasis added).

4. The emphasis on hand-spelling spoke to the film's contemporary audiences, as it presaged the postwar spelling-based phonics movement that was gaining popularity in the wake of Rudolph Flesch's *Why Johnny Can't Read* (1955). Interestingly, Horace Mann, one of the early proponents of deaf education in the US, was staunchly opposed to phonics. Helen Keller attended Horace Mann's program in Boston as preparation for her matriculation at Radcliffe.

5. Ironically, soon after the "w-a-t-e-r" incident, the two young women moved to Perkins Institute for the Blind in Boston, after which Helen attended several deaf education programs in New York and Massachusetts before going on to earn a bachelor's degree from Radcliffe. Her father rarely saw her once she obtained language.

6. In the vast catalog of mainstream Hollywood racial uplift films, the twenty-first century *Radio* (2003) and *The Blind Side* (2009) both stand out as pairing cognitive difficulty or disability with blackness, allowing the narrative to cure one or the other—but only to the level needed by a person of color. Radio (Cuba Gooding, Jr.) can be functional but never not black; Michael (Quinton Aaron) can be adopted by a white family but never not dyslexic.

7. Season 9, episode 22, airdate March 11, 1957. Throughout his career, Mann gravitated toward stories involving social justice; even his earliest work tackled alcoholism, payola, Nazism, and adultery. His teleplay for *Judgment at Nuremberg* had been made into a feature film the year before *A Child*, and garnered a Best Screenplay Oscar.

8. The proliferation of millennial and twenty-first-century Hollywood comedies in which the "retard" is the butt of jokes, teasing, and "comical" hazing is proof that this is not merely an historical prejudice. So with the widespread use of the R-word and shameful jokes about the short bus and Special Olympics, even by the president of the United States (2009). See Akers.

9. This film predates then-senator Robert Kennedy's 1965 reference to the Willowbrook State School on Staten Island as a "snake pit" and Frederick Wiseman's famous exposé of the Bridgewater (MA) State Hospital, *Titicut Follies* (1967).

Works Cited

Akers, Mary Ann. "Obama Likens His Bowling Game to Special Olympics." *Washington Post*, 19 March 2009, http://voices.washingtonpost.com/sleuth/2009/03/obama likens his bowling game.html.

Blau, Abram. "The Nature of Childhood Schizophrenia: A Dynamic Neuropsychiatric View." *Journal of the American Academy of Child Psychiatry*, vol. 1, no. 2, 1962, pp. 225–35.

Carney, Raymond. *American Dreaming: The Films of John Cassavetes and the American Experience*. U of California P, 1995.

Cassavettes, John. *Cassavetes on Cassavetes*. Edited by Raymond Carney, Faber and Faber, 2001.

A Child Is Waiting. Directed by John Cassavetes, screenplay by Abby Mann, performances by Judy Garland, Burt Lancaster, and Bruce Ritchie, United Artists, 1963.

A Child Is Waiting. *Studio One*, season 9, episode 22, directed by Vincent J. Donehue, television play by Abby Mann, CBS Television Network, 11 March 1957.

Crowther, Bosley. Review of *A Child Is Waiting*. *New York Times*, 14 February 1963, https://www.nytimes.com/1963/02/14/archives/the-screen-a-child-is-waitingsocial-drama-is-painful-but-compelling.html.

Dewey, John. "Creative Democracy: The Task Before Us." *John Dewey: The Later Works, 1925–1953*, edited by Jo Ann Boydston, vol. 14, Southern Illinois UP, 1981.

———. *The Later Works, 1925–1953*. Edited by Jo Ann Boydston, rev. ed., vol. 5, Southern Illinois UP, 2008.

Fine, Marshall. *Accidental Genius: How John Cassavetes Invented American Independent Film*. Hyperion, 2005.

Gibson, William. *The Miracle Worker*. *Playhouse 90*, season 1, episode 19, directed by Arthur Penn, with Teresa Wright and Patricia McCormick, CBS Television Network, 7 February 1957.

———. *The Miracle Worker*. Directed by Arthur Penn, performances by Anne Bancroft and Patty Duke, 19 October 1959–1 July 1961, Playhouse Theatre, New York.

———. *The Miracle Worker: A Screenplay*. Revision 8 May 1961.

———. *The Miracle Worker*. Directed by Arthur Penn, performances by Anne Bancroft and Patty Duke, United Artists, 1962.

Lekan, Todd. "Disabilities and Educational Opportunity: A Deweyan Approach." *Transactions of the Charles S. Peirce Society*, vol. 45, no. 2, 2009, pp. 214–30.

Mann, Abby. Interview by Gary Rutkowski. Part 1 of 6. *The Interviews: An Oral History of Television*, Television Academy Foundation, 18 August 2004, http://www.emmytvlegends.org/interviews/people/abby-mann#.

Maternal and Child Health and Mental Retardation Planning Amendments of 1963, Public Law 88-156, 88th Congress, H. R. 7544, 24 October 1963, www.archives.gov/research/americans-with-disabilities/transcriptions/naid-6050326-offprint-of-public-law-88-156.html.

McGuire, Anne. "Disability, Non-disability and the Politics of Mourning: Reconceiving the 'We.'" *Disability Studies Quarterly*, vol. 30, no. 3–4, 2010, http://dsq-sds.org/article/view/1282/1309.

Office of the White House Press Secretary. *Fact Sheet: President's Committee on Mental Retardation.* 28 March 1974. National Archives, http://www.archives.gov/research/americans-with-disabilities/transcriptions/naid-6037500-fact-sheet-presidents-committee-on-mental-retardation.html.

"Out of Darkness." *Print: America's Graphic Design Magazine*, vol. 16, no. 4, 1962, p. 40.

Perry, Barbara A. *Rose Kennedy: The Life and Times of a Political Matriarch.* W. W. Norton, 2013.

Schweik, Susan. "Disability Politics and American Literary History: Some Suggestions." *American Literary History*, vol. 20, no. 1–2, 2008, pp. 217–37.

Segaloff, Nat. *Arthur Penn: American Director.* UP of Kentucky, 2011.

"Statement by the President Regarding the Need for a National Plan in Mental Retardation." http://www.archives.gov/research/americans-with-disabilities/transcriptions/naid-6050301-statement-by-the-president-a-national-plan-in-mental-retardation.html.

Tube. Review of *The Miracle Worker*. *Variety*, 2 May 1962, p. 6.

Weusten, Josje. "Narrative Constructions of Motherhood and Autism: Reading Embodied Language beyond Binary Oppositions," *Journal of Literary and Cultural Disability Studies*, vol. 5, no. 1, 2011, pp. 53–70.

7

Passion and Delirium

Representing Madness in *Spider* and *Asylum*

Jim Leach

According to Patrick Fuery, in his book *Madness and Cinema*, "madness is that which resists representation" (44). Despite this resistance, "imaginative writers from the fifth century BC to the present have always been concerned with madness as a revelation of processes of the human mind, indeed processes not limited to the minds of the insane" (Feder xi). Madness has also preoccupied filmmakers from the very beginnings of the medium, and Fuery even argues that there is a special relationship between madness and film, because "when we watch a film . . . there are elements in the narration that purposefully allow for a resistance to interpretation" (44). As this formulation suggests, from Fuery's psychoanalytic perspective, film is closer to madness than literature because "the mad, as Lacan tells us, exists in the Imaginary, and cinema is dominated by the Imaginary" (104). More precisely, "cinema is a language that occupies both the discourse of the rational . . . and of madness, and what it requires from its spectator is the capacity to constantly move between both forms" (76).

This capacity necessarily involves the possibility of succumbing to the discourse of madness, but, as Sander Gilman argues, "how we 'see the insane' is determined by our psychological need for coherence, for a boundary between ourselves and the Other" (*Disease* 63). While Gilman's concern is with painting and the visual arts, he comes to much the same conclusion as Fuery, arguing that, while both visual and verbal representations of madness may construct the opposition between madness and sanity, "the special signification of words" means that the act of writing is "the sign of the rational in our society" (*Disease* 63). While writers and filmmakers may, of course, work against the grain of their medium, it would seem that cinematic representations of "passion and delirium" are likely to be more unstable, and thus closer to the "experience of unreason" (Foucault 85, 198), than literary ones.

In his book, Fuery is less concerned with films that depict states of madness than with "the madness involved in becoming a spectator" (4). This spectatorial madness, stemming from the mixture of "meaning, reality, and delusion" involved in the film experience (159), must also be present in films about madness, potentially creating an even greater instability. On the other hand, films—even those, like Luis Buñuel's *Un chien andalou* (1928), which use surrealist distortions to convey the experience of madness—"must necessarily commence from the Symbolic," that is, from the "cultural order" within which they are made and screened (24). If cinema is, as Fuery claims, the liminal site between madness and reason" (18), its mechanisms bring it close to Foucault's observation that "the ultimate language of madness is that of reason, but the language of reason enveloped in the prestige of the image" (95). As we shall see, novelists can subvert "the language of reason" in many ways, but novels dealing with the experience of madness must find coherent verbal ways of representing characters shaped by the "language of madness." Films, whether adapted from novels or not, inevitably exploit "the prestige of the image" but are clearly not exempt from the desire for coherence nor from the constraints of the cultural order.

In this chapter I will explore some of the implications of these arguments by focusing on two films adapted from novels by Patrick McGrath, a British author now living in the US, who has repeatedly explored the problems of defining "madness" and distinguishing it from sanity. As the author himself has explained, he inherited an interest in this question from his father, who "was medical superintendent of Broadmoor Hospital, a top-security mental hospital near London, once called Broadmoor Criminal Lunatic Asylum" ("Writing Madness" 1). His work has been frequently discussed as a modern development of the gothic tradition, and, as Sue Zlosnik has suggested, the gothicism of his novels *Spider* (1990) and *Asylum* (1996) "lies in the way they represent the unstable boundary between the sound mind and madness" (49).

My aim is not to praise cinematic representations of madness at the expense of literary ones but rather to explore how David Cronenberg's *Spider* (2002) and David Mackenzie's *Asylum* (2004), use film language to heighten the "unstable boundary" with which the novels are concerned. In so doing, both directors have created films that not only draw on the representation of madness in McGrath's novels but also contribute to their own personal visions as filmmakers.

Cronenberg's film was his first made outside Canada, but his earlier work had already established his international reputation as an auteur with a vision centered around body horror and states of madness. While *Spider* lacked, as many critics pointed out, the images of visceral horror found in most of his films, the performance of Ralph Fiennes as the title character, as he shuffles and mutters throughout the film, clearly embodies the director's concern with "the way a mental state manifests itself in a body" (quoted in James 19). In earlier films, such as *The Brood* (1979) and *Videodrome* (1983), Cronenberg depicted characters whose emotions and obsessions gradually take over their bodies, so that Nora Carver, in the former, gives birth to a brood of monstrous children and Max Renn, in the latter, develops orifices that can store videotapes and guns. More recently, *A Dangerous Method* (2011), a biopic about the origins of psychoanalysis, suggests that Freud and Jung were no more stable than many of their patients but also that Freud's methods were preferable to Jung's, because he "insisted on the reality of the human body at a time when the body was covered up by many stiff layers of clothing" (Cronenberg, quoted in Ratner 23). McGrath wrote the screenplay for *Spider*, but it succeeded as both a quite faithful adaptation of the novel and a characteristic Cronenberg film.

At the time he made *Asylum*, his third feature film, Mackenzie had not received the kind of critical attention that established Cronenberg's status as an auteur, and his films continue to fly under the radar, to the point that one critic has suggested he "might just be Britain's most undervalued filmmaker"(Johnston 28).[1] He has worked in several different genres, in Britain and in Hollywood, but all of his films depict characters driven to the edge of madness as a result of the social constraints in which they are living. *Asylum* is the middle film in what Mackenzie calls his "sex trilogy" (quoted in Barkham), three films in which sexual passion leads to acts of madness.[2] McGrath was not involved in creating the screenplay for *Asylum*, and, as we shall see, the film was often seen as failing to capture the spirit of the novel, but, in its own deceptive way, it offers an unsettling representation of madness akin to those in the author's novels.

The two key issues that I will focus on are narration—how the films frame the conditions of madness with which they deal and try to make sense of them—and identification—the extent to which the films encourage us to identify with characters who seem completely "other." These questions may be best approached by looking first at how they are handled in two earlier Hollywood films on madness, also adapted from novels, which may have had some influence on McGrath.

Madness in Hollywood

The Snake Pit (Anatole Litvak, 1948), made at the height of the classical period of Hollywood cinema, would seem at first to reverse the processes just described. It is an adaptation of a novel by Mary Jane Ward, published in 1946, narrated in the first person by Virginia, a woman confined in an underfunded mental hospital, with her account of her situation filtered through her uncertainties and misunderstandings. In the film, however, after an opening sequence that leaves the spectator to make sense of her fragmented voice-over musings, her voice is shared with male voices, notably that of her doctor, which gradually become more dominant. Whereas the novel ends with Virginia's release with little sense of what caused her condition, the film provides a Freudian "cure" and an apparently happy ending, although one that spectators may find not totally convincing, given the presence of another story, drawn from the novel, that coexists with the psychoanalytic one. In this story, Virginia (Olivia de Havilland) is subjected to electric shock and drug therapy before being assigned to the worst ward, which she calls a "snake pit" (217), where she is shocked into sanity.

In the novel, a sexual cause for her madness remains largely unspoken, hinted at only in Virginia's occasional references to her past. These allusions are more prominent in the film, reinforced by a flashback showing her relations with a former boyfriend who died in a car crash. The implication is that her condition in some way relates to her inability to respond to her husband, which seems connected to her feelings of guilt for the death of the boyfriend. The doctor's "cure" takes her even further back, also with the help of flashbacks depicting her unearthed memories, and hinges on convincing her that she was made to feel guilt as a result of a childhood incident with her father.

Lilith (Robert Rossen, 1964), adapted from J. R. Salamanca's 1961 novel, which is narrated by Vincent, a young occupational therapist in a private asylum, who falls in love with an attractive female patient. Reading the novel, we learn a great deal about the process by which Vincent's obsession with Lilith, who is diagnosed as an incurable schizophrenic, drives him to the verge of insanity himself. In the film, there is no voice-over narration, and we only see Vincent (Warren Beatty) from the outside, much as he sees Lilith (Jean Seberg), and must infer his inner thoughts from his actions. Whereas in the novel he returns to the "normality" of the small Maryland town in which he lives, in the film he starts to leave the asylum and then turns back towards the building and says, to the camera, "Help me." Compared to the one in *The Snake Pit*, the more well-endowed asylum here treats the patients with sensitivity and care, but the doctor is much less of an authority figure.

The differences between these films reflect the changing attitudes to madness in the 1960s, with psychologists such as R. D. Laing, for example, arguing that schizophrenia is essentially a healthy response to a mad society. They also reflect changing conditions in the film industry, with the decline of the Hollywood studio system and a more adventurous approach to storytelling. In their very different ways, both films offer representations of madness that, however contained by narrative conventions, have a more visceral effect than the verbal descriptions of their source novels. Even in films that, like *The Snake Pit*, conform to the narrative codes of classical Hollywood cinema, as Janet Walker argues, "the narrative oscillation between inside and outside, illness and health, reveals these terms to be highly unstable" (92).

Although McGrath has never mentioned seeing either of these films, it is likely that he did, given his interests, and they may have left residual traces in his writing. Just before the ending of *The Snake Pit*, the film expands on a brief scene in the novel in a sequence depicting a dance in the asylum, attended by male as well as female patients (250), which anticipates a key episode in *Asylum*. The film version of *Lilith* draws on a brief reference in the novel to experiments that induced schizophrenia in spiders (226), when the credits appear over shots of spiders' webs that prefigure Lilith's seduction of Vincent, perhaps providing the inspiration for the imagery in McGrath's *Spider*.

Narrating Madness

The main way in which McGrath's novels seek to undermine the symbolic power of language is through the use of unreliable narrators. Both novels in question here shape the reader's experience through the perceptions of narrators—the schizophrenic patient himself in *Spider* and a doctor who specializes in "sexual pathology" in *Asylum*—whose perceptions are gradually undercut so that it becomes difficult to distinguish reality from delusion. The novels thus adopt viewpoints from which, as Christine Ferguson puts it, "the world of health and reason . . . becomes subject to the scrutinising gaze of madness" (235). The two films adapted from these novels do not seek to replicate the novels' first-person address through the use of voice-over narration, a device that is often regarded as uncinematic. This decision means that they must develop ways using film language to create a similarly unstable distinction between madness and sanity.

The only other adaptation to date of a McGrath novel, *The Grotesque* (John-Paul Davidson, 1995), does retain brief passages of voice-over narration delivered, as in the novel, by Sir Hugo Coal (Alan Bates). However, his narration in the novel is rendered unreliable by frequent reminders that he has been paralyzed by a stroke and that his memories may be, as he himself admits, "the delusions of a diseased imagination" (73). The entire novel thus represents his version of the bizarre events that he narrates, but, in the film, the narration begins before his stroke, which only occurs near the end, so that these events seem unquestionably real. Although McGrath wrote the screenplay, he described the film as "a bit of a muddle. . . . They laid it on a bit thick" (quoted in Mackenzie). As Suzie Mackenzie suggests, however, this explanation is not very convincing, "since the book is a boldly surreal monologue by the crazed Sir Hugo, who has murdered his prospective son-in-law, fed him to the pigs and then served him up to his bereaved daughter as sausages for dinner." The main reason for the film's inability to capture the tensions in the novel stems less from its grotesque narrative than from the lack of an equivalent to the unreliable narrator.

The Grotesque was McGrath's first novel, and in his later work—including *Spider* and *Asylum*—he is careful not to lay it on so thick, creating a more plausible narrative whose "realism" is gradually eroded as we lose confidence in the narrator. Even without voice-over narration, Cronenberg's *Spider* creates similar doubts about the reliability of its narration by depicting the adult protagonist (known as Spider) as an observer of his younger self, visibly present within what appear to be his memories of the past. Although *Asylum* may seem to fall into the same trap as *The Grotesque*, using the techniques of "filmic realism" (Zlosnik 86) to depict its self-destructive protagonist, I will argue that it inflects narrative codes to create a disturbance that unsettles the distinction between madness and normality.

The reception of *Spider* was inevitably colored by an awareness of Cronenberg's auteur persona from his previous films. Some critics expressed surprise at the way "the film systematically departs from the novel in those areas of the book that seem most 'Cronenbergian'" (Beard 479), but most agreed that the film manages to be "both faithful to the novel and a distinctly Cronenbergian work" (Taubin 37). While McGrath's first draft of the screenplay did include Spider's voice-over narration, Cronenberg persuaded him to remove it and to rely on the innovative device of having the adult character appear with his younger self in what would otherwise be simple flashbacks recounting the cause of his present condition (Jackson 12). As a result, "the film depicts a divided diegesis that contains simultaneously two different temporalities occupying the same space" (Celeste 4).[3] Spider, in effect, becomes the unreliable narrator of his own past.

The film's opening credits, which appear over Rorschach blotches, set up the spectator as an analysand who is required to interpret the ambiguous imagery that the film will present. In the first shot after the credits, a modern train enters a railway terminus, with passengers getting off and rushing along the platform, much as they did in the Lumière brothers' *The Arrival of a Train* (1895), a film that supposedly initiated the realist tradition in cinema. Only after they have all left, a door opens, and a scruffy-looking man exits and starts to shuffle after them. This is Dennis Cleg (nicknamed Spider), and we then see him walking through streets, mumbling unintelligibly to himself. While we have now clearly entered the realm of fiction, the camera adopts an observational distance that keeps us on the outside and thus leaves us unprepared for the gradual process by which it comes to adopt his subjective vision. The barrier between outside and inside is evoked as he walks past a row of houses with their windows blocked up. When he enters a house, to a rough greeting from Mrs. Wilkinson (Lynne Redgrave), who appears to be the landlady, he is shown looking around as he takes in his new surroundings. It is only when another tenant (John Neville) refers to Mrs. Wilkinson as the "tyrant queen" who can send them back to the asylum that we realize that this is a halfway house for former patients.

Spider's journey from the railway station seems like a trip back in time, but this can be rationalized as his movement into an older part of the city. Cronenberg has explained that he and McGrath "chose a period that was slightly different from the book—in the book it's closer to the war" (quoted in Jackson 12), and indeed in the novel Spider's time at the asylum began before World War II.[4] Yet the time period in the film remains vaguely defined so that what we are eventually confronted with is a "mindscreen," to use the term devised by Bruce Kawin to answer the question, "If a film, which is already the dream of its maker and the dream of its audience, can present itself as a dream of one of its characters, can it, finally appear to dream itself?" (5). In this case, as in some of Kawin's examples, the mindscreen is distorted and one in which present and past are folded together, in an apparent attempt to visually represent Spider's journal entries, which we see him write in an undecipherable language.

The point where the temporal distortion first becomes apparent occurs early in the film when Spider, on one of his many walks through the neighborhood, looks through the window of a house and sees his younger self (Bradley Hall) at the table with his parents. What we then see through the adult Spider's eyes is his delusional memory of his father (Gabriel Byrne) murdering his mother (Miranda Richardson), whose place in the family home is taken by Eva (also played by Richardson), the blonde "tart" with whom the father has been having an affair. In the depiction of these events, the adult Spider is present as an observer (even in scenes where the boy is not present), while the camera both observes him and shows what he thinks he sees. After the boy refuses to accept Eva as his mother, he rigs up an elaborate arrangement of string and pulleys to turn on the gas oven in the kitchen where the drunken

Figure 7.1. Spider (Ralph Fiennes) at the window envisions a scene from his own family's past in *Spider*.

woman has passed out. He (and we) see that the body his father pulls from the house is that of his mother, but this realization does not end the delusion. The past even bleeds into the present when Eva takes the place of Mrs. Wilkinson, and Spider makes another murder attempt, prompting his return to the asylum.

It was his mother who gave him his nickname, and he remembers her telling him of her own memory from her childhood in the country of seeing spiders' webs in the trees, which looked like wheels and from which the spider walked away after laying her eggs. Shortly after he hears this story, he sees his father pushing his mother against the wall in the yard, and he starts to build webs of string in his bedroom. The web is thus associated with his reluctance to accept his parents' sexuality, and it becomes the means by which he eliminates Eva, his vision of the sexual mother. But the storyteller is caught in his own webs. He is haunted by the smell of gas, and the gasworks near his home looms over him during his walks along the canal. When he smells gas in the halfway house, he wraps himself in paper and string, but it is not clear whether he thinks he is protecting himself against the gas in his room or trying to prevent the gas inside himself from getting out.

If "the experience of watching Spider often leaves us as confused and fragmented as Spider himself must be" (Sklar and Sabbadini 430), the narration in *Asylum* seems to make no such demands on the viewer, and the film apparently conforms to the codes of mainstream narrative cinema, lending plausibility to Sue Zlosnik's claim that it is "the least successful of the three adaptations to date" (86). On the other hand, Philip Kemp thought that the filmmaker had "captured the essence of McGrath's novel and skilfully rethought it in cinematic terms" (54), and Glenn Heath, Jr., has argued that "Mackenzie's aesthetics are more avant-garde than they seem" and that his films "envision life as a never-ending whirlwind of experience, a cyclone of emotion constantly spinning out of control."

The differences between the two films reflect, at least to some extent, the differences between the narrators in the novels. In McGrath's *Spider*, the narrator, like Virginia in the novel of *The Snake Pit*, is a "madman" whose perceptions are fragmentary and skewed, despite the elegant language in which he conveys them; the narrator in *Asylum* is a doctor who, initially, seems to be a sympathetic and knowledgeable observer presenting the events in an orderly manner. Similarly, what differentiates Stella in Mackenzie's *Asylum* from Cronenberg's Spider is precisely that she seems normal. Whereas, in the novel, the doctor-narrator quickly makes clear that Stella is his patient and that her case is an example of "the catastrophic love affair characterized by sexual obsession," which has been a "professional interest" of his for many years (3), in the film, Stella Raphael (Natasha Richardson) initially seems like a well-adjusted wife and mother. The apparently objective narration depicts the process by which her passionate affair with Edgar Stark (Marton Csokas), a patient, drives her mad.

Like *Spider*, *Asylum* is set in the past, and Kemp argues that the "asylum, with its stratified hierarchy of doctors, attendants and patients, clearly reflects the restrictive, class-conscious society of 1950s Britain" (54). While this is true, the film does not explicitly identify its period setting, and the emphasis is on the mechanisms that push Stella across the unstable boundary between normality and insanity. Although he does not function as a voice-over narrator, Peter Cleave (Ian McKellen) manipulates the other characters, and it gradually emerges that he is as mad as his patients, even though he is in a position of power and speaks "the language or reason." He first appears at a reception to welcome Stella and her husband Max (Hugh Bonneville) who has been appointed deputy superintendent, a position Cleave clearly thinks should have been his. After Stella meets Edgar, Max tells her that he was an artist who brutally murdered his wife, and that he is now Cleave's "favorite patient." Once the affair comes to light, Max points out that it was Cleave who "passed him fit" to work on repairs to the derelict greenhouse in the garden of the house the family occupies within the grounds of the asylum, where the lovers first see each other. Cleave's apparent motive is to discredit Max for not being able to control his wife, but, at the end, after she has been committed, he offers to marry her and reveals a desire as obsessional as hers for Edgar.

At the reception, Jack (Joss Ackland), the head of the asylum, welcomes the new deputy superintendent and refers to "the confined and confused," joking that he means the guests rather than the patients, foreshadowing the precarious position Stella finds herself in, simultaneously inside and outside the asylum. When she meets Cleave, he tells her that he treats the extreme patients and specializes in "sexual pathology," spending his life "immersed in the passions of others." Unmarried himself, he distinguishes between marriage and passion, and it is clear that Stella's marriage to Max is not a passionate one. She is bored by the life she must lead as a doctor's wife and is immediately attracted to Edgar when she sees him through shards of broken glass in the greenhouse. They begin a passionate affair that continues even after she learns why he is in the asylum, and, when he escapes, she goes to him in London.

Her passion destroys her, but her downfall has been engineered by Cleave, and the film suggests she is caught in a web much like Spider's. Recurring images create the impression of a fatal entrapment. Thus Charlie (Guy Lewis), Stella's son lies under water in the bath while his mother is supposed to time him, and then, after her behavior has caused Max to lose his job and they move to rural Wales, she accompanies Charlie on a school trip and sits passively beside the river into which he has fallen, ignoring his cries for help. After his death, she is driven by car into the dark shadows of the asylum, recalling the arrival of the family in their car in the opening sequence. She finally escapes from Cleave's control by jumping from a tower in the asylum, falling through the glass roof of a conservatory, and dies among broken glass, evoking her first meeting with Edgar. At the end, Cleave examines the statuette for which Stella posed in Edgar's London studio and which now stands on his desk.

Identifying Insanity

According to Gilman, "the madman is that individual seen as 'other' by a culture" (*Seeing* xiii), but Ferguson points to the alternative of seeing "the diseased as variant members of the mainstream" (241). In this latter case, images of the insane will not simply construct a secure "boundary between ourselves and the Other" (Gilman, *Disease* 63) and will leave spectators vulnerable to fears about becoming unbalanced themselves. Films about madness tend to fluctuate between these two ways of seeing mad

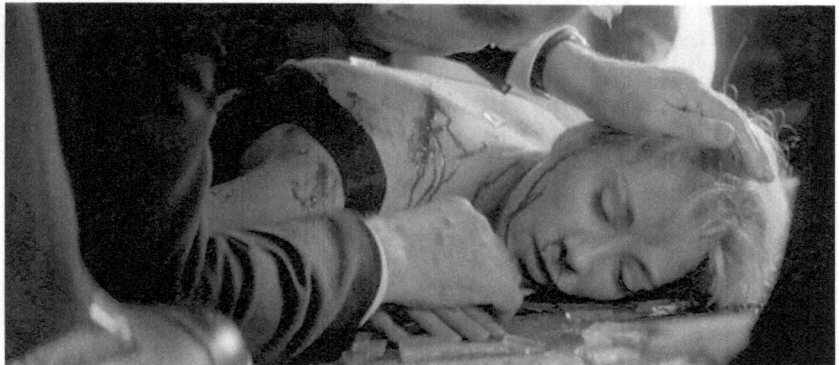

Figure 7.2. Stella (Natasha Richardson), after plummeting through the glass of a hothouse, to get away from Dr. Cleave (Ian McKellen) in *Asylum*.

characters, and this makes identification with such characters a complex, and often disturbing, process. For many film theorists, identification with the protagonist is a key element in the ideological apparatus by which popular cinema reinforces dominant cultural values, but, in the case of a mad protagonist, identifying with this character tends to undermine the cultural assumptions that distinguish madness from sanity.

However, the effectiveness and significance of the processes by which films ask us to identify with characters have been called into question by more recent theoretical work, including that of psychoanalytic theorists who argue that their predecessors misrepresented the thinking of Jacques Lacan.[5] These revisionist theorists argue that "the blurring of boundaries between self and other is an essential part of *any* identification" (Murphy) so that, "as with psychoses, the act of becoming a spectator involves a continual negotiating of the self and Other" (Fuery 98). Clearly, this negotiation becomes especially complicated in films like *Spider* and *Asylum*, in which the central characters are depicted as mad.

In *Spider*, Cronenberg's strategies would seem to have the effect of distancing spectators from the main character, to the extent that they disturb the transparency expected of mainstream narrative cinema, in which the processes of narration are not supposed to call attention to themselves. However, the director has emphasized his own identification with the character, insisting, "Spider, *c'est moi*. I'm not condescending to this character from a distance. I feel like I am this character" (quoted in Alioff 14). As in many of the director's other works, we are drawn into identifying with the point of view of a character whose hallucinations seem real to him but also, increasingly, to us; thus when Spider "sees" another woman take his mother's place, we share his delusion because the two characters are played by the same actress, an experience that is more unsettling than that of the novel in which Spider's version of his past is expressed in words that we are unlikely to trust.

Just as the spectator struggles to make sense of his behavior, so Spider seems to be engaged in putting his own experiences together so that they make sense to him. He works on a jigsaw puzzle, and in one of the "flashbacks" to his time in an asylum, he finds a shard of glass from a circular window that another patient has broken, which he returns to the doctor. The doctor thanks him for providing the last piece of the mirror he has been looking for and inserts it into a reconstruction that looks like a spider's web. After Spider sees that the woman he has killed is not Eva but his mother, he discovers that the woman he is trying to kill in the halfway house is not Eva but Mrs. Wilkinson. His (and our) return to "normal" vision leads, ironically, to his return to the asylum, to which he quietly acquiesces. Like Virginia in Litvak's *The Snake Pit*, he accepts the authority of his doctor but, unlike her, his "cure" does not lead to his release. As the car taking him away drives off, there is a cut to the boy looking out of the window. The film has thus encouraged the spectator to identify with his view of the world without diminishing the sense of his otherness. The distinctions between self and other, sanity and madness, are called into question.

The sense that the mad are radically "other" became a major problem in the reception of *Asylum*, with many viewers complaining that they could not identify with a woman who has a passionate affair with a homicidal inmate and then sits idly by while her son drowns. This complaint rests on the assumption that the spectator should identify with the main character in a mainstream narrative film, which, as we have seen, is a rather simplistic way of describing the experience of audiences in most films. While different spectators will identify (or not) in different ways with characters in a film, Fuery argues that the idea of "straightforward character identification" ignores "the delusional quality" involved in film viewing (97). To argue, as one Internet reviewer does, that "we are never able to identify with the heroine" in *Asylum*, because "she so clearly brings catastrophe upon herself through her own stupidity" presupposes a very narrow view of what is possible for film spectators.[6] This argument would preclude identification with characters such as Oedipus or King Lear (or Vincent in *Lilith*). It would seem that identification in any film is liable to be a shifting and unstable response and that, in the case of characters regarded as mad, the blurring of the distinction between madness and sanity may lead to the recognition that spectators may easily slip from one state into the other or to a resistance to this recognition.

There is no doubt that Stella is the main character in the film, as we witness her dissatisfaction with life in the asylum and then follow her disastrous affair with Edgar. In the novel, these events are filtered through Cleave's narration, which resorts to speculation when describing those that take place outside the asylum. However, the objection that the film is "a drab and depressing tale of self-destruction" (Zlosnik 86) depends on the erasure of the pointers to the doctor's role in exploiting her situation. While he claims to be only concerned to "preserve the integrity of the hospital," both Edgar and Stella fall victim to his possessive attitude to his patients, which clearly derives from personal motives. He has a photo of Edgar on his desk, and he describes him to Stella as "a failed artist," insisting, "He's mine, and he needs my help."

At the end of the film, Edgar is locked up in a cell in the asylum, and realizing that Cleave is now more interested in Stella, tells him, "I thought you wanted me." After Cleave learns that Stella has been staying with Edgar in London, he goes to their apartment where he fondles Stella's underwear and takes the statuette for which she has posed. Earlier, when Stella is (falsely) suspected of aiding Edgar's escape, Cleave and Jack agree that Max is "not for us," since he has "no control over her." Inevitably, Cleave becomes Jack's successor, and he places the statuette on his desk when he moves into his office. At Charlie's funeral, Stella watches from a police car and does not hear Jack telling Cleave, "Arranging things is your forte, isn't it Peter?"

The two annual balls that Stella attends bring out the doctor's, but also Max's, role in manipulating Stella. On the way to the first of these, shortly after their arrival at the asylum, Max comments ironically on her "interesting dress" and asks if it is not "too revealing." Cleave then watches her as she dances with Edgar. After she is admitted to the asylum and becomes his patient, he invites her to the next ball, and she asks if Edgar will be there. He assures her that he will, and, when she attends the ball, in the same dress as on the earlier occasion, she sees Edgar walking towards her, but then realizes it is Cleave (the only occasion on which the film represents her subjective vision). He tells her that Edgar changed his mind, but there is a quick cut to Edgar weeping in his room. Stella has apparently resigned herself to his control over her, and, in one of their sessions, when he asks her to "think rigorously about what it means to love," she tells him that her affair with Edgar was "never real. It was only an obsession." He tells her she is "very brave," and she docilely replies, "Thank you, Peter." When he asks her to marry him, he gives her a ring and tells her it was his mother's, hinting at a psychological disturbance that may be (like Spider's) driving his obsessions. The film leaves us to imagine his mental state, as it does with Stella's when she marches up the stairs to throw herself off the tower.

Conclusion

Neither of these films can claim to have achieved the impossible by fully overcoming the resistances to representing madness. Yet both, like McGrath's novels, expose "the porous borderline between sanity and madness" (Kemp 54). In so doing, the film versions exploit the specific properties of a medium whose images place the spectator in "a deeply unstable and tumultuous position" (Fuery 2–3), akin to a state of madness. Of course, this is a temporary state, and one that most films seek to contain by framing the experience within parameters that ultimately endorse the normal functioning of the society that produced them. As Ferguson suggests, "it is through the creation of orthodox, distinct ways of seeing that the mainstream subdues the threat of the monstrous" (241), but we need not assume it is always successful in these endeavors. In this respect, "cinema . . . becomes both, and at the same moment, a part of the asylum and a force against it" (Fuery 29). At the end of the films, Spider goes back to the asylum and Stella commits suicide to escape from it, the spectator remains outside but with an uneasy sense that the opposition between outside and inside the asylum is by no means a fixed and certain one.

Notes

1. This situation may be changing with the success of *Hell or High Water* (2016), Mackenzie's Hollywood-made heist film/contemporary western.
2. The other films in the trilogy are *Young Adam* (2002) and *Hallam Foe* (2006).
3. The idea for this device may have been inspired by *The Hanging Garden* (1997), a Canadian film directed by Thom Fitzgerald, in which three versions of the same character at different ages inhabit the same space.
4. In the novel, Spider's father died during a bombing raid that destroys the family home. In the film, the house is still standing.
5. The earlier work on film as an ideological apparatus is often referred to as *Screen* theory, after the journal in which it first appeared in English. It drew on the dramatic theory of Bertolt Brecht as much as on Lacan, and both were filtered through the perspective of political theorist Louis Althusser.
6. The quotation is from Christopher Tookey's review that appeared in *Movie-Film-Review*, which has now disappeared into cyberspace. It should be noted, however, that the film did receive many very positive Internet responses.

Filmography

The Arrival of a Train. Louis and Auguste Lumière, 1895.
Asylum. David Mackenzie, 2004.
The Brood. David Cronenberg, 1979.
Un chien andalou. Luis Buñuel, 1928.
A Dangerous Method. David Cronenberg, 2011.

The Grotesque. John-Paul Davidson, 1995.
Hallam Foe. David Mackenzie, 2006.
The Hanging Garden. Thom Fitzgerald, 1997.
Hell or High Water. David Mackenzie, 2016.
Lilith. Robert Rossen, 1964.
The Snake Pit. Anatole Litvak, 1948.
Spider. David Cronenberg, 2002.
Videodrome. David Cronenberg, 1983.
Young Adam. David Mackenzie, 2002.

Works Cited

Alioff, Maurie. "Stripped to the Bone: David Cronenberg's *Spider*." *Take One*, vol. 11, no. 40, Dec. 2002–Jan. 2003, pp. 8–14.

Barkham, Patrick. "I've Done Sex. Now I'm Doing Money." *Guardian*, 29 Aug. 2007, https://www.theguardian.com/film/2007/aug/29/1.

Beard, William. *The Artist as Monster: The Cinema of David Cronenberg*. 2nd ed., U of Toronto P, 2006.

Celeste, Reni. "In the Web with David Cronenberg: *Spider* and the New Auteurism." *CineAction*, no. 65, 2005, pp. 2–5.

Feder, Lillian. *Madness in Literature*. Princeton UP, 1980.

Ferguson, Christine. "Dr. McGrath's Disease: Radical Pathology in Patrick McGrath's Neo-gothicism." *Spectral Readings: Towards a Gothic Geography*, edited by Glennis Byron and David Punter, Macmillan, 1999, pp. 233–43.

Foucault, Michel. *Madness and Civilization: A History of Insanity in the Age of Reason*. Translated by Richard Howard, Vintage, 1973.

Fuery, Patrick. *Madness and Cinema: Psychoanalysis, Spectatorship and Culture*. Palgrave Macmillan, 2004.

Gilman, Sander L. *Disease and Representation: Images of Illness from Madness to AIDS*. Cornell UP, 1988.

———. *Seeing the Insane*. Wiley, 1982.

Heath, Glenn, Jr. "Surviving Desire: The Cinema of David Mackenzie." *Notebook*, MUBI, 20 Oct. 2014, https://mubi.com/notebook/posts/surviving-desire-the-cinema-of-david-mackenzie.

Jackson, Kevin. Review of *Odd Man Out*. *Sight and Sound*, vol. 13, no. 1, 2003, pp. 12–15.

James, Nick. Review of *Analyse This*. *Sight and Sound*, vol. 22, no. 3, 2012, pp. 16–20.

Johnston, Trevor. Review of *Between the Walls*. *Sight and Sound*, vol. 24, no. 4, 2014, pp. 28–30.

Kawin, Bruce F. *Mindscreen: Bergman, Godard, and First-Person Film*. Princeton UP, 1978.

Kemp, Philip. Review of *Asylum*. *Sight and Sound*, vol. 15, no. 9, 2005, p. 54.

Mackenzie, Suzie. "In Pursuit of Sublime Terror." *Guardian*, 3 September 2005.
McGrath, Patrick. *Asylum*. Vintage, 1998.
———. *The Grotesque*. Vintage, 1996.
———. *Spider*. Poseidon, 1990.
———. "Writing Madness." 2013, https://www.leggendometropolitano.it/pdf/testi/ megrath/writingmadness8.pdf.
Murphy, Paula. "Psychoanalysis and Film Theory, Part 2: 'Reflections and Refutations.'" *Kritikos*, vol. 2, 2005, http://intertheory.org/psychoanalysis2.htm.
Ratner, Megan. "Dangerous Methodology: Interview with David Cronenberg." *Film Quarterly*, vol. 65, no. 3, 2012, pp. 19–23.
Salamanca, J. R. *Lilith*. Heinemann, 1962.
Sklar, Jonathan, and Andrea Sabbadini. "David Cronenberg's *Spider*: Between Confusion and Fragmentation." *International Journal of Psychoanalysis*, vol. 89, no. 2, 2008, pp. 427–32.
Taubin, Amy. "Webbed Wonder," *ArtForum*, February 2003, p. 37.
Walker, Janet. *Couching Resistance: Women, Film, and Psychoanalytic Psychiatry*. U of Minnesota P, 1993.
Ward, Mary Jane. *The Snake Pit*. Random House, 1946.
Zlosnik, Sue. *Patrick McGrath*. U of Wales P, 2011.

8

Scorched

Landscape, Trauma, and Embodied Experience in *Incendies*

TARJA LAINE

INCENDIES (DENIS VILLENEUVE, 2010) tells the story of twins, Jeanne (Mélissa Désormeaux-Poulin) and Simon Marwan (Maxim Gaudette) from contemporary Quebec, unravelling the mysterious past of their recently deceased mother Nawal (Lubna Azabal). Adapted from Wajdi Mouawad's play of the same name, the story is set in a fictitious Middle East country, which is clearly meant to be Lebanon in the 1970s and 1980s, divided by civil war. "Incendie" is the French word for destruction by fire, whereas in English "incend" means to inflame or to excite. The film's title is sometimes translated as "Scorched," perhaps a reference to the marks left behind by traumatic war experiences, from which not only survivors suffer, but also frequently their offspring. Trauma itself is clinically described as a mental and physical disorder that is triggered by either experiencing or witnessing a terrifying event, which manifests itself in uncontrollable and distressing memories, flashbacks, and nightmares about the event. As a cinematic disorder it has often been explored as a "cultural syndrome" (Kaplan 27) that keeps the individual locked up in the paralyzing repetition of trauma. Thomas Elsaesser defines this paralysis as "the failure of the protagonists to act in a way that could shape the events and influence the emotional environment [in which] the characters are acted upon" (55). In *Incendies*, this emotional environment presents itself literally as physical landscape that simultaneously entraps the protagonist in the incapacitating experience of trauma, and estranges her from the lifeworld in which she is located. Like John Ford's *The Searchers* (1956), discussed by Janet Walker, *Incendies* thus exemplifies the power of cinema to "transform physical landscape into a mental traumascape for characters and spectators alike" (219). In a similar vein, Rupert Ashmore argues that landscape imagery can embody the traumatic human experience of a changed lifeworld, not only on a personal, but also on a collective and intersubjective level. Landscape and human experience are related, insofar as what happens to people within the landscape also happens *to* the landscape (290). And vice versa, for our sense of being in the world is continuously affected by our interaction with different landscapes. Thus, the relationship between people and landscapes is an affective one, and human-landscape encounters are charged with issues related to identity, belonging, displacement, and embodiment.

As far as trauma is concerned, the human-landscape relationship can be characterized by "a radical estrangement" (Trigg 90), in which the subject's embodied spatial experience in the present remains essentially alienated from the materiality of the landscape. It is precisely this tension between the experience of place in the present, and the emergence of traumatic memories from the past that is conveyed in *Incendies*. Its landscape establishes a troubled stage between the past and the present. In trauma studies the emphasis is ever so often placed on temporality and the omnipresent return of the traumatic event, accompanied by the feeling of being cut off from the flow of time (Riley 14). This chapter attempts to situate trauma in space rather than in time, analyzing the way in which *Incendies* epitomizes landscape as symptomatic of trauma not only by means of its temporal but especially by means of its spatial logic, upon which the traumatic subject is unable to act.

In film studies, the concept of "landscape" has been important for the exploration of cultural mediation between place, space, nature, and the human subject (Gandy 218–29). In cinema, not only does landscape regularly function as a physical location for human action, but often it becomes a setting for psychological exploration of the disorderly mental states of the films' protagonists. For instance, the cinema of Michelangelo Antonioni develops the theme of mental alienation expressed through landscapes, in which his protagonists experience the world, while physically disoriented (224). *Incendies* too might open itself up for an interpretation in which the landscape implies a process of profound and traumatic alienation from one's country, one's culture, and one's roots. However, I shall argue that in *Incendies* the landscape also exists independent of the film's main protagonist Nawal (and her children), insofar as the landscape itself can be considered a narrative agent that entraps Nawal viscerally in the realm of trauma. This communicates a vision whereby trauma is not contained within human subjects, but extends materially into the surrounding world (Jill Bennett 49). Visually, this is realized in the film through the panoramic establishing shots that literally immerse Nawal in a representation of space that exceeds an allegorical relationship between a human subject and the landscape. The depiction of landscape in *Incendies* thus suggests that subjective and historical trauma is intertwined, both on a temporal and on a spatial level.

In *Incendies*, the landscape itself is subject to fires, road blocks, and destruction, thus, consequently, burnt, dry landscapes play a dominant role in the visual design of the film. They provide the seedbed or a bodily habitat for the protagonists' embodied experience: trauma of identity, trauma of motherhood. Another element prominently present in the film's mise-en-scène is water, which functions both as an environment for death and a source of redemption or (re)birth. Thus fire and water establish trauma as an experience similar to death and resurrection. This emerges out of the violent rupture that divide Nawal's life "before," in the rural Middle East country, from her life "after," in urban Quebec. Later, her children attempt to overcome that trauma through spatial remapping of her life. It is as if this temporal structure functions as disjunction between two selves divorced in time but united in place, through the traumatic landscape. This in turn attends to both the "unclaimed experience of trauma" (Caruth 181), and the act of its testimony through which a transformed future is created.

The film thus suggests that trauma can be overcome through a search for truth, as a way of fitting the trauma into a narrative continuum of past and present, even if carried out by those who have not experienced the trauma at first hand. This chapter thus analyses the way in which the complex narrative structure of *Incendies* is inextricably intertwined with mapping and narrating (rather than repressing) traumatic memories. By so doing, the narrative logic of the film suggests that trauma can be claimed (rather than refused) as if it were one's *own* memory. The temporal and spatial disarray of the film's narrative renders its organizational logic similar to the figuration of trauma itself: chronologically fragmented and spatially spectral. The effect of fragmentation in the film both disrupts and soothes the sense of being unified in time and space, and the landscape plays an important role in realizing this effect. Furthermore, it functions as the site and the soil of embodied experience, thus forming the basis for both understanding trauma and for working through trauma. For Nawal's life after the "resurrection" is a rebirth into a traumatic existence of "arrested, frozen time" (Riley 14) characterized by "intimate detachment" (Tanner 243) from the world.

According to trauma theory, a traumatic event resists cognitive processing because it is stored in somatic memory in a way that subjects the event to uncontrolled repetition, until the traumatized person learns to work through the trauma by creating a coherent narrative of the experience which can be integrated in the semantic memory. Jill Bennett defines this process as follows:

> In the normal course of events, experiences are processed through cognitive schemes that enable familiar experiences to be identified, interpreted, and assimilated to narrative. . . . Traumatic or extreme affective experience, however, resists such processing. Its unfamiliar or extraordinary nature renders it unintelligible, causing cognitive systems to balk; its sensory or affective character renders it inimical to thought. . . . Trauma is not so much remembered as subject to unconscious and uncontrolled repetition. . . . The subject is often incapable of making the necessary narrative which we call memory regarding the event. (23)

The film suggests that Nawal is unable to make the necessary narrative out of her trauma, which leads her to a spiritual and ultimately physical death. It is only after her children's (more or less) successful testimonial journey that Nawal "looks back from her grave" and completes her story with her letters to her children, read by her own voice at the end of the film. It is significant that the film uses Nawal's voice-over in the ending scenes, since this gains the function of what Michel Chion calls *acousmêtre*, a voice that is neither inside nor outside the film's diegesis, and therefore has no clearly defined limits to its power (129). The status of Nawal's voice as an acousmêtre suggests that she is now able to react to her traumatic experience, regain a sense of agency, and rediscover her own voice, her own self.

Trauma, then, is the emotional core of *Incendies*. The complex narrative structure of the film is best described as retrospective and circular, progressing through a storyline in the past, which alternates with the present. This strongly indicates that not only is the protagonists' trauma rooted in their ancestral heritage, but that it also prevails in the present, calling for immediate resolution. This is already suggested in the opening scene of the film, which is a flashback functioning as a watching instruction. This gives us a sense of what the inner dynamics of the film will be. The flashback starts with an establishing shot of a landscape, in which some vegetation is seen at the foreground, while in the background of the image desert hills loom in the horizon. A rift separates these different terrains, which insinuates a divided, war-torn country. To a song by Radiohead, "You and Whose Army,"[1] the camera tracks backwards and pans from right to left, revealing an interior in which guerrilla soldiers shave the heads of dirty, wounded children. The shaving gesture is significant, since this group of orphan boys is literally groomed to become soldiers themselves, as will be revealed later on in the film. The camera shows us a close-up of the tattooed heel of one of the boys, followed by an extreme close-up of the same tattoo, which consists of three black circles. The three circles function as a visual metaphor for the enigma presented in the film, which not only concerns its circular logic of trauma, but also with its mathematical premise. This premise is the devastating truth conveyed by Simon to Jeanne at the end of their investigation, in the form of an equation: "One plus one . . . can it really make one?" The opening ends with a tracking shot into a close-up of the boy's face, intensely gazing directly into the camera. Finally, the scene cuts to an interior shot of a notary's office in present-day Quebec, from where the story starts to unfold.

Incendies consists of ten episodes or chapters, the titles of which are announced by means of large letters in a heavy font and an aggressive red color, often standing out in harsh contrast to the earthy tones of the remaining filmic image. The narration unfolds in a nonlinear fashion through two circularly interwoven temporal layers. There is the past with Nawal searching for her son, becoming a terrorist, and serving her prison sentence. And there is the present with first Jeanne and then Simon travelling in Nawal's native country, carrying out her final wish and discovering the secrets Nawal kept from her children during her lifetime. Nawal's final wish involves two sealed envelopes, one of which is for Jeanne to deliver to the twins' father. The other envelope is for Simon to deliver to their brother. The narration "in the past tense"—for the sequences in which we follow Nawal cannot be labelled regular flashbacks, as they take up most of the screen time—is triggered by the twins' meetings and their conversations. This clearly signifies that their present life and their mother's past are parts of the same continuum, overshadowed by trauma. This is reinforced by the way in which the film abruptly cuts between the two temporal layers, so that the spectators get regularly confused about the current moment in time, which seems exactly the point. Furthermore, the visual style of the film is dominated by establishing shots of various landscapes, and these landscapes themselves function as nodes, connection points through which past and present meet.

This emphasis on landscapes epitomizes John Wiley's idea that places are not merely reminiscent of the past, but that they form a continuum between the past and the present in which (traumatic) memories continuously take place (173). Furthermore, the landscapes embody trauma as an experience of bodily disconnection, the disembodied feeling that "I have a body," instead of an embodied experience that "I am my body" (Zeiler 335). Shot in Jordan and Quebec, the landscape in *Incendies* has direct affective quality, and Villeneuve himself has said in an interview that he wished to focus on the inner experience of the characters instead of making sensational action scenes, for instance. Furthermore, he stressed that "it was important that there was a relationship between the landscapes and the inner feelings of the characters walking through them" (Dawson). This renders the landscape into something more than a mere allegory of the protagonists' embodied experience of being in the world, or an allegory of a nation in distress. It becomes what Jane Bennett terms "vibrant matter," a nonhuman source of action that flows through and around humans, aiding, thwarting, enriching, disabling, enhancing or degrading them as it does (viii–x).

In his *Landscape and Memory*, Simon Schama writes that even though we are accustomed to considering landscape and human experience as two distinct realms, they are inseparable nevertheless. This means that human experience is not a question of self-contained existence, but that it emerges through its relationship with its surroundings. Similarly, W. J. T. Mitchell writes that landscape is not so much an object to be seen or a text to be read, but a process through which one can find oneself, through which subjective identities are formed: "Landscape is a dynamic medium, in which we 'live and move and have our being'" (4). And according to Guiliana Bruno, the exterior landscape always conveys an interior one, the geographical and human landscape sharing a "tangible territory" (207). This is why the landscape embodies what and how we feel about places, and there is an overlapping, often complex relationship between landscape and our sense of identity. In trauma this relationship is disturbed, though, and the landscape becomes a place to lose, rather than to have one's being. In *Incendies*, this is not only conveyed in the way in which landscapes are depicted as inhospitable, desolate spaces that one has to struggle against, but also in Nawal's instructions to Jeanne and Simon considering her funeral arrangements: "Bury me with no casket, no prayers, naked, face down, away from the world. . . . I want no gravestone, nor my name engraved anywhere. No epitaph for those who don't keep their promises." Furthermore, Nawal's traumatic experience is transmitted to Jeanne and Simon, of which the Montreal cityscape becomes an ideal manifestation. The city is regularly portrayed as a cold, grey, disconsolate place, an environment to suppress trauma passively, rather than to deal with it actively. Towards the end of the film the editing creates a visual juxtaposition between Nawal in her prison cell and the drab, industrial block of flats in Montreal where Simon resides. This juxtaposition suggests that the twins are as much entrapped in their mother's trauma as Nawal is a prisoner not only physically in her prison cell, but also in her own (dis)embodied existence. In one early scene Jeanne stares at a swimming pool, which was the location of her mother's final traumatic realization, which ultimately triggered her death. It is autumn, and the pool is emptied, which is a traumatic image that combines the metaphor of motherhood in absence, with the metaphor of emptiness that Jeanne needs to fill in by discovering the truth about her mother. The image dissolves into a flashback of Jeanne swimming under water, and finally surfacing only to find her mother paralyzed, catatonic even. The flashback ends with Nawal being admitted to a hospital, where later she dies.

Nawal's storyline starts with an establishing shot of craggy rock formations on the right side and thin shrubbery on the left side of the image, separated by a narrow path. As in the opening shot, this suggests a fundamental cultural gap through which Nawal attempts to navigate, depicted as a tiny figure making her way down the path. Nawal, who is a Christian, wants to flee her environments together with her Muslim lover Wahab, by whom she is pregnant. But they are stopped by Nawal's brother, who emerges from among the cliffs. The brother subsequently kills Wahab and intends to kill Nawal too. But her grandmother intervenes and confines Nawal to a small hut until she has given birth. In one scene, Nawal's brother sits in solitude on top of a cliff with his back to the spectators, ignoring her inconsolable cries while contemplating the landscape. Positioning the character in this way in the landscape immediately communicates to us his cultural attitude, which is as unyielding as the rock on which he sits.

After Nawal has given birth, and her son has been taken to an orphanage, she flees to the fictional city of Daresh, which is also the title of the next chapter in the film, presented to us with an establishing shot of the colorful, chaotic, densely populated cityscape. At this point the narration shifts to the present, with Jeanne arriving in the country. The city of Daresh embodies two different narrative meanings. In Jeanne's storyline, the chaotic setting of the city could be seen as equivalent to the complicated mathematical equation she is determined to solve, without having an idea where to start from. In Nawal's storyline, the city becomes a potential space of tolerance, cultural diversity, and possibilities, as well as of political resistance. That is, at least until the civil war breaks out and Nawal returns to her region of origin, in an attempt to rescue her son from the throes of war. It is at this point that the film becomes nomadic—to use Teshome Gabriel's terminology—alternately tracking Nawal and Jeanne on their arduous tours through the rugged landscapes in the south of this imaginary country.

In one characteristic scene, Nawal crosses a safeguarded bridge that both connects and divides the torn-up country. The camera follows Nawal as she passes barbed wire at the military checkpoint and forces her way through the refugees coming from the opposite direction. As from this point onwards she has to travel on foot, her journey is depicted as an endless, solitary struggle in oppressive heat against the rugged, craggy landscape, through which she labors her way. There is one moment of serenity, when Nawal passes through a small grove where she stops to embrace a tree, while mourning her dead lover Wahab. The tree stands for what could have been, a possibility lost forever. This is what Steve Neale has defined as the traumatic temporality of "if only," which leads us and the characters to wish "if only they had met in different circumstances in a different time, in a different place" (12). After this short moment of relief she has to return to the landscape that is more hostile than ever. When she arrives at the first village of her destination, she finds that it has been bombed and burned to the ground. In the second village the destruction is even more complete, and here she finds out that Muslim guerrillas have taken all the boys from the orphanage her son was left in. At this point we do not see the destruction itself, we only see only its consequences. It is as if the unseen threat holding this region in its spell had deepened the notion of hostility that is the dominant feature of its landscape. The landscape of her life that used to be "one of familiarity, certainty, and the known" (Offord 6) has now become a territory full of danger and the unknown.

Thus the fire and smoke surrounding Nawal as she seeks a moment of rest in the ruins of the village are shown as emanating from her surroundings, suggesting the traumatic, disturbed relationship between her bodily experience and the physical landscape, which in turn reflects her trauma of loss without resolution (fig. 8.1). As many theorists of trauma, including Pierre Janet and Charlotte Delbo, have suggested, trauma resists rational processing by its nature, provoking ambiguity, incongruity, and incomprehension. This is why trauma is experienced on the affective level of *deep* or *somatic* memory, instead of on a more cognitive level of *common* or *semantic* memory. If this were otherwise, the traumatic event could be remembered, narrated, and worked through. So while the image of Nawal within the ruins surrounded by the smoke drifting across the scenery does not narrate her trauma directly, it embodies that aspect of trauma that *resists* narrativization. It prompts affective, visceral experience, which is incompatible with narrative processing. Furthermore, as Jill Planche describes this while discussing postapartheid landscape photography in South Africa, it evokes a powerful, claustrophobic sense of the body restrained by the landscape, resulting in a loss of identity, loss of spirit, and a loss of agency (cited in Corrigall 333).

Dylan Trigg, on the other hand, approaches ruins, such as the ruins of gas chambers in Auschwitz-Birkenau, as a location of memory that can haunt the subject of trauma effectively through spectral or "negative spatiality." Ruins are empty of memory, and bring about "a non-memory, a puncturing in spatio-temporal presence" (95). The image of Nawal

Figure 8.1. Nawal within the ruins in *Incendies*.

within the ruins is a powerful one, drawing a parallel between a ruined subject and the spectrality of the ruins themselves, for there is a suggestion of Nawal being out-of-place here, as if she came to the scene too late, "as though the presence is defined by what fails to materialize in the present" (98).

Incendies emphasizes a crisis of identity resulting from traumatic experience, but it refuses to depict Nawal solely as a victim lacking spirit or agency, as she is determined to proceed on her journey even beyond her grave. At the same time, throughout the film Nawal is so deeply steeped in traumatic despair, that the only continuation possible is in the present, where the trauma can be resolved, be it by Jeanne and Simon as her superseding agents. In the series of events that trigger her trauma, Nawal first gets a ride on a bus carrying Muslim passengers to the refugee camp of Deressa. Taking in the panoramic views of the landscape, she dozes off, only to find the bus ambushed by militant Christian soldiers when she wakes up. They shoot the driver in the head, riddle the bus with bullets, and mercilessly proceed to pour petrol into the bus, while Nawal manages to stumble to the door, taking out her crucifix and proclaiming loudly that she is a Christian. As she is being taken outside, she grabs the daughter of a Muslim woman, who also had survived the bullet attack, but whose horrible fate it is to be burned alive. The bus goes up in flames and the child breaks loose from Nawal, running towards her mother inside, only to get shot in the back by a soldier, after which Nawal is shown to collapse next to the burning bus. On the right side of the frame there is Nawal's desperate expression facing left, where on the left there is the burning bus on the background. The sequence ends with an establishing shot of the scorched, rocky landscape with Nawal as a tiny spot on the left hand side of the image and the bus emanating fire and black smoke on the right. With this final shot of the bus in flames with Nawal as a tiny detail in a larger surrounding wasteland the film suggests that the burning landscape consumes Nawal, as she experiences the devastating effects of returning trauma, after the sensory bombardment of violent events.

Up to this point Nawal's journey is a spiraling decline deeper into the trauma, and her ever-aggravating struggle against the landscape conveys her inability to achieve any embodied foothold in her surroundings. The film suggests that this traumatic condition can only be resolved on a second level, as soon as Jeanne undertakes the geographically exact same journey as her mother. The film contains numerous shots of

Jeanne's struggling progress to the south that are almost identical to the shots from Nawal's journey. For instance, there is an establishing shot of a bus travelling a road in the present that is indistinguishable from an earlier shot showing the same road and bus in the past. In addition, this shot is cut to a similar shot of Jeanne sitting in the same posture as we previously have seen Nawal in, even using the same framing. This parallelism strongly suggests that Jeanne is sent to fulfill her journey in order to experience her mother's trauma from within, after which it can be worked through.

Thus the geographical and mental journey that Jeanne (like later on Simon) undertakes in order to deal with her secondhand trauma implies her purgatory urge to shape a coherent identity by recreating her mother's journey. Therefore, both journeys reveal the entanglement between different temporalities (past/present), spatialities (Canada/Lebanon), memories, and identities. In trauma terms, perhaps it could be said that Jeanne and Simon's journeys are attempts to bridge the rift between deep memory and common memory, the journeys functioning as a mediating process that trace their quest to conquer both Nawal's traumatic experience and their own. That is because journeying is a way to incorporate the very *structure* of their mother's trauma—even when never *fully* inhabiting her experience—a precondition for the ability to work it through. Marianne Hirsch calls this phenomenon a postmemory of trauma, an inheritance of traumatic memory that burdens trauma survivors' children who are not the ones who suffered the primary loss (5). Yet it must be stressed that this is not a question of appropriating the parents' pain by empathetically putting oneself in their position, but in the recognition of similarities across personal histories, past and present. This in turn becomes a question of claiming responsibility for the past, since, as Mieke Bal puts it, "we are in the present of what happened in the past, we are also in the 'here' of what happened elsewhere" (25). Similarly, Nurith Gertz and George Khleifi argue that by attempting to construct a historical continuity that leads from the (traumatic) past to the present and the future, cinema can depict a repressed past, not by replacing the image of the present, but rather by seeing the present through the past (15).

Jeanne and Simon "inheriting" their mother's trauma—quite literally, enclosed in sealed envelopes—seems especially relevant, as for Nawal no closure of trauma was ever available. In fact, she remained in search of her son even after she had found him, that is, even after her death. Yet after her traumatic experience with the Christian militia, Nawal seemingly abandons her decision to find her son "swallowed by the war," in order to join a radical Muslim group and "teach the enemy what life has taught" her. She arrives at Deressa in the dark only to find the refugee camp burning and destroyed to the ground, again the metaphorical scenery of her own scorched bodily existence. Her ensuing actions perhaps serve as strategies to hold her trauma at bay, but they eventually preserve and reinforce it, since her intentions are borne out by hatred and torment turned inwards. When she is imprisoned and tortured at the notorious penitentiary of Kfar Ryat, in which she becomes known as "the woman who sings," it is as if there is an analogy between her physical circumstances and the traumatic state of her embodied existence.

Laura Tanner speaks of trauma as entrapment in the urgent bodily experience of pain, on the one hand, and a sense of bodily separation from the world in which one is located, on the other. As one simultaneously lacks the agency to participate in this same world, she calls this experience "intimate detachment" (243). It is this entanglement of pain and bodily separation that is depicted in *Incendies*. Shots of the interior of Nawal's isolated, empty cell, in which she is held in solitary confinement, are juxtaposed with shots of the exterior of the prison, safeguarded by a dilapidated barbed-wire fence and surrounded by a bleak desert landscape, dotted with withered bushes (fig. 8.2). This is truly a landscape of pain and desolation, the oscillation between shots demonstrating Cathy

Figure 8.2. Landscape as prison.

Caruth's claim that traumatic stories ultimately address "the oscillation between the crisis of death and the correlative crisis of life: between the story of the unbearable nature of an event and the story of the unbearable nature of its survival" (7). And, finally, Nawal's own body becomes a landscape of life and death to fight against as she becomes pregnant from her torturer, after which she is unable to be at home in her own body: yet another traumatic event that alienates her not only from the rest of the world, but also from her own embodied existence.

After Nawal has given birth to twins, a prison guard takes the newborns to a river to drown them, but the prison nurse saves the infants, saying she will take care of them because "these are the children of the woman who sings." At this point in the film it becomes clear to the spectator that Jeanne and Simon are about to discover the truth, not only about their mother's past, but also about their own. The shot in the past with two light spots on the river surface illuminated by two torches is cut through a graphic match to a shot from within a tunnel, from which Simon emerges to arrive at Daresh in the present. Witnessed from outside, a tunnel is customarily seen as a metaphor for phallic penetration,[2] but seen from the inside it is suggestive of the birth canal, implying the possibility of rebirth into the land where the twins had already been born. This suggestion is reinforced in the scene in which the twins jump into a hotel pool after they have learned the truth about their father, with Simon floating under water in foetal position for several moments before surfacing. But this rebirth is traumatic and can only be resolved if Jeanne and Simon are able to hand deliver their mother's envelopes to the addressees.

In the final part of the film, Simon sets off for Deressa in search of the Muslim warlord Chamseddine, who can provide the last piece for this jigsaw puzzle of the traumatic mystery. Indeed, the establishing shot of the rugged hills surrounding the winding road along which Simon progresses, strikingly resembles such a jigsaw puzzle piece, strongly hinting that all pieces will soon fall into place. The film cuts to Nawal's storyline in the past one final time, with two cars parked on a bridge. This is done so abruptly that one cannot be sure whether it is Simon or his mother in the second car meeting the warlord. The bridge brings the circular logic of trauma to a close, as the film presents us a flashback of Nawal at the swimming pool, staring at the heels of her son standing by this pool in exactly the same framing as used in the flashback the film opened with. After the encounter, the film shows us a close-up of

Nawal's face, which consequently becomes a landscape in itself: once full of life but now "dried up" and defeated (fig. 8.3). Gilles Deleuze and Félix Guattari have made this association between face and landscape in their *A Thousand Plateaus*: "The face is a surface: facial traits, lines, wrinkles. . . . The face is a map. . . . The face has a correlate of great importance: the landscape" (170).[3]

Incendies realizes this association by juxtaposing the close-up of Nawal's face with an establishing shot of a harsh desert landscape, replete with barren hills and imposing rock formations, as an allegorical environment for Nawal's traumatic experience (fig. 8.4). In other words, the wrinkly jagged ditches cutting thorough the rocky hills become an allegory for Nawal's trauma that is mirrored in her physical, almost scar-like facial lines.

In his *Landscape Allegory in Cinema*, David Melbye argues that landscapes in cinema can obtain significance beyond the function of the setting, becoming "outward manifestations of characters' troubled psyches" (1). In other words, the landscape can become an allegory, which reflects the protagonists' psychological state of mind as they interact with their surroundings. According to Melbye, this takes place as soon as "the film positions the landscape as independent subject" (1), after which we come to understand the protagonists through the landscape instead of other way around. That *Incendies* positions the landscape as an independent subject is already evident from the very first shot of the film. But instead

Figure 8.3. Face as landscape.

Figure 8.4. Landscape as face.

of merely reflecting the protagonists' psychological state, the film shows how their whole embodied existence is inextricably intertwined with the landscape, in such a way that we become directly engaged with the effects, if not the experience, of their trauma. In moments like this the film itself becomes a landscape that is fundamentally *more* than an allegory, insofar as through its operational logic, the landscape as the site of trauma and the spatiotemporal experience of trauma form a "structurally parallel unity" (Trigg 88).

Furthermore, there is the suggestion that a journey through a demanding landscape towards the truth can become a means to resolve trauma. In the end, the twins' journey functions as a testimony of their resolve to understand and overcome the effects of not only their mother's but also their own trauma. It is a common understanding that testimony is a way to confront and work through trauma in order to get beyond it. That the testimony is realized "by proxy" seems to be of no concern in *Incendies*. Like Art Spiegelman's graphic novel *Maus* (vols. 1 and 2), the film presents the narrative of a trauma victim's tale and the transference unto her offspring with ultimate healing effects. Indeed, there is a strange consolation in the film's final shot of a graveyard, with Nawal's final resting place now supplied with a tombstone and an epitaph. This final image embodies the general desire to make up for a traumatic past, a process which *Incendies* illustrates particularly well.

Notes

1. From their 2001 album *Amnesia*.
2. See for instance the famous Alfred Hitchcock citation from *Cahiers du Cinema* in 1959: "There are no symbols in *North by Northwest*. Oh yes! One. The last shot, the train entering the tunnel after the love scene between Cary Grant and Eva Marie Saint. It's a phallic symbol. But don't tell anyone" (cited in Wood 131).
3. At the same time the close-up of Nawal's face is an example of an "affection-image," stimulating a direct engagement between the spectator and the image by distorting scale and suspending time (Deleuze 87).

Filmography

Incendies. Denis Villeneuve, 2010.
North by Northwest. Alfred Hitchcock, 1959.
The Searchers. John Ford, 1956.

Works Cited

Ashmore, Rupert. "'Suddenly There Was Nothing': Foot and Mouth, Communal Trauma and Landscape Photography." *Photographies*, vol. 6, no. 2, 2013, pp. 289–306.
Bal, Mieke. *Thinking in Film: The Politics of Video Installation according to Eija-Liisa Ahtila*. Bloomsbury, 2013.
Bennett, Jane. *Vibrant Matter: A Political Ecology of Things*. Duke UP, 2010.
Bennett, Jill. *Empathic Vision: Affect, Trauma, and Contemporary Art*. Stanford UP, 2005.
Bruno, Giuliana. *Atlas of Emotion: Journeys in Art, Architecture, and Film*. Verso, 2002.
Caruth, Cathy. "Unclaimed Experience: Trauma and the Possibility of History." *Yale French Studies*, no. 79, 1991, 181–92.
Chion, Michel. *Audio-Vision: Sound on Screen*. Edited and translated by Claudia Gorbman. New York: olumbia UP, 1994.
Corrigall, Malcolm. "Beyond Trauma: Landscape, Memory, and Agency in Photographs by Cedric Nunn and Sabelo Mlangeni." *Safundi*, vol. 15, no. 2–3, 2014, pp. 329–51.
Dawson, Thomas. "Blood Lines: Denis Villeneuve on *Incendies*." *BFI Film Forever*, 2 Jan. 2015, http://www.bfi.org.uk/news-opinion/sight-sound-magazine/interviews/blood-lines-denis-villeneuve-incendies.
Deleuze, Gilles. *The Movement Image*. Translated by Hugh Tomlinson and Barbara Habberjam, Minnesota UP, 1986.

Deleuze, Gilles, and Félix Guattari, *A Thousand Plateaus: Capitalism and Schizophrenia*. Translated by Brian Massumi, Minnesota UP, 1987.

Elsaesser, Thomas. "Tales of Sound and Fury: Observations on the Family Melodrama." *Home Is Where the Heart Is: Studies in Melodrama and the Woman's Film*, edited by Christine Gledhill, British Film Institute, 1987, pp. 43–69.

Gandy, Matthew. "Landscapes of Deliquescence in Michelangelo Antonioni's *Red Desert*." *Transactions of the Institute of British Geographers*, vol. 28, no. 2, 2003, pp. 218–37.

Gertz, Nurith, and George Khleifi. *Palestinian Cinema: Landscape, Trauma and Memory*. Edinburgh UP, 2008.

Hirsch, Marianne. *Family Frames: Photography, Narrative, and Postmemory*. Harvard UP, 1997.

Kaplan, E. Ann. *Trauma Culture: The Politics of Terror and Loss in Media and Literature*. New Brunswick: Rutgers UP, 2005.

Melbye, David. *Landscape Allegory in Cinema: From Wilderness to Wasteland*. Palgrave Macmillan, 2010.

Mitchell, W. J. T. Introduction. *Landscape and Power*, edited by W. J. T. Mitchell, U of Chicago P, 2002, pp. 1–4.

Neale, Steve. "Melodrama and Tears." *Screen*, vol. 27, no. 6, 1986, pp. 6–22.

Offord, Baden. "Landscapes of Exile (and Narratives on the Trauma of Belonging)." *Landscapes of Exile: Once Perilous, Now Safe*, edited by Anna Haebich and Baden Offord, Peter Lang, 2008, pp. 5–18.

Riley, Denise. *Time Lived, without Its Flow*. Capsule, 2012.

Schama, Simon. *Landscape and Memory*. Vintage, 1996.

Spiegelman, Art. *Maus*. Vol. 1, Pantheon, 1986.

———. *Maus*. Vol. 2, Pantheon, 1992.

Tanner, Laura E. "'Looking Back from the Grave': Sensory Perception and the Anticipation of Absence in Marilynne Robinson's *Gilead*." *Contemporary Literature*, vol. 48, no. 2, 2007, pp. 227–52.

Trigg, Dylan. "The Place of Trauma: Memory, Hauntings, and the Temporality of Ruins." *Memory Studies*, vol. 2, no. 1, 2009, pp. 87–101.

Walker, Janet. "Captive Images in the Traumatic Western." *Westerns: Films through History*. Edited by Janet Walker, Routledge, 2001, pp. 219–52.

Wiley, John. "The Spectral Geographies of W. G. Sebald." *Cultural Geographies*, vol. 14, no. 2, 2007, pp. 171–88.

Wood, Robin. *Hitchcock's Films Revisited*. Columbia UP, 2002.

Zeiler, Kristin. "The Phenomenological Analysis of Bodily Self-awareness in the Experience of Pain and Pleasure: On Dys-appearance and Eu-appearance." *Medicine, Health Care and Philosophy*, vol. 13, no. 4, 2010, pp. 333–42.

9

Ghostly and Ghastly Desires and Disorders in *Young Adult*

KenTacoHuts in Mercury

JULIE GROSSMAN

In *Young Adult*, Jason Reitman's reprise collaboration with screenwriter Diablo Cody after *Juno* (2007), Mavis Gary (Charlize Theron) returns to Mercury, Minnesota, a hometown she detests, to reclaim her high-school lover Buddy Slade (Patrick Wilson), who is happily married and a new father. Mavis is a ghost-writer for a soon-to-be defunct young adult book series, and like the adolescent characters she writes about, Mavis gropes painfully for affirmation, exploiting her former prom queen persona with everyone but Matt Freehauf (Patton Oswalt), the marginalized and damaged geek she befriends. Despite Mavis's much-remarked-upon physical beauty, she feels cheated and invisible, literalizing her status as a ghost-writer and driving her obsessional behavior, which includes alcoholism and trichotillomania (hair-pulling). Hair-pulling functions for Mavis "to modulate an averse affective state, such as anxiety, sadness, or boredom" (Shusterman et al. 637). Like the traumatized serial killer Aileen Wuornos, whom Theron won an Academy Award for portraying in *Monster* (2003)—or even Betty Elms and Diane Selwyn (Naomi Watts) in David Lynch's *Mulholland Drive* (2001)—Mavis is presented in some sense as a cultural phantom—an ectoplasmic precipitate of warped socialization practices and deranged gender roles. These female characters are symptoms of a damaging acculturation into the American dream experienced as a nightmare, the films' depiction of their traumas itself a rebellion against an ameliorative cinema. *Young Adult* explores the sources, symptoms, and effects of female trauma born of a lunatic cultural obsession with surfaces.

In the production notes for *Young Adult*, Patton Oswalt astutely observes that, like *Monster*, "in a weird way, [*Young Adult*] is also a horror movie in that Charlize is kind of this maniac stomping through the quiet countryside leaving this trail of destruction behind her." A. O. Scott agrees, saying Patty Jenkins's title "might suit *Young Adult* just as well." As in *Monster*, the oppression of Charlize Theron's character registers most forcefully in the uncanny physicality of her performance. In both films, the female body is keyed to the "monstrous" cultural process by which women become consumable bodies (like the action figures Matt Freehauf builds), whose education takes place within the world of romance. As Scott rightly observes, *Young Adult* "systematically demolishes a china shop full of shopworn sentimental touchstones about—for starters—high school, small-town life, heterosexuality, Minnesota and the capacity of human beings to change, learn and grow."

These sentimental fictions are just the kind of books Mavis authors ("Just as Kendall hit send, a message from Ryan popped up like magic," Mavis writes), while young Aileen Wuornos tries to escape domestic abuse by imagining Marilyn Monroe being discovered at the soda shop. Despite belonging to different cinematic genres, *Monster* and *Young Adult* both expose the brutality of a consumer-based means of valuing women. Further, *Young Adult* upsets cinematic conventions, occasioning the *New Republic*'s David Thomson to write that "[it] is highly unusual for an American film to drop us with so little reassurance or escape." That this film is a comedy exacerbates its marginalized position and constitutes its "mad" generic status, while also explaining its unpopularity at the box office.

Mavis Gary ranks among the least likable characters in recent cinema history. She parties like a disaffected teenager with her recalcitrant new friend, the hobbled-up nerd Matt Freehauf, whom she remembers from high school as "that hate-crime guy" and who walks with a cane (Matt was savagely beaten by school bullies who thought he was gay). "Could you walk any slower?" Mavis taunts. She insults Matt for being a loser, although the two bond over disdain for Mavis's disabled cousin Mike Moran. Mavis recalls, "Car wreck. God, he got so much attention. . . . That dick ruined my sweet 16. Same weekend." Mavis's extreme narcissism is uncomfortably funny, at the same time as the film gradually reveals her despair, culminating in a momentary but anguished admission to Matt Freehauf, "I'm crazy and nobody loves me."

Mavis Gary's dissociation can be understood in relation to her hair-pulling. An appropriate symptom of Mavis's personality disorder, trichotillomania suggests the character's "experiential avoidance" (see Begotka et al.): Mavis refuses to confront the reality of her experience, relying instead on ideation that combines clichés from the young-adult fiction she writes, overemphasis on her beauty and specialness inspired by the reality television she watches, and an upbringing within a dysfunctional family in Mercury that we're meant to assume has cultivated her narcissism. Often a symptom of "identity problems related to feelings of emptiness or lack of purpose" (Wetterneck et al. 68), Mavis's hair-pulling, alongside her lack of impulse control and binge eating, signals the character's feelings of worthlessness.

Mavis's desperation expresses itself from the beginning of the story in her delusional plan to win back her high-school sweetheart. Trichotillomania has been linked by psychologists to the avoidance of emotion and experience generally, indicating an inability to accept change. Mavis wears Buddy Slade's sweatshirt (Matt telling her that "you look completely insane wearing it") on which is embroidered "Mercury Injuns." If times have changed (the team is now called the "Mercury Indians"), Mavis hasn't. Even the city's name ironically denotes this lack of change (the "mercurial"), as well as the idea that Mavis is coming back to a place that is, for her, like another planet. Mavis's failure to move beyond adolescent ideation might call for treatment in the form of acceptance and commitment therapy, often assigned in cases of experiential avoidance. Such treatment helps patients in "developing psychological flexibility: defusion, acceptance, contact with the present moment, the observing self, values, and committed action" (Harris 2). Reitman's film refutes such treatment, however, seeing in Mavis and the world she inhabits few possibilities for change, little belief in the flexibility of character and personality.

Mavis returns to Mercury to reclaim her high-school boyfriend, despite all signs that Buddy Slade is happily married with a new baby. She demonstrates sociopathic disregard for others when she visits Buddy's home and reminisces with him and his wife Beth (Elizabeth Reaser) about high school: "I used to sleep in [Buddy's] t-shirts and boxers," Mavis tells Beth. Matt tries to convince Mavis that her attempt to steal Buddy back is delusional, but Mavis is determined, inviting Buddy out for drinks, kissing him while intoxicated after they've watched Beth's band play at the bar. Mavis's imperviousness to Buddy's contentment with his life is painful to observe, like Travis Bickle's deluded attempts to woo Betsy in *Taxi Driver*, about which more below.

As painful as Mavis's self-absorption is, hardly a scene in contemporary mainstream cinema exists like the tragicomic one in *Young Adult* in which Mavis confronts Buddy at a naming party for the Slades' baby. In a back room, Mavis tells Buddy that together, they can overcome the fact that he's married; they can "beat this thing," Mavis notably equating marriage with a disease. Buddy rejects Mavis, who, drinking excessively at the party, verbally attacks Beth after they bump into one another, and a glass of red wine is spilled on Mavis's cream-colored tweed suit. "Fuck you. You fucking bitch," she screams at Beth. Mavis's emotional chaos is registered with a handheld camera tracking her movement to the front yard, where everyone in attendance watches Mavis unravel in embarrassed horror. Angry and humiliated, cursing at Beth, Mavis consummates her transformation from prom queen to pariah. It is no wonder that *Young Adult* floundered at the box office, as the scene of Mavis's self-immolation and lashing out is more than just cringe-worthy. It directly flouts the feel-good Hollywood narrative pattern, "breaking the rules of safe Hollywood storytelling" (Debruge).

Reitman's *Up in the Air* (2009) laid some of the groundwork for the director's grim satire of American efforts to achieve happiness in *Young Adult*. In the earlier film, Ryan Bingham (George Clooney) glides through life as a professional downsizing expert, committed only to reaching the landmark number of five million frequent flyer miles as he transports trauma to America's work force, a trauma to which he is inured. Despite his unconcern about the feelings of others and his aversion to intimacy, Ryan falls for a businesswoman, Alex Goran (Vera Farmiga), he meets during his travels, eventually choosing to abandon his solipsism in favor of "true love." When Ryan shows up at Alex's townhouse to whisk her away, he learns that she has a husband and children; their affair has been, for her, pure pleasure-seeking. Alex, as her androgynous name suggests, is a stereotypically masculine "Mad Man," seeking narcissistic enjoyment in pretending while she's with Ryan that her adulterous sex is meaningful romance. The film offers the prospect of the self-involved Ryan being saved by meeting the woman of his dreams, only to disillusion Ryan and viewers who expect a happy ending. Instead, Alex's double life reflects a society in which both sexes practice an exploitative masculinity masked as individual bids for success.

Such social pathology characterizes the demystified world of Mavis Gary too, though casting a woman as the deluded egotist expecting the world to submit to her desires changes the dynamic and has further implications for viewer abjection in the face of these characters' failures. *Young Adult* rebels against "the nice girl," or the "nice film," in which women accede to acceptable stereotypes of their powers, ambitions, desires, and rebellions. In a warped paeon to strong female cinematic characters, Mavis screams and curses at Beth Slade, who has what Mavis wants. Beth watches Mavis self-destruct with pity, which further angers Mavis, who yells at Beth to "Stand up for yourself!" then, "I fucking hate you." The film experiments with giving us a bad girl antihero, a female version of the "man-child" (see Debruge). As in *Up in the Air*, the viewer is given no narrative resolution to the dysfunctional life of its emotionally adolescent protagonist.

In one of the final scenes of *Young Adult*, Mavis has a confessional conversation with Matt Freehauf's lonely sister Sandra (Collette Wolfe), who tries to buoy Mavis up when she tells Sandra that she "has trouble being happy": "I need to change, Sandra." Sandra insists that this is all wrong: that Mavis is special and everyone in Mercury is "fat and dumb." Mavis is Sandra's American Idol. In their first conversation, Sandra reminds Mavis that when they were in high school, Sandra got the key to Mavis's locker from the vice principal to put Rice Krispie treats in her locker on Mavis's birthday. Still in thrall to Mavis, Sandra pleads with her idol at the end of *Young Adult*, "Take me with you"—back to Minneapolis. As Cody observes, "[Sandra's] attitude is what feeds Mavis' flaws" ("Talk with the Makers," 81). Theron affirms that "Sandra is the character who causes the most damage in a way and she does it so innocently" (*Young Adult* production notes). Reassured by Sandra that she is still more precious than anyone in Mercury, Mavis responds with affected sympathy, "You're better here." Learning nothing from her journey to rock bottom (back home), Mavis returns to Minneapolis. Sandra calls Minneapolis "The Mini-Apple," an inflated reading of anywhere outside of Mercury as an idyllic urban mecca.

At the end of *Young Adult*, Mavis's narcissism is reinforced as a result of Sandra's deeply misguided pep talk. Locked in a selfhood that is adolescent and obsessional, Mavis is wearing the "Hello Kitty" T-shirt she wore at the film's start. The film provides no closure, and traps the viewer in a circular narrative in which Mavis's crisis has no consequences. Her life, we are left to assume, will carry on in much the same way it always has. Such arrested development in the narrative, as well as in Mavis's character, is predicted not only in jump cuts of Mavis applying her makeup and getting manicures and pedicures earlier in the film, but also in the audio jump cuts of "Mad Love," the song she believes is her private shared song with Buddy until her fantasy is disrupted by hearing his wife Beth's band play it at the bar.

The film also represents the idea of stasis in the repetition of an image of Mavis waking up in bed with a man whose arm is draped across her. While sleeping with Matt Freehauf late in the film potentially signifies a meaningful encounter with someone with whom the attraction goes beyond the surface, the poignancy of their intimacy is belied by this shot's reference back to the beginning, when she slept with a date whose stories of volunteer teaching in Southeast Asia ("one of the most rewarding things I've ever done") bored her. The mise-en-scène suggests

Figure 9.1. Mavis (Charlize Theron) in bed with insignificant lovers in *Young Adult*.

that sex with Matt will have as little value for Mavis as the sex that followed her earlier date.

Eight years before Charlize Theron played *Young Adult*'s monstrous "psychotic prom queen bitch," the name she earns from high-school peer Mary Ellen Trantowski (Kate Nowlin), Theron won an Academy Award for her portrayal of Aileen Wuornos in Patty Jenkins's bracing feminist serial-killer movie *Monster*. In roles that seem diametrically opposed, Theron similarly deconstructs contemporary beauty ideals. Mavis and

Figure 9.2. Mirroring warped feminine personalities of Aileen Wuornos (Charlize Theron) and Mavis.

Aileen struggle within their very different dysfunctional families, Aileen's a much more severe case of devaluation, as she escapes an abusive father to seek attention as a young prostitute. The warped processes by which both women search for happiness and, in the case of Aileen, money for survival, are displayed in mirror imagery.

An intertextual comparison of Theron's performance as a destitute serial killer with her role in *Young Adult* as a narcissistic beauty equally lacking in self-esteem reveals the female body to be a site for the projection of society's diseased fetishization of surfaces. When Mavis applies a fake hair piece in one montage of her cosmetics regime, we are reminded that in high school, Mavis won an award for "best hair." At one point, Buddy tells Mavis that she looks the same as she did in high school, a compliment that also telegraphs Mavis's Dorian Gray failure to mature.

If *Young Adult*'s horror story is about false faces and empty surfaces, *Monster* also explores the fragile veneer of female socialization, revealed to lead inevitably to a series of traumas that Aileen and Shelby (Christina Ricci) strain to navigate within bars and cheap hotels. For her part, Mavis watches American Idol and reality TV and eavesdrops on teenagers sharing vapid stories about social media and romance at fast-food restaurants. Cody is quoted in Paramount's production notes for *Young Adult*: "I feel like Facebook and all the social networking that exists has enabled us to stay in touch in a way that may not be healthy." Mavis's habits exemplify trends of arrested development in older Americans recently commented upon by the *New York Times*: "There is something inherently juvenile about social media. To begin with, it elevates superficiality, speed and the image—all youthful preoccupations—over depth, deliberation and text, which we associate with mature adults" (Wayne). Underneath the attractions of social media for most people in contemporary culture, where people's value, as Cody has observed, is measured by "how many friends you can amass on social media" ("Talk with the Makers" 81), both *Young Adult* and *Monster* address the false seductions of fame, illusory beauty ideals, and the American dream. We are introduced to Aileen Wuornos as a child, "I always wanted to be in the movies. When I was little I thought for sure, one day, I'd be a big big star. Or maybe just beautiful. Beautiful and rich, like the women on TV. Yeah, I had a lot of dreams." At the beginning of Ezra Edelman's ESPN documentary about another American dream turned lurid, *O. J.: Made in America*, O. J. Simpson says in the voiceover, "As a kid growing up in the ghetto, one of the things I wanted most was not money. It was fame." *Monster* and the O. J. documentary chart the true stories of a man and woman who wished to escape their gender, class, and race. Although these stories differ, they share a legacy of American film's fictional representations of sociopathic behavior—from Rico's (*Little Caesar*) insistence that he's going to "be somebody" to *Goodfella*'s overture: "As far back as I can remember," says Henry Hill (Ray Liotta) in voiceover, "I always wanted to be a gangster." The conflation of dreams, fame, and violence in American film often reveals the seductions of celebrity that drive individuals to criminality.

If American film has always been preoccupied with illicit behavior committed by male characters who lack the resources to gain power in conventionally sanctioned ways, Jason Reitman, Patty Jenkins, and David Lynch have explored how female agency is thwarted as a result of cultural obsessions with surfaces. Like its inspiration, Billy Wilder's *Sunset Blvd* (see Grossman ch. 5), *Mulholland Drive* reveals the crises in store for women whose dreams are constructed by false obsessions with popular images and then destroyed by the madness such adulation brings about. Lynch's film represents this madness in the presence of mirrors and images of alternate selves that figure heavily in *Mulholland Drive*, as in *Monster* and *Young Adult*. In *Mulholland Drive*, Rita (Laura Harring), Diane's dream image of a damsel in distress she, Diane, can save, derives her identity from a poster of Rita Hayworth as Gilda she sees through a mirror in the bathroom of Betty Elms's aunt. There Rita observes the poster tagline, "There never was a woman like Gilda." Like Mavis, Aileen, and Diane's imagined selves, the character of Gilda, and the idealized woman she represents (whose power comes from her sexuality and appearance), isn't real but a projection: "There never was a woman like Gilda." All three films show women seeming to gain self-esteem by identifying with images of success that are revealed to be seductive deceptions. The tortured battle between Mavis Gary, Aileen Wuornos, and Diane Selwyn and their fantasy selves leads to mental illness or alcoholism and trauma. The characters ward off such confrontation through performance—a layered production of alternate identities made possible by the remarkable presence of Charlize Theron and Naomi Watts. These performers poignantly demonstrate an art and flexibility that their characters cannot achieve.

Another major link among these three films is that they entreat viewers to empathize with characters without condoning their actions or encouraging us to like the characters. This is, once again, distinctive in these films' presentation of female antiheroes. Indeed, Reitman and Theron have both commented on how much easier it is for audiences to accept a bad-boy than a bad-girl narrative, unless, I would add, the bad girl falls easily into genre expectations, as in film noir's femme fatale. Even in this case, the bad girl is often the object of inquiry ("who is this mysterious, probably fatal, woman?") rather than the subject of identification for the viewer. As Theron has observed, "The greatest characters are the unlikable ones, but mainly men get to play them. Rarely do women" (Sperling).

The earlier reference to *Taxi Driver*'s Travis Bickle is thus not incidental, since Mavis shares traits with this iconic antihero. Mavis and Travis are most closely connected not to lovers, friends, or families, but to their mirrors. Mavis's fantasies, like Travis's self-enclosed delusions, land her in a crisis, which teaches her nothing and places her back at the beginning of the same story. While both films deny viewers the pleasure of a denouement assuring redemption and change and a happy ending, this unameliorative trajectory is more common in Hollywood when men are the central characters. Says Reitman, "You used to see that in quite a few movies from the 70s" (Whipp). Reitman similarly observes in Paramount's production notes in 2011 that there are "actually very few female characters that we love to hate." Those who do appear are rarely main protagonists. They are foils or femmes fatales, like Alex Forrest (Glenn Close), saying famously to Michael Douglas's character in *Fatal Attraction*, "I will not be ignored." In *Taxi Driver*, while recognizing the irony of Travis Bickle having been celebrated a hero, we wonder about his mental condition at the end of the film. Travis is likely wedded still to illusions and delusions, figured in Scorsese's double takes of Travis's view in the rearview mirror of the chimeric Betsy (Cybill Sheperd). To push the comparison a bit further, we might think back to Scorsese's striking scene in a hallway, in which Travis is on the phone, trying to convince Betsy to go out with him again after he took her to a pornographic movie on their first date. Scorsese pans away from Travis at the phone booth to a shot of the long hallway, marking Travis's failed efforts and his loneliness as too painful to watch. Jason Reitman makes us witness to Mavis's degradation, saying that in *Young Adult* his intention was to challenge audiences, to "try to make them increasingly uncomfortable to a point where they actually have to look in the mirror and ask, 'Am I like this person?'" (Whipp). *Young Adult* offers viewers no refuge from Mavis's humiliating meltdown, and she is no male icon like De Niro's Travis Bickle. Earlier in *Young Adult*, when Mavis first reaches out to Buddy from her room at the Hampton Inn, she sits on the vanity by the sink, speaking with him on her cell phone. Reitman brings the camera back to reveal more empty space in a desolate room at a chain hotel, creating a sense of Mavis's entrapment and isolation, as she crouches by the mirror near the bathroom. The shot reveals the character's alienation, even as she tries to (re)unite with Buddy, just as Scorsese links a dreary empty hallway with Travis's attempt to connect with Betsy.

Figure 9.3. Empty hallways as visual metaphors for Mavis.

In keeping with *Young Adult*'s anti-ameliorative tone is its critique of superficiality of all sorts, from Mavis's parents' shallow cheerfulness, even to Mavis's wheelchair-bound cousin Mike, mentioned earlier, who finds powers coming from his disability: "What is up, girly-friend? Holy shit, cuz. This is such a rad surprise. . . . I'm great! Kim and I just had our six-year anniversary. . . . Work is a trip but I play hard too. I've been doing a lock of rock climbing. . . ." Matt responds, "You mean rock crawling, right?" and Mike says, "No I'm vertical, bro, believe it or not. We can do anything a normal can do. Probably more, because we've had to reboot for extra positivity. You know what I'm saying? You should try it, Matt."

Mike's overzealous "positivity" and oppressive optimism has an analogue close to home for Mavis, in a domestic space devoted to surfaces. It is no wonder that Mavis sees no value beyond the cosmetic cover of things, given her parents' hollowness. Consider their breakfast conversation about Mavis's ex-husband, whose picture she asks her parents to remove from the wall. Insisting that it carries nice memories for them, her parents ignore Mavis's objection that the marriage was a failure. Instead, Hedda Gary (whose name resonates with Ibsen's unhappy married woman, Hedda Gabler) replies, "Well the wedding wasn't a failure. Remember the tiramisu?" In this scene, when Mavis tells her parents she thinks she's an alcoholic, they dismiss her confession as "very funny," assuring viewers that their pleasantness stands in for an emptiness and narcissism that has no doubt contributed to the making of the monster that is Mavis Gary.

But Mavis's lack of connection to any depth of experience is also symptomatic of the bland society she represents, the superficiality, once again, that the film finds in contemporary culture. Diablo Cody has remarked that *Young Adult* is about obsessions with youth and reality television. The writer apparently sent Charlize Theron copies of "Keeping Up with the Kardashians," "My Super Sweet 16," and "The Hills." Cody calls such shows "creatively bankrupt," with their characters "in full makeup when they're supposed to be waking up" ("The show *Kendra* is a fascinating case study because it's about people who are past their prime, and they're only in their 20s" ["Talk with the Makers" 80]). Cody suggests that Mavis is wrong to think that "having a job and kids and friends is so little. That used to be considered a very full life. Now we're bombarded with the message that each us of is a special snowflake and deserves to be found by E's cameras" (81).

Cody's remarks raise questions of tone: we are surely supposed to sympathize with Matt Freehauf, who finds Happy Mike too giddy for being wheelchair-bound. And we are supposed to see the limits of even good guy Buddy, who is everyone in town's buddy and is simple, though perhaps not superficial. Buddy speaks in uninspired language, telling Mavis when he learns that she has divorced Alan, "It sucks to be Alan." Buddy is a good guy with little depth, but he is content with his job at General Mills, where he has lunch with his dad every day. Buddy and Beth, however, have empathy for Mavis, and that—alongside an ability to live in the moment—is their virtue, despite the limits of their imagination. In different ways, Sandra, Matt, and Mavis cannot accept their limits. Like Mavis, Matt is arrested developmentally, with his superhero toys and man cave in a house that the film's production designer Kevin Thompson confirms is meant to be "stuck in time": "The house was so depressing and it completely set the tone" (*Young Adult* production notes). Opposed to the unhappy Sandra Freehauf, who idolizes Mavis Gary, is Beth Slade, the moral center of the film. Beth is happy with her life, though surely aware of its limits: that her girl band Nipple Confusion, for example, is bad, while it affords her pleasures and an opportunity to hang out with friends. Beth wears flannel, reinforcing her unconcern with glamor and affectation. As Kevin Thompson notes, "Clothing to these people [in Mercury] is strictly for function and to keep comfortable and warm" (*Young Adult* production notes).

Though the film questions its characters who, unlike Beth, thrive on artifice and don't live in the moment, it also satirizes a life of normalcy, especially when tied to rampant consumerism and the bland products being hawked or otherwise foregrounded.

At the bar where Mavis and Buddy first reunite, a mashup of the American sports bar and an Irish pub, "Champion O'Malleys," the restaurant server says, "You're going to want to try the popcorn shrimp." Sandra reminds Matt not to open a "bottle of Ranch" before the last one is finished. Creativity stifled in a culture defined by its enthrallment with cosmetics, department stores, and fast-food, Buddy tells Mavis with giddy enthusiasm, "We're getting a new Chipotle at the mall." Mavis purchases burp cloths for the Slade baby at the Buy Buy Baby store, whose title

Figure 9.4. Day and night at the BUY BUY BABY mart.

and mise-en-scène point to a twisted commodification of emotions associated with family. Mavis's illness is surely in part a symbolic rebellion against the appropriation of feeling by capitalism that is also uncritically embraced by suburban middle-class ideology.

Young Adult satirizes American fetishes with consumption and franchise culture, from the presence of the soon-to-be defunct young-adult book series for which Mavis ghost-writes to the omnipresence of fast food in Mercury, including the KenTacoHut strip mall, where those from town can enjoy Kentucky Fried Chicken, Taco Bell, and Pizza Hut all in the same place. Extending the film's critique of the low expectations of Mavis's home town, Mercury's work force shows the town to be a cultural wasteland, exemplified by the book seller who overzealously prevents Mavis from contaminating copies of her book by signing them because she isn't the *real* author, or the clerk at the Hampton Inn, whose depression and monotone deserve pause.

The clerk calls to mind Louise Finch, the bleak server in the bar Uncle Charlie (Joseph Cotton) takes young Charlie (Teresa Wright) to in *Shadow of a Doubt* (1943). Hitchcock's film takes place in a town, like Mercury, portrayed as static and metaphorically dead. The clerk at the hotel in *Young Adult* seems beaten down, lacking the will to confront Mavis on the obvious presence of a dog in her purse, which, though allowed by the hotel, would force the stubborn Mavis to admit that she lied about having a pet. There is reason to rebel against the corporati-

Figure 9.5. A world-weary, beaten down hotel clerk who could have been Mavis.

zation of experience, the tone of the film justifying Mavis's final gesture in the lobby of the Hampton Inn, stealing a donut that's "for Honors members only."

The omnipresence of franchise culture not only defines the landscape of Mercury in *Young Adult*. It refers to young-adult fiction and cultural production that trades on repetition and sameness and sells adolescent clichés: When Mavis tells Buddy, "Buddy, you're my moon. My stars. You're my whole galaxy," she is quoting a teenager she earlier overheard at the fast-food restaurant. Reitman and Cody want to counter the adulation of vapid cultural production by making a film whose tone is decidedly not the same as most films, but ironically whose message is depressingly all about sameness, since, as Reitman avers, "People don't change" (*Young Adult* production notes). The film invites viewers to be uncomfortable with that sameness and with the film's own disruption of ameliorative filmmaking, suggesting a value in such disruptions. They challenge viewers to extend empathy beyond its normal bounds, to the likes of female characters who are neither angels in the house nor sexy bad women, but flawed, bewildered women whose disorders are a mirror of the unhealthy society they founder within.

Filmography

Fatal Attraction. Adrian Lyne, 1987.
Goodfellas. Martin Scorsese, 1990.
Juno. Jason Reitman, 2007.
Little Caesar. Mervyn LeRoy, 1931.
Monster. Patty Jenkins, 2003.
Mulholland Drive. David Lynch, 2001.
O. J.: Made in America. Ezra Edelman, 2016.
Shadow of a Doubt. Alfred Hitchcock, 1943.
Sunset Blvd. Billy Wilder, 1950.
Taxi Driver. Martin Scorsese, 1976.
Young Adult. Jason Reitman, 2011.
Up in the Air. Jason Reitman, 2009.

Works Cited

Begotka, Andrea M., et al. "The Relationship between Experiential Avoidance and the Severity of Trichotillomania in a Nonreferred Sample." *Journal of Behavior Therapy and Experimental Psychiatry*, vol. 35, no. 1, 2004, pp. 17–24.

Debruge, Peter. Review of *Young Adult*. *Variety*, 4 Dec. 2011, http://variety.com/2011/film/markets-festivals/young-adult-1117946687/.

Grossman, Julie. *Rethinking the Femme Fatale in Film Noir: Ready for Her Close-Up*. Palgrave Macmillan, 2009.

Harris, Russell. "Embracing Your Demons: An Overview of Acceptance and Commitment Therapy." *Psychotherapy in Australia*, vol. 12, no. 4, 2006, pp. 2–8.

Scott, A. O. "Once a Prom Queen, Still a Spoiled Princess." *New York Times*, 8 Dec. 2011, http://www.nytimes.com/2011/12/09/movies/charlize-theron-in-young-adult-review.html.

Shusterman, Anna, et al. "Affective Regulation in Trichotillomania: Evidence from a Large-scale Internet Survey." *Behavior Research and Therapy*, vol. 47, no. 8, 2009, pp. 637–44.

Sperling, Nicole. "An Unlikable 'Adult' Role." *Los Angeles Times*, 1 Dec. 2011.

"A Talk with the Makers of *Young Adult*." *Time*, 5 Dec. 2011, pp. 79–81.

Thomson, David. "An Unsparing Portrait of American Breakdown." *New Republic*, 12 Dec. 2011, https://newrepublic.com/article/98424/young-adult-theron-oswalt-monster.

Wayne, Teddy. "Social Insecurity? Internet Turns Boomers into Twits." *New York Times*, 5 May 2017, https://www.nytimes.com/2017/05/05/style/seniors-social-media.html.

Wetterneck, Chad T., et al. "Personality Characteristics and Experiential Avoidance in Trichotillomania: Results from and Age and Gender Matched Sample." *Journal of Obsessive-Compulsive and Related Disorders*, vol. 8, 2016, pp. 64–69.

Whipp, Glenn. "Jason Reitman on *Young Adult*." *Variety*, 14 Dec. 2011, http://variety.com/2011/film/news/jason-reitman-on-young-adult-1118047305/.

Young Adult production notes. Paramount Pictures, 2011. Margaret Herrick Library.

10

Criminal Biographies and Visual Culture

HOMER B. PETTEY

One sign of modernity has to be popular culture's fascination for criminals. Audience fixation with criminal tales extends to the beginnings of film, such as *The Life of Charles Peace* (1905), the infamous Sheffield burglar and murderer. Of course, television and now the Internet early on saw the potential of crime dramas, with particular emphasis on true crime. Problems, however, persist in attempting to define this pervasive, yet complex genre of the criminal biopic. The publication of criminal tales, often with accompanying sketches, found its initial heyday in the eighteenth century, especially with the *Newgate Calendar*, which presented biographies of thieves, highwaymen, and murderers. From then, the exploits of criminals, beyond journalistic accounts, became a formula of sorts for nineteenth-century fiction, often with ties to real crimes, such as Vidocq's mostly fabricated memoirs, accounts of Burke and Hare, Dostoevsky's obsession with crime, Balzac's re-creation of crimes, Dickens's accounts of Old Bailey trials, Thomas de Quincey's famous "On Murder Considered as one of the Fine Arts," and, of course, numerous accounts and retellings of the hideous exploits of Jack the Ripper. The proliferation of crime fiction, films, and television in the twentieth century explains considerably a cultural obsession with serial killers, mass murderers, family murders, conmen, bank robbers, and white-collar criminals. Truman Capote's nonfiction novel, *In Cold Blood*, has been adapted for three major films, Richard Brooks's *In Cold Blood* (1967), Bennett Miller's *Capote* (2005), and Douglas McGrath's *Infamous* (2006), as well as a television miniseries, *In Cold Blood* (1996). Of course, the Manson family has spawned numerous films, television miniseries, and documentaries that were mostly based upon Vincent Bugliosi's *Helter-Skelter* (1974). Criminal biopics became part of the American, and to some extent the British, television wasteland, with exploitative half-hour, but primarily hour-length episodes of series on true crime. Still, criminal biographies also had a satiric, often very darkly comic portrayal in film, among them *Catch Me If You Can* (2002), *Bronson* (2008), and *I Love You Phillip Morris* (2009). A generic description of criminal biopics, then, does little justice to the variety of genres that represent graphic depictions of crimes for an always-eager public. Criminal biographies are not limited to the exploits of a criminal, but extend to narratives about forensic procedures (crime as biography), psychoanalytic profiles (hypothetical narrative), and the place of the crime (visual narrative of the scene). Again, modernity, however one wishes to define it, must always include society's insatiable appetite for the aberrant criminal mind, the details of the crime itself, and the capture, trial, and punishment of the criminal. In all, that narrative pattern sustains itself in some degree or another in criminal biopics, if only to appease the formula-seeking audience's need for graphic details and safely distanced media retribution. After all, the history of modernity resides in its capacity to consume the truly horrific and its resulting insistence on political or social revenge. Modernity, from the early modern period to the contemporary world, often seems as deviant as the criminals it finds fascinating.

The image of the highwayman, his biographies, and his appearance in eighteenth-century fiction became a staple of the period, as did tales, dramas, and novels of prostitutes, pickpockets, and rakes. For all, the gibbet or else religious salvation appeared to be the teleological end of criminality, the former appeasing sociopolitical ends, the latter, no matter how pious a fraud, restoring piety to the nation. The archaeology of the criminal biopic has its roots in previous centuries. The visual spectacle before the populace often appeared as a kind of criminal performance, especially for the highwayman, the fallen gentleman:

> After having squandered a large fortune, he turned gamester, then pimp, and then highwayman; in which last occupation he was soon detected, taken, and thrown into *Newgate*. . . . When

he came to gallows, instead of the psalm he sung a bawdy catch, threw away the book, and bid *Jack Ketch* tuck him up like a gentleman. Many of his relations were present at the execution, and shook their heads repeating the words of *Mat* in the *Beggar's Opera*, "Poor fellow! we are sorry for you, but it is what we must all come to." (Colman and Thornton 366)

Clearly, the evocation of Jack Ketch, Charles II's favorite, but often botching executioner, and of John Gay's play suggests a public visual and dramatic understanding of criminality. *Blackguardiana* (1793) lists numerous highwaymen, including the remarkable Walter Tracey, a university man, who "became extravagant, and turned highwayman, among other robberies, he robbed Ben Johnson, and the Duke of Buckingham, and for the last, he was executed at Winchester" (Caulfield 155). Criminal biographies sustained annual publications, including the *Newgate Calendar*, which began in the mid-eighteenth century, and included life depictions that follow a now-familiar pattern from birth to execution, such as an account of a John Price, "otherwise Jack Ketch" (or the Devil), "who was hanged for *Murder*, with some Particulars of his Life." The graphic and gory details of the account of the crime certainly correspond to twenty-first-century desires for details, crime scene photos, and court descriptions:

> In the course of the evidence it appeared that Price met the deceased near ten at night in Moorfields, and attempted to ravish her; but the poor woman (who was the wife of a watchman, and sold gingerbread in the streets) doing all her power to resist his villainous attacks, he beat her so cruelly that streams of blood issued from her eyes and mouth, broke one of her arms, beat out some of her teeth, bruised her head in a most dreadful manner, forced one of her eyes from the socket, and otherwise so ill-treated her that the language of decency cannot describe it. (Jackson 239)

While "decency" prohibited description of the sexual assault, the author hardly winced at providing graphic details of the furious brutality of the beating, which, again, corresponds to contemporary popular culture's fascination with details of even the most heinous crimes.

Here, the visual quality of the language, the reenactment of the crime in words, effects an ekphrastic account not unlike those reenactments in contemporary film and television. One outstanding difference, however, remains that the narrator provides first the crime and the sentence followed by the biographical details of the criminal's life, whereas the reverse narrative order sustains most true crime features. According to this account in the *Newgate Calendar*, Price suffered the horrors of an upbringing now commonly used as excuse for criminal behavior. Price's father was blown up during an explosion in Tangier, his mother had limited means to provide him with a proper education, he worked for a rag dealer before going to sea, and, very darkly ironically, upon his return he applied for the newly vacant position of executioner and profited from the coins and articles of those newly executed in order to pay off mounting debts. Of course, like the moralistic tone of contemporary criminal biopics, the *Newgate Calendar* provides a lesson, "to moderate our passions of every kind" (241). A sketch of Price as *Jack Ketch Arrested* in the text reveals the gibbet cart's wheels being turned by manpower, as a constabulary figure holds a cudgel and proffers the verdict to Price, as the accused pulls backs, scowling in defiance to protest his innocence. Such a biopictographic scene often occurs in the concluding moments of televisual criminal biopics, with the newly sentenced felon led away from the court as bystanders, family members, and especially the press offer up their jeers.

Perhaps the most well-known highwayman of the period was Richard Turpin, executed for horse-stealing, whose "genuine history" went through several editions. Its title page also lists nine sections of this thirty-five page biography of a scoundrel, the first seven being episodes from the rogue's adventurous life. This almost picaresque tale follows a biographical account from Turpin's birth through his profligate life, his joining a gang of robbers, his famous exploits in his new gang's cave, to finally his apprehension, trial, and execution. That cave became Turpin's sanctuary away from the arm of the law, and a sketch of seated Turpin with his shotgun, bottle of wine, and some bread in the cave serves as the standard frontispiece for this criminal biography. Significantly, the rendering of Turpin shows him as an aristocrat, with tricorn hat, overcoat, long vests, breeches, and high riding boots: upon his face, there appears a calm, if not ironic expression. For his execution, Turpin kept up these airs to the last: "He behav'd himself with amazing Assurance, and bow'd to the Spectators as he pass'd: It was remarkable that as he mounted the Ladder, his Right Leg trembled, on which he stamp'd it down with an Air, and with undaunted Courage look'd around about him; and after speaking near Half an Hour to the Topsman, threw himself off the Ladder, and expired in about five Minutes" (*Genuine History* 33). Lincoln B. Faller, in his analysis of seventeenth- and eighteenth-century criminal biographies, provides exceptional details about the audience for these popular accounts, which reveals that both aristocracy and the lower classes found interest in these works, about, according to Smith's *Highwayman* of 1719, a variety of classes of victims: "Thus there are some ninety-five references to victims whose chief importance is their status as gentry or nobility; ninety-four to the middling sort, ranging from the professions down to tradesmen and artisans; and approximately twenty-five to the lower classes" (Faller 205). In terms of contemporary film and television, the proliferation of crime-solving and crime-biography indicates a class and socioeconomic interest across a spectrum of the audience.

The basic pattern of eighteenth-century criminal narratives can be found in contemporary teledocumentaries of murders. The case of the spinster Elizabeth Jeffryes, who was executed along with her coconspirator John Swan for the murder of Jeffryes's uncle, Joseph, takes the familiar form of a memoir. It begins with an account of Elizabeth's family, her parents living "a reputable Way of Life," as opposed to "this un-christian-like Criminal," whose "Misbehavior" caused her uncle to threaten to alter his will, in response to which she hatched the murder scheme to Swan: "Miss, however, by setting before the Necessity of the Thing, and that if her Uncle was not destroyed, she herself, as well as Swan, must be ruined and beggared, as would be the necessary Consequence of her Uncle's altering his Will, which he (Swan) was as much concerned to prevent as herself; she made the Promise to *Swan* of Marriage on her being possessed of the Money, which the Uncle was dead" (*Authentick Memoirs* 2, 3). Elizabeth's troubles began at age fifteen when this same uncle "debauched her," "destroyed her Honour in its Bud, and laid the Foundation of all her after misspent Life" (5). Uncle Jeffryes sent Elizabeth away to Portsmouth, where she miscarried; undeterred it seems, Elizabeth confronted her uncle again with her new pregnancy, which he, not wishing the expense of another country trip, "procured and gave her some Things to cause an Abortion, which had the Effect he desired, and she miscarried" (6). On the night of the murder, Elizabeth, in order to avoid suspicion, called out to neighbors that the house had been robbed and her uncle murdered, but "there seemed to have been an Interval of near an Hour" between the uncle's death and her outcry. That interval afforded Elizabeth and Swan time to "put up in a Sack the Brass, Pewter, Tankard, Spoons, &c. that were found in a Pond hard by, in order to induce People to believe that some Rogues had robb'd the House" (4). The narrative follows the pattern of arrest, imprisonment with fits of delirium tremens from a young life devoted to drinking, the trial, verdict, her confession, and execution. Most television documentaries follow this narrative with the exception of considerable eighteenth-century detail of the execution. Elizabeth, riding in a death-cart, had a tremendous fit that almost threw her out of the cart. At the place of execution for the pair, attended by thousands, Elizabeth had another fit of sorts:

> The Executioner then put on a Sort of Hood, made like a Purse, prepared on Purpose in *Chelmsford* Gaol, which drew together with Strings, and tied behind; when this was put on her head, she swooned away, nor did she recover from it, before she was turned off. She was put upon a Chair in the Cart, to put the Halter about her Neck, but *Swan* being very tall, the Halter was put round his Neck, he standing in the Cart. When they were both fixed in their Halters, Mr. *Griffith*, in a short Prayer, recommended their Souls into the Hands of the Almighty God, and then the Cart drew away. (14)

Elizabeth's body was placed in a coffin, but Swan's was placed in irons and hung up as an example to others.

William Hogarth's appeal in the eighteenth century certainly attests to such a broad class interest in crime. Both print series *A Harlot's Progress* (1732) and *A Rake's Progress* (1735) align themselves well with any concept of a criminal "biopic." To begin with, both reveal a sequential visual narrative akin to film and television biopics; moreover, both accentuate the graphic nature of the crimes and propose the moral for the viewer. Unlike most prose discussions of criminals during this era, even with limited illustrations, Hogarth's artistic narratives stand out as the first visual demonstrations of criminal behavior—animated in the sense that the viewer must follow from panel to panel in order to observe the record of criminal debauchery. *A Harlot's Progress* relies upon actual events in the pattern of debauching fresh-to-the-city country girls into lives of prostitution by the notorious procuress Elizabeth Needham, an associate of the infamous Colonel Francis Charteris. While John Gay's *The Beggar's Opera* (1728) and Daniel Defoe's *Moll Flanders* (1722) might well have served as influences, London newspapers presented tales of the patterns of procuring prostitutes that only thinly disguised the culprits, as indicated in *Fog's Weekly Journal* of December 6, 1729: "It is reported about the Town, that a certain noble colonel lately attempted to rob a young Woman, a Servant Maid, of her Honour, and that to frighten her into a Compliance with his filthy Desires, he drew a Pistol upon her—He is to be sued for the Assault, and it is thought considerable Damages will be given against him, not only for putting the Young Woman in Fear of Her Maidenhood, but for using a Weapon altogether unlawful upon such an Occasion" (as quoted in Paulson 241). Of course, in the idiom of the eighteenth century, one wonders which "Weapon" *Fog's Weekly* refers to here. Hogarth's plates reveal a visual narrative of the decline and death of the harlot: 1) the arrival of the young Moll in London, greeted by pox-ridden Elizabeth Needham, while Colonel Charteris watches from a nearby doorway; 2) Moll entertains an old, wealthy merchant in her bedroom, decorated with paintings of sexuality; 3) Moll has fallen into common harlotry in poor lodgings, while a magistrate comes through the door with bailiffs to arrest her; 4) in Bridewell Prison, a jailer threatens Moll to begin beating hemp, probably for nooses, while a woman, probably the jailor's wife, steals clothing from her bag; 5) Moll in a dismal room is dying of syphilis, as quacks prepare to bleed her and a charwoman steals her possessions; 6) Moll's wake with her coffin in the middle of the frame surrounded by thieves and prostitutes. Extraordinary was Hogarth's ability to convey in these frames a devolving, complex narrative of the sociopathology and immorality of London's underworld.

In addition to visual narrative structures, criminal biographies construct a cartography or topography of murder, both imaginary and contemporary, as a way of defining modern urban and national landscapes (Biressi 171). So prevalent have been accounts of locales for homicides and for executions, that murder-tourism has become a type of historical attraction: examples include the Whitechapel district of Jack the Ripper's murders in 1888, which London newspapers, like the *Daily Telegraph*, covered with sketch maps of the area, maps readily available today for site exploration; the OK Corral in Tombstone, Arizona, downloadable from the Tombstone Historama Corporation; a map of Los Angeles County designating the Tate-Polanski and LaBianca residences, as well as Spahn Ranch; John Waters photographing himself outside the People's Temple in San Francisco; or maps for the self-guided in criminal biographies, one of which this author followed to the sites of Aileen Wuornos's vicious Florida crimes.[1] Of course, all of these notorious scenes of violence have been made into films, some with several adaptations, such as the extensive

Jack the Ripper and O K Corral films, as though those moments captured and identified national fascinations. The pervasive newspaper maps of crime scenes found their way into popular detective fiction and would include maps of rooms, locales, and city blocks, such as the map of the apartment house facing Riverside Drive between 75th and 76th Streets, behind which is the archery range fronting the Drukker house and the residence of Professor Dillard in a famous Philo Vance case (Van Dine 28–29). Precise domestic and anatomical topography would determine Lizzie Borden's ability to commit murder within such a short time span and with her servant present in the residence. Edwin H. Porter, in *The Fall River Tragedy: A History of the Borden Murders* (1893), includes graphic maps of the murder scene: "A Plan of the Border House and Yard," "Ground Plain of the Border Residence," and "Second Floor of Borden House," as well as shocking photographs of "Position of Mrs. Borden's Body When Found" and "Position of Andrew Borden When Found" (51, 113). Perverse seekers of the hidden cause for these murders visited the Borden home and supplied the queerest of reasons, according to Edmund Lester Pearson, the New York Public Librarian and among the first writers of actual murder cases in a nonfictional novelistic manner: "Spiritualists, clairvoyants, crystal-gazers, and other seers had discovered strange things under flooring of the Borden house, or concealed in the stuffing of the "sopha." The Ouija board had been invoked, and had answered a long series of questions in its maddening fashion—half devil and half child. Its control was much interested in "Lizzie's cat," that doubtful animal, which, according to cruel and unfounded bit of gossip, had been carried down cellar, by Miss Borden, and beheaded, with an axe" (Pearson 75). Along with these charlatans of crime solving, the Borden case attracted political attention of the time to women, as Pearson notes:

> Advocates for suffrage for women came energetically to the defense of Miss Borden, almost as if her sex alone proved her innocence . . . that all women accused of grave crimes should either be cleared in advance of trial, or if convicted, should not be liable for punishment. . . . In 1892, Mrs. Mary A. Livermore, an estimable lady of very vigorous character, Mrs. Susan Fessenden, president of the Women's Christian Temperance Union, and Miss Lucy Stone, all distinguished in the struggle for what were then termed "Woman's Rights," came to the aid and comfort of Miss Borden. They did it so

ecstatically as to leave doubt whether they were acting from logic or from emotion. (66–67)

The Borden case and the suffragettes' insistence on the innocence of womankind seems strikingly au courant for contemporary America in 2020. Both the sham seers and the suffragettes desire to impose their reading upon the Borden case, again showing a provocative tendency to spin the narrative in a particular direction that is not lost in controversies to this day.

The psychological portrait of criminals expanded during the nineteenth century. As detailed accounts of the etiology of criminal activity coincided with the development of photography, so, too, did the fascination for interpreting the visual and physical narratives of crime scenes. The narrative landscape of murder can certainly be related to the rise of journalistic depictions of crime, such as the early New York crime work of Weegee, particularly the urban sites transformed brutally due to Murder Inc. (Coplans 13). Of course, television true crime tales rely extensively on mise-en-scène, particularly positions of bodies and objects within rooms or the surrounding area of an exterior homicide. Retracing the crime, both in time and in space, set the standard for homicide investigation, so much so that it has become visual formula for accounts of murder in crime documentaries, murder case files, and forensic shows. More than just a visual formula, these sites of killing also create recognizable cartographic narratives of both anatomy and place. Personality can very well become a dual narrative of contact and trace, as suggested by French criminalist Edmund Locard's "theory of interchange," in which the offender leaves something at the scene and takes something from the victim with him (Brookman 247). In fact, crime scenes contain visual biographies of both offender and victim, as forensic criminologist Dr. Laura G. Pettler explained: "Crime scene dynamics are a reflection of the personality, behavior, emotions, ways of thinking, and the totality of how an offender experiences his or her environment, how he or she experiences society, and how he or she experiences his or her culture" (59).

In addition to the biographies of the culprit, the scene of the crime, and the dual narrative of offender and victim, another biography of criminality emerged in the nineteenth century: a narrative merging culprit with detective. Eugène François Vidocq's four-volume *Memoires* recounts his criminal life, exploits, and societal rise from a once-infamous rogue to become the chief of the Sûreté. Vidocq also provides insight into his own psychology as a criminal. His accounts of his adventures and misadventures read like a cheap mock Dumas or Hugo melodrama, filled with fantastic characters in and out of prison, daring escapes, and infiltrations of crime rings. In fact, both Alexandre Dumas *père* and Victor Hugo were great admirers and defenders of Vidocq. Dumas's Edmond Dantès in *The Count of Monte Cristo* (1844) and M. Jackal in *Les Mohicans de Paris* (1854) were modeled after Vidocq, as were Jean Valjean and Javert in Hugo's *Les misérables* (1862). His *Memoires* also influenced Edgar Allan Poe in his creation of the first great fictional detective, Auguste Dupin, whose powers of observation and deduction emulate Vidocq's account of his own abilities. The dangerous criminal turned police agent Vautrin of Honoré de Balzac's *Comedie humaine* certainly has the dual characteristics of Vidocq, as observed most famously in *Le père Goriot* (1834), *Illusions perdues* (1837–43), and *Splendeurs et misères des courtisanes* (1838–44). Eugène Sue's *Les mystères de Paris* (1842–43) details the adventures of the Vidocq-like Rodolphe, Duke of Gerolstein, who can infiltrate any stratum of society, including the urban poor and criminal classes. Emile Gaboriau's murder investigator Monsieur Lecoq (rhyming with Vidocq) employs in his first major case some of the tactics and tools first adopted by Vidocq, such as preserving footprints for evidence in *Monsieur Lecoq* (1869). Of course, Arthur Conan Doyle contrasted the criminal mastermind and the sleuthing acumen of Vidocq in the alter egos of Professor Moriarty and Sherlock Holmes. Vidocq's *Memoires* provide psychological insight into both criminal and police tactics, but also the society that enables both to exist.

According to Vidocq, his criminal career began in the military, from which he deserted and then joined a band of charlatan soldiers who performed various confidence games on unwitting wealthy citizens and obtuse figures of the byzantine French military complex. His crimes also included forgery, although Vidocq claimed to be surprised at being "complicité de faux en écritures authentiques et publiques" (complicitous for falsely creating authentic and public works; 53). While in prison, Vidocq attempted several escapes, often donning a variety of disguises, and succeeded only for brief periods before being returned to the cells. In one particular confinement, he met a lifetime bandit named Desfousseux, who introduced him to several other convicts who belonged to a gang that took orders from Sallambier, a famous underworld figure. He learned about their trade and also paid attention to the recounted exploits of smugglers, burglars, and cutthroats, from all of whom Vidocq acquired intimate knowledge of how the criminal mind worked. Because of his association with notorious criminals and because of his involvement with numerous crimes, Vidocq gained a nefarious reputation, as he was designated by the gendarmerie:

> SURVEILLANCE SPECIALE
>
> Vidocq (Eugène-François) condamné à mort par contumace. Cet homme est excessivement entreprenant et dangereux.
>
> Special Surveilland
>
> Vidocq (Eugène-François) condemned to death in absentia. This man is extremely enterprising and dangerous. (179; translation mine)

After several incarcerations and escapes, Vidocq's exploits became the stuff of underworld legend, but his conscience, at least according to his *Memoires*, had become disgusted with this life of crime. This realization came to Vidocq at Bicêtre, where he could have held court among the criminal class:

> Mais mainteant toute cette gloire des prisons m'était odieuse; plus je lisais dans l'âme des malfaituers, plus ils se mettaient à découvert devant moi, plus je me sentais porté à plaindre la société de nourrir dans son sein une engeance pareille.
>
> But now, all that prison glory was odious to me; the more I read in the souls of the malefactors, the more they revealed themselves to me, the more I sensed my pity for the society that nurtured within its breast such a mob. (269)

To assuage his conscience, Vidocq decided to become a police informer. The rumor that he was a murderer Vidocq used to his advantage, achieving credible confidence among convicts for twenty-four months. The result was his release from confinement, although the authorities claimed he had escaped. As a fugitive in Paris, Vidocq freely circulated among thieves, who hid him, fed him, and told him their plans for robberies. In fact, Vidocq saw himself taking on a military role as a moral spy: "Je faisais la guerre à tout de coquins qui infestaient la capitale" (I made war on all of the rascals who infested the capital; 285). He was able to rid Paris of

Boudin and Saint-Germain, two of the greatest scoundrels of the period. Not only did he mingle among the criminal classes and find out their schemes, but he also discovered the fences, all due to his knowing that thieves are such stupid creatures that they accepted anything he told them, no matter how absurd ("Les voleurs sont en general des êtres si stupides, qu'il n'y avait pas d'excuse absurde que je ne pusse leur fair admettre . . ."; 294). Even the few clever and bold criminals, including women, found Vidocq's efforts to eradicate crime far too compelling not to become police spies themselves. His interest in fingerprints, in footprints, in special paper and ink to discover forgeries—all pointed to a criminal mentality that had turned against itself for the sake of its conscience. His measures against counterfeiting were not solely for remittance of his soul; Vidocq took out patents on special paper and ink developed by chemists in his employ, built a factory for their production, and encouraged bankers and companies to use his paper and ink for their security bonds; by the mid-1860s, the French government printed its currency using Vidocq's paper and ink (Edwards 63).

Along with early fictional portrayals of Vidocq, French silent cinema produced four films about the former thief turned police agent. Harry Baur, best known for portraying Beethoven in Abel Gance's 1936 biopic *Un grand amour de Beethoven*, starred as Vidocq in three short films: *La jeunesse de Vidocq ou comment on devient policier* (1909), *L'évasion de Vidocq* (1910), and *Vidocq* (1911). In 1922, Jean Kemm made a film based upon the *Memoires*, which starred René Navarre of *Fantômas* fame. Jacques Daroy directed the French sound feature, *Vidocq* (1939). In 2001, Gérard Depardieu took on the mantel of Vidocq in an entirely CGI French sci-fi account of the master criminalist.

Douglas Sirk's *A Scandal in Paris* (1946), very loosely adapted from Vidocq's memoirs, stars George Sanders as a sardonic rogue and Akim Tamiroff as his untrustworthy criminal sidekick, Emile. In a preposterous twist on even the outrageous self-acclaim in Vidocq's own words, the film has the pair of crooks posing for a church portrait of Saint George (Sanders) defeating the dragon (Tamiroff), which inspires a kind of fetishistic adoration in Therese (Signe Hasso), the daughter of the minister of police (Alan Napier). The crooked duo eventually become houseguests of the minister, where they steal the jewels of his mother, the Marquise De Pierremont (Alma Kruger), only to hide them nearby on the manor grounds, and to return them by means of Vidocq's confidence game of pretending to employ logical deduction and to unearth clues, all of which he laid himself. For much of the film, Sanders portrays Vidocq as devoid of any morality, as superficially able to negotiate social situations, and as a charming, erudite gentleman—in short, as a sociopath.

Complications increase in an already unrealistic plot, including Vidocq becoming the new chief of police, ousting Richet (Gene Lockhart), whose wife Loretta (Carole Landis) once had an amorous encounter with Vidocq, the criminal who stole her signature garter. When Loretta later accidentally sees Vidocq in Paris, she blackmails him and he pursues plans for another robbery with Emile. Richet, obsessed with losing Loretta, intends to confront her and Vidocq and kill himself, but the hapless man ends up killing Loretta instead. Thérèse, however, informs Vidocq that she has deduced that he originally stole her grandmother's jewels, but she forgives him out of undying love. Vidocq's conscience overrides his heart of larceny, and he withdraws from the robbery, warning Emile that he will hunt down any thief who attempts to steal the jewels. In a mirroring plot of the Richets' mishap, Emile tries to murder his former partner, but Vidocq kills him instead. Vidocq, a changed man, confesses his crime to the minister's family, receives due forgiveness, and becomes the groom to young Thérèse.

Typically, violent behavior falls under general clinical rubrics, such as conduct disorder, antisocial personality disorder, intermittent explosive disorder. Estimates of prison populations indicate that between 70 and 80 percent of inmates exhibit tendencies toward antisocial personality disorder, as might be expected by the nature of their crimes (Séguin et al. 190). The Psychopathic Personality Inventory reveals two "uncorrelated factors": "The first factor (*Fearless Dominance*) reflects the interpersonal-affective traits of psychopathy and is marked by social dominance, stress immunity, and fearlessness. The second factor (*Impulsive Antisociality*) may be characterized more in terms of high negative emotionality (i.e., alienation and aggression) and low constraint (i.e., self-control and traditionalism)" (Blonigen and Krueger 298). Antisocial personality disorder remains as common in the general population as "panic disorder, obsessive-compulsive disorder (OCD), and attention-deficit/hyperactivity disorder (ADHD)," and only depression outranks it in terms of frequency.[2] Such frequency of psychopathological disorders ensured the seemingly endless true accounts for television crime series.

The reboot of *Dragnet* (2003) begins with the familiar caveat about the veracity of the crime and the ensuing investigation about to unfold: "The story you are about to see was inspired by actual events. The names have been changed to protect the innocent." In the original of 1951–59 and its resurrection of 1967–70, the show follows Sergeant

Friday and his partner as they conduct interviews, follow leads, meet with crime lab personnel, and eventually apprehend the culprit. All *Dragnet* series conclude each episode with line-up of the culprit and the resulting sentence handed down in the Superior Court in and for the County of Los Angeles. This narrative arc established a formula for investigative procedurals on the small screen, a storyline that follows a crime as though it had its own life cycle, even if liberties are taken to reveal the human side of the detectives through Friday's moral tirades in syncopated patter about the dismal state of the world. As television shows developed, *Dragnet*'s caveat became less important than more realistic details, and the narrative shifted to a much more exacting biography of a crime or of an investigation.

A&E's *American Justice* (1992–2005) with host Bill Kurtis, which had a syndicated run fittingly on the *Biography Channel*, began with notorious cases, such as, from the first season, serial killer Jeffery Dahmer's demented sexual cannibalism; Joseph Valachi and Sammy Gravano as hitmen who violate the code of *omertà*; Lorena Bobbitt's literal emasculation of her supposedly abusive husband; and the FBI assault on the Branch Davidian compound outside of Waco, Texas. Kurtis narrates the documentary biography of crimes, focusing not just on the crime itself, but on the motivations, often told by victims' and criminals' family members, police and attorneys, and at times the criminal himself, in the form of a chronology of misdeeds and missteps that led to tragedy. Often, the moment of the crime occurs almost inexplicably, as though a rational analysis eludes this biography and results in a murky psychological assessment. This type of documentary relies upon biographical narrative development for both the crime itself and for the perpetrator. So successful was *American Justice* that it spawned numerous docubiographies of crimes, including Kurtis's own *Cold Case Files* (1999–2017). This docu-reality show contains all the essential narrative elements for biography, actually two lives are constructed: the crime in the past and the reconstruction and renewed investigation that leads to an arrest, trial, and conviction. The past crime involves memories of the detectives assigned to the case, local newspaper and news program coverage, gathered evidence—usually DNA in older cases before polymerase chain reaction testing—and photographs and videos of the crime scene that are significant visual narrative. *Cold Justice* (2013–present) picked up this pattern of two crime biographies—past and present—and replaced the voice-over narrator with the actual experience of two seasoned female investigators, former Texas prosecutor Kelly Siegler and former Las Vegas Metro crime scene expert Yolanda

McClary. The visual narrative of the original crimes scene, locales, and media images propel the drama of the new unfolding biography of a crime, whose culprit often appears among those witnesses and suspects from the initial investigation. The female angle remains key to this show's success on the Oxygen channel.

In popular culture, cable television has long affirmed this equal opportunity disorder for women, as evident in the numerous shows, either real life stories or fictional tales, devoted to women who murder, especially on Lifetime, which have the ironic tagline "Television for Women." Women in crime biographies have a contemporary appeal for audiences and fairly consistent ratings. As television docu-reality crime shows developed, so, too, did shows focusing exclusively upon female murderers. Former FBI profiler Candice Delong hosted *Deadly Women* (2005–present) on the Investigation Discovery Channel. Unlike the hour-long Bill Kurtis vehicles and *Cold Justice*, these episodes were short twelve- to fourteen-minute reenactments of vicious crimes by often psychopathic female murderers, who often targeted family members. These episodes relied upon accounts collected over a considerable time span and from around the world. Having commentary from a female forensic profiler adds more psychopathological depth than most procedural crime series, with evaluations that include satisfying excessive narcissism, sadistic desires, dangerous and uncontrollable seething rage, and erotomania. The episodes invariably conclude with the actress melodramatically playing the role of the female killer looking into the camera, lowering her brow, and staring almost wide-eyed as if to heighten her mental derangement.

Wicked Attraction (aka *Couples Who Kill*, 2008–2013), like many of these crime biopics series, has a YouTube presence of previously aired episodes, as well as a YouTube following. *Wicked Attraction* also employs criminal psychological profilers and psychiatrists to provide insights into the couples' psychopathological state of mind. "My Girl" (2008) explores a taboo subject, although all too prevalent in terms of violence, about a complicated, teenaged, lower-class lesbian love triangle, with two of the parties married to men, that results in a savage lesbian-jealousy murder. Newlyweds Michelle Hetzel and Brandon Bloss stab to death Michelle's erstwhile lover Devon Guzman, who resides with her lesbian lover, Keary Renner. The episode intersperses reconstructed acting of the relationships and the crime with interviews with real-life lesbian partners, primarily Renner, who admits that their relationship involved domestic violence. On the night of the murder, Hetzel and Bloss arrive at Renner's apartment under the pretense of looking for Guzman, whom Renner assumes is out drinking. Eventually, Hetzel leads Renner to search the streets for Guzman, only finding her abandoned car, which Hetzel asks Renner to approach and talk to Guzman, most likely passed out. Renner sees Guzman's body in the back seat, opens the car door, realizes something is wrong, and yells for Hetzel to call 911. Like a visual intertitle, Guzman's smiling photograph punctuates much of this episode, as a way to convey her youth and tragic loss of life. When police and paramedics arrive, time passes before a paramedic informs the other lovers that Guzman is dead, the news prompting Hetzel to vomit and Renner to cry uncontrollably. A jacket had been placed over Guzman's body, which criminalists refer to as a "psychological undoing," meaning that the killer knew the victim and wants her to appear natural and without any trauma. Little blood at the scene even with a large throat gash, however, pointed to the murder occurring elsewhere—again a standard piece of information that any audience member would understand. A bogus syringe lay next to the body, although there were defensive wounds to indicate a struggle prior to death. Under police questioning, prime suspect Renner admits to the domestic violence between the two lovers, allowing for a search warrant for Renner's apartment, which did produce small amounts of blood in the living area and bathroom. The lesbian sexual biography that unfolds is very complicated: Renner was dating Hetzel when she first met Guzman, then Renner moved in on Guzman and they became lovers, which brought about a psychopathological game of violent power struggles for dominance over and possession of "my girl," Devon Guzman. Guzman and Renner dropped out of high school, as Hetzel went into foster care and developed a relationship with a somewhat older Brandon, son of her foster-mother, which eventuated in a marriage proposal. That, the clearly borderline personality disorder Guzman could not abide, with frequent telephone calls to Hetzel and stalking incidents. Jealousy, domestic violence, financial problems, infidelity, multiple partners—all orchestrated by the borderline personality, Guzman, who always had a lover waiting for her between Hetzel and Renner. After a late night ride by Renner and Guzman to Hetzel's home provoked the murder, with an emasculated Bloss and a sadistic Hetzel prepared to commit the crime, Guzman bit Bloss in the struggle, and that proved to be their undoing. When these crime biographies appear on YouTube, viewer commentary reflects national sentiments about such television shows. Among the most pertinent comments for "My Girl" is one that came from a psychopathology knowledgeable wag, who offered the following: "I caught a personality disorder just trying to understand these people." With the proliferation of such criminal biography shows, small wonder that such contact syndromes, no matter how facetious and parodic, occur.

While the vast majority of crime biographies in film and on television deal with murderers, a new trend in cinema reveals other types of crimes as the basis for oddly humorous analysis. *Catch Me If You Can* (2002), based on Frank W. Abagnale's autobiography with Stan Redding; *Bronson* (2008), based on Charles Bronson's prison autobiography; and *I Love You Phillip Morris* (2009), based on Steve McVicker's biography of Steven Russell—all present criminals who have never committed murder, but have received odd prison terms for their multiple offenses. Steven Russell currently serves in solitary confinement for a 140 year sentence for insurance fraud, embezzlement, and multiple escapes from prison, a retaliatory sentence imposed by the State of Texas primarily because he quite successfully faked his own death from AIDS in order to escape. Charles Bronson remains in prison, having served a majority of his thirty-one years for armed robbery in solitary confinement, primarily for his extremely violent behavior and hostage takings over the years while incarcerated. Frank W. Abagnale, Jr., who illegally posed as an airline pilot, physician, and attorney, committed forgery, bank fraud, and elaborate confidence swindles, served a total of five years in prison—six brutal, horrible, and filthy months in France, six humane months in Sweden, and four years of a twelve year sentence in a United States federal penitentiary—before his release, only to become an anti-fraud consultant for the United States federal government. Their biopics, with the same titles as their biographies, take new approaches to cinematic representations and aesthetics of criminality, thereby recasting portrayals of felonious psychopathology.

Steven Spielberg's *Catch Me If You Can* chronicles con man Frank Abagnale (Leonardo DiCaprio) from his mid-teens as a check kiter, through his late teens as he impersonated a Pan Am Airlines copilot, to his early twenties in other guises in order to exploit funds from corporations and banks through complex schemes of fraud and forgery. Spielberg obviously recognized that Abagnale's autobiography perfectly fit a number of Hollywood genres, mixing heist and chase film elements with a rom-com formula in the a-go-go 1960s. Motivation for Abagnale's confidence schemes always comes back to his excuse that he possessed a weakness for women and for acquiring sufficient material possessions—expensive cars, tailored clothes, and jewelry—to impress women: "An inflamed sex drive has no conscience"; "My one sensuous fault was women" (Abagnale 16, 77).

Figure 10.1. Fake copilot, con man Frank Abagnale (Leonardo DiCaprio), follows the objects of his desire in *Catch Me If You Can*.

His sociopathy for bunco games, according to Abagnale, derived from a hyper-libido, which the film does not dispel. In fact, DiCaprio's unchecked lust seems playful at first, not unlike Abagnale's account, but soon, in a sea of fraudulent checks, he leaves many duped bank tellers and stewardesses in his wake. He also dates them to find out information about banking and airline procedures and their various lingos. To accommodate this Don Juanism on screen, *Catch Me If You Can* employs a number of long shots with attractive stewardesses moving through airports, occasionally followed by DiCaprio in his copilot's uniform. Everywhere in the film beautiful women dot the landscape, even a poolside long shot of a timer going off to remind a row of chaise-lounged, bikini-clad beauties to turn over. So obsessed with women and his con, Abagnale set up a sham contest at the University of Arizona to enlist eight coeds to join him on a summer European Pan Am promotional and photographic tour as flight attendants to-be. Spielberg intercuts the long shot of the college girls in tight-fitting stewardess outfits sashaying through the Miami International Airport, with DiCaprio now camouflaged by them, with reaction shots of male rubbernecking by police, detectives, and FBI agents supposedly pursuing Abagnale. Of course, agent Carl Hanratty (Tom Hanks) finally captures his man in a small French village, where the con man is printing up thousands of fake checks. Like Don

Juan, Abagnale receives a pardon from a superior being, Hanratty, who subsequently enlists his aid in tracking down con men across the country. Unlike the visual crime narratives of Hogarth's day, the reprobate here lives to be reformed.

Not all criminal biopics entertain a morality of reform. Through a surrealistic aesthetic and often dark humor, *Bronson*, starring Tom Hardy, offers insights into the complex, often irrational psychopathology of Michael Peterson, a small-time Luton villain before he took the moniker Charles Bronson, after the US action-film actor. Interspersed throughout the film, Bronson, in prison blues and facing the camera, narrates events of his life in prison. Several transitional scenes show Bronson, always in a three-piece suit, on a theatrical stage as he addresses an audience, dimly captured in evening clothes. These shifts represent Bronson's maniac phases, his fantasy for achieving fame and recognition, and patterns related to a forensic psychiatrist's diagnosis of Bronson: "He said I was psychopathic, with very sensitive ways that caused paranoia" (Bronson 65). The stage represents Bronson's emotional psyche during his explosions of laughter, for which he wears a white face of a clown with tear drops on one cheek and a cloverleaf the other, as well as white gloves, which he

Figure 10.2. Bonson's (Tom Hardy) stage profile as himself arguing for his release in *Bronson*.

splays à la Jolson. These scenes, very much like a Genet play or moments from Kubrick's *Clockwork Orange*, always precede graphic, disturbing acts of violence by Bronson. Just before his removal from prison to Broadmoor Hospital, a high-security psychiatric institute for the criminally insane, Bronson addresses the audience in severe right-profile as himself and switches to severe left-profile as a nurse with painted black hair on his bald head, eyelashes, lipstick, and red fingernails, only observable from this perspective. Bronson informs the audience of this crucial turning point: "I would like to re-enact 'What happens when murder goes wrong.'"

Bronson refers to a previous scene in which he thought his only recourse out of Broadmoor was to kill an admitted pederast. Bronson remained at Broadmoor, however. During the infamous Broadmoor riot, Bronson and other inmates assailed the rooftop, threw off slate tiles, and started a conflagration that caused over a quarter of a million pounds in damage. Back on stage, Bronson introduces the short fifteen-second film, "Charlie versus Broadmoor," which contains actual color newsreel footage of the chilling incident. Much of the film relies upon interjections of pop and classical music, montage sequences of Bronson fighting guards, and a short sequence of his surrealistic drawings, which appear to have influences from Salvador Dalí and René Magritte.

Bronson certainly fits within *script theory*, a clinical model that explicates how cognitive scripts shape behavior. For an aggressive person, scripts

Figure 10.3. Bronson, reverse profile, as the nurse who denies his request.

that lead toward aggressive actions are "more accessible across a wider variety of situations, meaning that an aggressive behavior will be more likely to be generated as an appropriate response" (Sestir and Bartholow 159). In both his autobiography and the portrayal in the biopic, Bronson admits to acts of violence that follow a kind of theatrical or film script. In fact, his violence within prison occurs with such regularity when confronted by official denials and after long periods within solitary confinement that he appears to be following a script. He also later evaluated his actions in ways that suggest script theory, such as relying upon memories of violence and being cued to react in similar situations and environments, particularly "when the previous experience was considered successful" and noticing when violence became automatic "without much thought or weighing of consequences" (Fagan et al. 691). This psychological theory shows immediate correlations to cinematic scripting.

The same year as *Bronson*, the French industry produced its own version of its most notorious criminal. Bank robber and murderer, Jacques Mesrine penned his autobiography, *L'instinct de mort* (*The Death Instinct*), in 1977, which made him a cultural antihero and the book an overnight sensation. A two-part film adaptation, *Mesrine: Killer Instinct* and *Mesrine: Public Enemy #1* (2008), charts the sociopath's odyssey of crime. Along with his lover Jeanne, Mesrine commits armed robberies in France, kidnaps a Canadian billionaire in Quebec who later escapes, gets arrested in Arizona, sent to and escapes from a Canadian prison, returns to France to commit more robberies, and ends up killing two forest rangers who have recognized him. That was just part 1! The second part follows Mesrine's exploits of more bank robberies, his media presence and his kidnapping and attempted murder of journalist Jacques Tiller, whose articles Mesrine disapproved of, and, finally, his death on a Paris street after his car, also containing his wife and dog, is blasted with bullets, nineteen of which end Mesrine's life. Like Bronson, Mesrine scripts his own media existence and narrative arc from a kind of Robin Hood to political revolutionary, all the while confessing in his autobiography that he was nothing more than a remorseless gangster:

> I was going to become a killer. One of those criminal beasts that in cold blood eliminates a human being made of flesh and blood without the slightest twinge of guilt. I would kill these men out of honor, interest, or simply to defend my life. . . . The only crime I never forgave myself for is that of a little blue-feathered bird that I shot down in our garden

when I was thirteen. Because I had killed it out of stupidity while its only fault was to have serenaded me with its song. That is the only remorse I ever knew, as monstrous as it sounds. (Mesrine 44–45)

The release of the films ushered in a wave of 1970s nostalgia and lifted Mesrine to a cult status, one surely he did not deserve for his narcissistic sociopathy.

The mixed-genre *I Love You Phillip Morris* plays out a comic sexual bromance and rom-com about two con men who meet by accident in a prison library and inescapably fall in love. The film begins with Russell as a child with three friends, two boys and a girl, on their backs watching clouds. Both the girl and Russell notice an obvious phallic cloud, but the other boys are blind to it. That homosexual joke of insight and blindness underlies much of *I Love You Phillip Morris*. Like McVicker's biography, the film chronicles a narcissistic Steven Russell's faux Christian marriage, his decision to be openly gay following a near-fatal traffic accident, and his new gay lifestyle with a handsome lover in Miami; however, an unfortunate epiphany occurs to Russell: "Being gay is really expensive." Russell (Jim Carey) resorts to what will become a criminal pattern of confidence games of check kiting to buy expensive watches and stays at upscale hotels and spas. He also works insurance frauds, presented in a montage of physical humor, particularly Carey's slipping on oil in a supermarket aisle and his head dive down an escalator. On discovering that the police want to arrest him, Russell follows another pattern of suicide attempts to avoid apprehension and jail time. He downs prescription drugs and Vodka, but awakens in the hospital, as his ex-wife Debbie (Leslie Mann), his lover Jimmy (Rodrigo Santoro), and a policeman discuss his physical and criminal situation in the hallway. Expressing societal misunderstanding about the gay lifestyle, Debbie asks Jimmy if being homosexual and stealing go hand-in-hand! Even as the others talk in the corridor, Russell tries to flee, ending up on the roof of the hospital in what appears to be another suicide attempt. Still woozy from the overdose, Russell, in slapstick comedy fashion, puts his hands together as though ready to dive. The camera cuts to large, open garbage bin below, cuts back to Russell jumping as Debbie and Jimmy scream, and then cuts to the garbage bin that Russell has missed and shows him lying facedown and bleeding on the pavement. Russell's blindness here also plays into the humor.

In prison, Russell and Phillip Morris (Ewan McGregor) share scenes of intimacy, such as slow-dancing in their cell to Johnny Mathis's "Chances Are," cuddling in bed, and having comic moments of sex. Outside the joint, they share an extravagant domestic life with expensive cars, his-and-his jet skis, and ostentatious accoutrements, all financed by Russell's corporate crimes. Russell has conned his way into an executive position as chief financial officer of a large medical management company in Houston, where he steals over $900,000 by cooking the books. So willing are they to increase profits that his company's officials blindly accept Russell's false credentials and his doctored books. Of course, he gets caught, and, again, tries to commit suicide, poking himself multiple times with Morris's insulin injections, in an final effort to avoid incarceration.

The film's centerpiece remains Russell's numerous escapes from prison in order to be with Phillip Morris. As is typical of crime biographies, montage demonstrates the main activities that define the criminal. In Russell's case, the film presents a montage of scenes of his outlandish escapes based upon appearance versus reality. After the suicide attempt by insulin shock, Russell awakens chained to a hospital bed. Taken to be processed in county jail, he slips into an elevator with janitors in one shot as the doors close, only to be in custody again as the doors reopen. With bail set at $900,000, Russell forges a bail bond reassessment and reduction, impersonates a judge, and walks out of lockup, only to be caught. Still awaiting trial, Russell pays a burly inmate to break his nose, and while in the emergency room, Russell swipes the attending physician's identity card. In his cell at night, as other prisoners watch in awe across the cellblock, Russell breaks open pens of green ink and dyes his prison clothes to match those of a physician. Again, he escapes, only to be caught again. After observing an undercover vice tap on the guarded glass exit door with a walkie-talkie, Russell steals one from an unwary secretary, grabs a bag of clothes from another inmate, and then the camera reveals Russell from behind, walking in red plastic hot pants with black plastic back pockets and a genital strip in front, fishnet stockings, and a dark leopard-patterned wife-beater shirt.

Of course, this scene plays as cross-dressing comedy, unlike the attire that the ingenious Russell donned in the real escape not from prison, but from county jail: "There he found a dumbwaiter used by female classification officers to send females' civilian clothes down to the basement. Better still, in front of the dumbwaiter he found a pile of women's clothing waiting to be sent down. Russell quickly rummaged

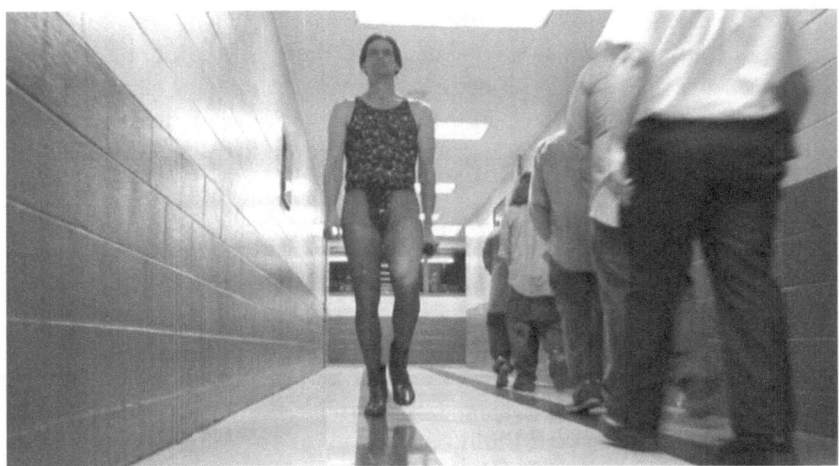

Figure 10.4. Steven Russell (Jim Carey) walking toward the prison exit as a vice cop in *I Love You Phillip Morris*.

through the skirts, blouses, and slacks until he came across a pair of red stretch pants that would fit him. . . . A day later, Russell has a brown stained T-shirt and a pair of red stretchpants. It was better than an orange jumpsuit" (McVicker 118–19). Arriving at Morris's house in a limo, with champagne and flowers in hand, Russell tries to convince Phillip of his regret and his love, and, at the moment that Morris relents, a SWAT team descends and arrests them both. As with most criminal biopics, montage sequences do more than condense time; they provide insights into personality and character deficits, as well as a visual narrative pattern that defines the criminal.

The film builds to Russell's most outrageous escape—by way of his own death from AIDS. Again, a montage of scenes reveals Russell's devious, even sociopathic plan to use public sentiment toward homosexuals afflicted with HIV and AIDS to obtain his freedom. From his deathbed in a prison hospital ward, Russell explains to the camera how he died. The first step required massive weight loss, eating half of his allotted meals, then half of that until he was down to a quarter of normal intake. He needed resultant loss of weight to corroborate with the false medical history and testing. As McVicker's biography establishes, step two required forging his medical records to indicate that "he had been infected with the HIV virus long before his sudden weight loss" and then to produce a "lab report from UTMB [University of Texas Medical Branch] showing a progressive decline in [his] T-cells. . . . [He] was eventually diagnosed with full-blown AIDS" (214). Step three required prison-assisted removal from incarceration to relocation in a nursing home. Russell knew that such a release would be granted only through a Special Needs Parole, which was monitored by "an obscure division of the state's criminal-justice division known as the Texas Council on Offenders with Mental Impairments" (212). He won his parole, and the film shows Russell in a slow pratfall from the ambulance to the curbside next to a wheelchair, again to reinforce the comedy of errors upon which this con relied. Step four required taking advantage of contemporary experimental protocols and treatments for AIDS. Using the name of Dr. Adam Rios, known since the mid-1980s for AIDS research, Russell requested a patient with the viral disease to serve in a clinical trial, knowing full well it would be he. His request was granted by the Special Needs Board. The final step was the announcement of his own death, which the good doctor (Russell assuming the role) did with sorrow. The film concludes with Russell, disguised as Morris's attorney, meeting a shocked Phillip in a prison conference room. Later, trying to secure Phillip's own release from prison, Russell is spotted in the men's room by a former nemesis at the swindled medical management company. He is caught and sentenced to an extremely lengthy prison term, one beyond natural life. The final scene that segues into the credit sequence represents the imprisoned Russell's complicated wish-fulfillment fantasy. In a long shot of the exterior prison walls and fencing with razor wire, sirens blare as Russell runs past the camera, laughing madly with guards in pursuit, and then the camera tilts upward through a rainbowed sky to stop at a phallic-shaped cloud formation, returning the visual narrative back to the opening scene of desire.

Criminal biopics exhibit genre shifts, particularly in the comic vein. Unlike the serious reenactments of violent domestic murders, mass murders, and serial killings, the new trend in criminal biopics encompasses the satiric docufiction. New films worthy of this latest subgenre include two dark comedies, *Bernie* (2011) and *I, Tonya* (2017). *Bernie* stars Jack Black as a devout Christian, assistant funeral parlor director in Carthage, Texas, where he is beloved by the townspeople, but in a moment of temporary insanity shoots his long-time, very domineering benefactress (Shirley MacLaine) four times in the back and then deposits her body in the garage freezer beneath the frozen vegetable and steaks. His trial must be moved for fear that he will get too much sympathy in Carthage. Interspersing the reenactment of Bernie's life are documentary inserts of conversations with actual community members, most of whom provide commentary in dialect and idiom that is pure East Texas, such as one man's assessment of the other town's jury members: "They have more tattoos than teeth!" *I, Tonya* also mixes documentary style with reenactment (mockmentary) as it chronicles the rise and fall of Tonya Harding, her complicated domestic relationships with her alcoholic mother (Allison Janney) and her profligate husband Jeff Gillooly (Sebastian Stan), her complicity in the 1994 assault on her skating rival Nancy Kerrigan, cooked up by her husband and his delusional CIA-wannabe friend Shawn Eckhart (Paul Walter Hauser), her trial, and the various career paths that ensue. *I, Tonya* remains a character study of lower-class America, its often bizarre ambitions, its lack of self-awareness, and its mendacious, even felonious struggles for an ever-elusive American dream. Both *Bernie* and *I, Tonya* represent a subgenre of mocking satire leveled at unfortunate people caught up in circumstances that are only partially within their control. With the onslaught over the past three decades of criminal biographies, biopics, television crime series, it seems altogether fitting that a darkly comic, somewhat mean-spirited genre would emerge to placate an overly saturated American audience seeking new ways to escape into its favorite psychopathological pastime—crime.

Notes

1. L. Perry Curtis, Jr., *Jack the Ripper and the London Press* (148). Vincent Bugliosi, *Helter Skelter* (150ff.). John Waters, *Shock Value: A Tasteful Book about Bad Taste* (122). Joseph Michael Reynolds, *Dead Ends: The Pursuit, Conviction, and Execution of Serial Killer Aileen Wuoros*: see inserts "Map of the Body and Vehicle Recovery Sites" and "The Murdered Men, the Cars They Drove, and Where They Were Found."

2. David W. Black, *Bad Boys, Bad Men: Confronting Antisocial Personality Disorder* (5). Black includes the gender statistics from a recent National Epidemiological Survey on Alcohol and Related Conditions (NESARC) that revealed out of 43,000 Americans, roughly 5.5 percent of men and 1.9 percent of women could be diagnosed as antisocial. Black suggests that, while the prevalence of this disorder "may sound remarkably high," in fact, the statistics "may not be high enough" (5).

Works Cited

Abagnale, Frank W., with Stan Redding. *Catch Me If You Can: The Amazing True Story of the Youngest and Most Daring Con Man in the History of Fun and Profit!* Broadway Books, 2000. Originally published 1980.

Authentick Memoirs of the Wicked Life and Transactions of Elizabeth Jeffryes, Spinster, Who Was Executed on Saturday, March 28, 1752 [. . .]. London, 1752.

Belfort, Jordan. *The Wolf of Wall Street*. Bantam Books, 2007.

Biressi, Anita. *Crime, Fear and the Law in True Crime Stories*. Palgrave, 2001.

Black, David W., with C. Lindon Larson. *Bad Boys, Bad Men: Confronting Antisocial Personality Disorder*. Oxford UP, 2013.

Caulfield, James. *Blackguardiana: Dictionary of Rogues, Bawds, Pimps, Whores, Pickpockets, Shoplifters, Mail-Robbers, Coiners, House-Breakers, Murderers, Pirates, Gipses, Mountebanks, &c*. London, 1793.

Blonigen, Daniel M., and Robert F. Krueger, "Personality and Violence: The Unifying Role of Structural Models of Personality." *The Cambridge Handbook of Violent Behavior and Aggression*, edited by Daniel J. Flannery et al., Cambridge UP, 2007, pp. 288–305.

Bronson, Charles. *Bronson*. John Blake, 2008.

Brookman, Fiona. *Understanding Homicide*. Sage, 2005.

Bugliosi, Vincent, with Curt Gentry. *Helter Skelter: The True Story of the Manson Murders*. W. W. Norton, 1994. Originally published 1974.

Coplans, John. "Weegee the Famous." *Weegee's New York: Photographs, 1935–1960*. Te Neues, 1982, pp. 7–14.

Curtis, L. Perry, Jr. *Jack the Ripper and the London Press*. Yale UP, 2001.

Colman, George, and Bonnell Thornton. *The Connoisseur, by Mr. Town, Critic, and Censor-General*. Vol. 1, London, 1755.

Edwards, Samuel. *The Vidocq Dossier: The Story of the World's First Detective*. Houghton Mifflin, 1977.

Fagan, Jeffrey, et al. "Social Contagion of Violence." *The Cambridge Handbook of Violent Behavior and Aggression*, edited by Daniel J. Flannery et al., Cambridge UP, 2007, pp. 688–723.

Faller, Lincoln B. *Turned to Account: The Forms and Functions of Criminal Biography in Late Seventeenth- and Early Eighteenth-Century England*. Cambridge UP, 1987.

The Genuine History of the Life of Richard Turpin, the Noted Highwayman, Who Was Executed at York for Horse-Stealing, under the Name of John Plamer, on Saturday Ap. 7, 1739. London, 1739.

Jackson, William. *The New and Complete Newgate Calendar; or, Villany Displayed in All Its Branches—Containing Accounts of the Most Notorious Malefactors, from the Year 1700 to the Present Time*. London, 1795.

McVicker, Steve. *I Love You Phillip Morris: A True Story of Life, Love, and Prison Breaks*. Miramax Books, 2003.

Mesrine, Jacques. *The Death Instinct*. Translated by Catherine Texier and Robert Greene, Tam Tam, 2014.

Paulson, Ronald. *The "Modern Moral Subject," 1697–1732*. Hogarth, vol. 1, Rutgers UP, 1991.

Pearson, Edmund. *Studies in Murder*. Modern Library, 1938. Originally published 1924.

Pettler, Laura G. *Crime Scene Staging Dynamics in Homicide Cases*. CRC Press, 2016.
Porter, Edwin H. *The Fall River Tragedy: A History of the Borden Murders*. Fall River, MA, 1893.
Reynolds, Joseph Michael. *Dead Ends: The Pursuit, Conviction, and Execution of Serial Killer Aileen Wuornos, The Damsel of Death*. St. Martin's Press, 2004.
Séguin, Jean R., et al. "The Neuropsychology of Violence." *The Cambridge Handbook of Violent Behavior and Aggression*, edited by Daniel J. Flannery et al., Cambridge UP, 2007, pp. 187–214.
Sestir, Mark A., and Bruce D. Bartholow. "Theoretical Explanations of Aggression and Violence." *Aggressive Offenders' Cognition: Theory, Research, and Practice*, edited by Theresa A Gannon et al., Wiley, 2007, pp. 157–78.
Van Dine, S. S. *The Bishop Murder Case: A Philo Vance Story*. Grosset and Dunlap, 1929.
Vidocq, Eugène François. *Mémoires: Les voleurs*. Edited by Francis Lacassin, Éditions Robert Laffont, 1998.
Waters, John. *Shock Value: A Tasteful Book about Bad Taste*. Thunder Mouth, 2005. Originally published 1981.

Contributors

Julie Grossman is Professor of English and communication and film studies at Le Moyne College, Syracuse, New York. With R. Barton Palmer, she is founding coeditor of a book series on adaptation and visual culture and coeditor of the collection *Adaptation in Visual Culture: Images, Texts, and Their Multiple Worlds* (2017). Other books include *Rethinking the Femme Fatale in Film Noir* (2009), *Literature, Film, and Their Hideous Progeny: Adaptation and ElasTEXTity* (2015), and *Ida Lupino, Director: Her Art and Resilience in Times of Transition* (coauthored with Therese Grisham, 2017). Forthcoming monographs include *The Femme Fatale* and *Major Performers in Hollywood Noir* (coauthored with R. Barton Palmer).

Susan Hayward, Emeritus Professor of cinema studies, University of Exeter, has written extensively on French cinema. Her publications include *French National Cinema* (2005), *Luc Besson* (1998), *Les Diaboliques* (2005), and *French Costume Drama of the 1950s* (2010). She is also the author of *Cinema Studies: The Key Concepts* (currently in its 4th edition).

Jennifer L. Jenkins is Professor of English at the University of Arizona and director of the Bear Canyon Center for Southwest Humanities. She is principal investigator on a National Endowment for the Humanities funded project to repatriate midcentury educational films about Native peoples by recording new, culturally competent narrations in a process termed "tribesourcing." She holds the 2019 Cátedra Primo Feliciano Vázquez Chair of History at the Colégio de San Luis in San Luis Potosí, Mexico, where she is developing a comparative study of theaters and cinemagoing behaviors in railroad towns in the US and Mexico, 1896–1930.

Tarja Laine is Assistant Professor in Film Studies at the University of Amsterdam, and Adjunct Professor in Film Studies at the University of Turku (Finland), as well as visual artist graduated from Wackers Academy, Amsterdam. She is the author of *Bodies in Pain: Emotion and the Cinema of Darren Aronofsky* (2015), *Feeling Cinema: Emotional Dynamics in Film Studies* (2011), and *Shame and Desire: Emotion, Intersubjectivity, Cinema* (2007). Her research interests include cinematic emotions, film aesthetics, and film-phenomenology.

Jim Leach is Professor Emeritus in the Department of Communication, Popular Culture and Film at Brock University, St. Catharines, Ontario. He is the author of books on filmmakers Alain Tanner and Claude Jutra, as well as of *British Film* (2004) and *Film in Canada* (2010). He has also published a monograph on *Doctor Who*, coedited a volume on Canadian documentary films and one on heist films, and developed a Canadian edition of an introductory film studies textbook. His latest book is *The Films of Denys Arcand* (2020).

Robert Miklitsch is Professor in the Department of English Language and Literature at Ohio University. His work on film and television has appeared in *Film Quarterly*, *Journal of Film and Video*, *Journal of Popular Film and Television*, *New Review of Film and Television Studies*, and *Screen*. He is the editor of *Psycho-Marxism* (1998) and the author of *From Hegel to Madonna* (SUNY Press, 1998), *Roll Over Adorno* (SUNY Press, 2006), and *Siren City: Sound and Source Music in Classic American Noir* (2011), which was named a Choice Outstanding Academic Title of 2011. His edited collection *Kiss the Blood Off My Hands: On Classic Noir* (2014) was nominated for an Edgar Allan Poe Award in Criticism by the Mystery Writers of America. *The Red and the Black: [American] Film Noir in the 1950s* appeared in 2017. *I Died a Million Times: Gangster Noir in Mid-century America* is forthcoming in 2020.

R. Barton Palmer is an independent scholar. He is the author, editor, or general editor of more than sixty academic books on various literary and cinematic subjects, as well as the author of more than seventy-five book chapters, journal articles, and encyclopedia entries. He serves as the general editor of book series on traditions in world cinema and traditions in American cinema, and as general/founding editor of four other book series.

Homer B. Pettey is Professor Emeritus of film and literature at the University of Arizona. He serves as the general/founding editor for three book series on global film studios, international film stars, and global film directors. With R. Barton Palmer, he has coedited several collections on film: *Film Noir* and *International Noir* (2014), *Hitchcock's Moral Gaze* (SUNY Press, 2017), *Rule, Britannia! The Biopic and British National Identity* (SUNY Press, 2018), and *French Literature on Screen* (2019). Currently, he is writing a book on *Transnational Silent Film*.

Murray Pomerance is an independent scholar living in Toronto. He is author of, most recently, *Virtuoso: Film Performance and the Actor's Magic*, *A Dream of Hitchcock* (SUNY Press), *Cinema, If You Please: The Memory of Taste, the Taste of Memory*, and the BFI Classics of *The Man Who Knew Too Much* (2016) and *Marnie* (2014). His *The Film Cheat: Screen Artifice and Viewing Pleasure* is forthcoming. He has edited numerous volumes, and is editor, as well, of the Horizons of Cinema series at SUNY Press and the Techniques of the Moving Image series at Rutgers.

Index

Adjani, Isabelle, 37–38, 44–45, 51, 57, 61–63
AIDS, 60, 62–63, 223, 230–231
Alzheimer's disease, 10–11
Amadeus (1984, Milos Forman), 3
American Justice (1992–2005), 220
Americans with Disabilities Act, 132, 150
amnesia, 8–9, 28, 32
Andrews, Dana, 11, 103
Anémic Cinéma (1926, Marcel Duchamp), 5
anorexia, bulimia films, 14–15
As Good As It Gets (1997, James L. Brooks), 16–17
Assassination of Richard Nixon, The (2004, Niels Mueller), 17–18
Asylum (2004, David Mackenzie), 157, 163–164, 167
asylum, asylums, 2–4, 9, 18, 38, 41, 53, 103, 145, 158–159, 161, 163–165
asylum films, 3–4
Ayres, Lew, 89–90

Bacon, Kevin, 21, 22, 26–27
Bancroft, Anne, 14, 129, 136, 139
Baur, Harry, 218
Bernie (2011, Richard Linklater), 231–232

Best Years of Our Lives, The (1946, William Wyler), 11
Big Heat, The (1953, Fritz Lang), 7, 123
Bigger Than Life (1956, Nicholas Ray), 12
bipolar, 2, 13, 15
Bird's Nest, The, 79, 81–82, 97
Boone, Richard, 84
Borden, Lizzie, 214–215
Born on the Fourth of July (1989, Oliver Stone), 12
Boys in the Band, The (1970, William Friedkin), 20
Boys in the Band, The (play), 20
Boys in the Sand (1971, Wakefield Poole), 20
Brahm, John, 66–67, 69, 73
Bronson (2008, Nicolas Winding Refn), 208, 223, 225–227
Bunny Lake Is Missing (1965, Otto Preminger), 21

Cabinet of Dr. Caligari, The (1919, Robert Wiene), 3, 4, 101
Cage, Nicholas, 14, 16–17
Camille Claudel (1988, Bruno Nuytten), 37, 38, 39–41, 44, 45, 52–57, 62
Captain Newman, M.D. (1963, David Miller), 4, 11

Carey, Jim, 228, 230
Cassavetes, John, 129–130, 141–144, 146–148
Catch Me If You Can (2002, Steven Spielberg), 208, 223–225
Charly (1968, Ralph Nelson), 18
Cheat, The (1915, Cecil B. DeMille), 20–21
Chéreau, Patrice, 37, 42, 45, 59–61
Chien andalou, Un (1929, Dali and Buñuel), 5, 156
child abuse, 21
child abuse films, 21–27
Child Is Waiting, A (1963, John Cassavetes), 129, 141–149
child molestation, 21–27
Clean Slate (1994, Mick Jackson), 9
cognitive studies, 30–31
Cold Case Files (1999–2017), 220–221
Cold Justice (2013–present), 220–221
Coming Home (1978, Hal Ashby), 12
Cooper, Bradley, 15
costume, 38, 46, 117, 124, 149
Cottage on Dartmoor, A (1926, Anthony Asquith), 4
Cregar, Laird, 66–70, 77
Cronenberg, David, 157, 160–161, 163, 166

Dark Mirror (1946, Robert Siodmak), 89–90, 92
Darnell, Linda, 66–67
Deception (1946, Irving Rapper), 69–70
Deer Hunter, The (1978, Michael Cimino), 11
delirium, 3–4, 18, 156–157, 161, 163
delirium tremens, 12, 212
De Niro, Robert, 12, 15, 200
Depardieu, Gérard, 218
depression, 8, 14, 17, 28, 204, 219
Dewey, John, 130–131, 139, 145, 147, 150

Diagnostic and Statistical Manual of Mental Disorders (DMS), 19–20, 79
DiCaprio, Leonardo, 223–224
disability films, 150
Dmytryk, Edward, 101–102, 110, 113, 115, 118, 122–125
Doctor X (1932, Michael Curtiz), 7
Dragnet (television series), 219–220
Dreyfuss, Richard, 15
Driving Miss Daisy (1989, Bruce Beresford), 11
Duke, Patty, 13, 136, 139
Dumas, Alexandre, *père*, 41–42, 45, 59, 216

Fatal Attraction (1987, Adrian Lyne), 200
Fawkes, Guy, 65–67, 72
female sexual predators, 22–23
female sexual predator films, 23
femme fatale, femmes fatales, 31, 38, 89, 109, 113, 199–200
femme fatale films, 8
Finnes, Ralph, 157, 162
Fleming, Rhonda, 106
Flight (2012, Robert Zemeckis), 13
Forrest Gump (1994, Robert Zemeckis), 19
Frankenstein (1931, James Whale), 6
Franz, Arthur, 109, 114
Freaks (1932, Tod Browning), 18, 143
Frenzy (1972, Alfred Hitchcock), 8
Freud, Sigmund, 8, 28–29, 81–82, 85–86, 93–94, 109, 157–158
Fu Manchu films, 6–7

Garland, Judy, 130, 141, 143

Haas, Hugo, 80–82, 84, 86, 88, 92
Hands of Orlac, The (1924, Robert Weine), 70
Hangover Square (1945, John Brahm), 65–77

Hard Candy (2005, David Slade), 21–22
Hardy, Tom, 225
Havilland, Olivia de, 9, 89, 158
Herrmann, Bernard, 66, 69, 72–73, 75
L'Histoire d'Adèle H (1975, François Truffaut), 37, 41, 43–52, 62
Hogarth, William, 212–213, 225
homosexuality, 16, 19–20, 228, 230
homosexual films, 19–20
Hugo, Victor, 39, 42, 44, 47–49, 51, 216

I Am Sam (2001, Jessie Nelson), 19
I Love You Phillip Morris (2009, John Requa), 208, 223, 228–231
I, Tonya (2017, Craig Gillespie), 231–232
In Harm's Way (1965, Otto Preminger), 14
Incendies (2010, Denis Villeneuve), 173–187
Informant!, The (2009, Steven Soderbergh), 17
insane, insanity, 1, 2–4, 6, 9, 18, 30, 37, 41, 53, 61, 75, 77, 105, 145, 155, 159, 165, 193, 226, 231
Invisible Man, The (1932, James Whale), 7
Iris (2001, Richard Eyre), 10
Island of Lost Souls, The (1932, Erle C. Kenton), 6

Jackson, Shirley, 92
Jekyll and Hyde motif, 5, 14, 80–81, 86, 93
Johnson, Nunnally, 80, 90–92, 95

Kinsey, Alfred, 92, 94, 98–99
Kiss of Death (1947, Henry Hathaway), 7

Lancaster, Burt, 129, 141–142

Lang, Fritz, 21, 101–109, 122–125
landscape, 32, 80, 113, 132, 174–187, 213, 215, 224
Lawrence, Jennifer, 15
Leaving Las Vegas (1995, Mike Figgis), 14
lesbian domestic violence, 23–24
Lizzie (1957, Hugo Haas), 80–90, 97
Lolita (1962, Stanley Kubrick), 21
Lost Weekend, The (1945, Billy Wilder), 12
lunatic, 52, 156, 192
Lupino, Ida, 107

Mackenzie, David, 157, 160, 163
madness, 3–4, 21, 30, 38–39, 42, 44, 46–49, 5, 62, 76, 155–161, 165–169, 199
manic, manic depression, 2, 15, 17, 28, 32, 195
Man with the Golden Arm (1955, Otto Preminger), 12
Mark, The (1961, Guy Green), 22, 25–26
Marnie (1964, Alfred Hitchcock), 8, 31
Matchstick Men (2003, Ridley Scott), 16–17
McKellan, Ian, 164–165
media and psychopathological symptoms, 30
mental disorder film texts, 30
mental retardation, mentally retarded, 9, 18–19, 32, 129–131, 141, 143–144, 146, 150, 151
Mesrine, Jacques, 227–228
Miracle Worker, The (1962, Arthur Penn), 129, 132, 133–141
Monster (2003, Patty Jenkins), 21, 191–192, 197–199, 202
Mulholland Drive (2001, David Lynch), 199
multiple personality disorder (MPD), 79–86, 90–94, 97, 99

murder, murderer, 3–4, 6–8, 12, 21, 23, 32, 41, 45, 60, 66–67, 69, 72, 76, 77, 89, 98, 103, 107–108, 113, 115, 122–123, 160, 162, 164, 207, 209, 211, 213–217, 219, 221–223, 226–227, 231
Murray, Bill, 15
"My Girl" (*Wicked Attraction* series), 221–223
Mystic River (2003, Clint Eastwood), 21–22

Napier, Alan, 73, 218
Navarre, René, 218
Nebraska (2013, Alexander Payne), 10
Nerves (*Nerven* 1919, Robert Reinert), 4
Nicholson, Jack, 16
Night of Terror (1933, Benjamin Stoloff), 7
Notes on a Scandal (2006, Richard Eyre), 23
Now, Voyager (1942, Irving Rapper), 82
Nuytten, Bruno, 37, 44, 47, 52, 54, 55–57, 61

obsessive-compulsive, obsessive-compulsive disorder (OCD), 2, 15, 16, 28, 219
Ordinary People (1980, Robert Redford), 14
Oscar Wilde films, 19
Oswalt, Patton, 191–192
Overboard (1987, Garry Marshall), 9

Parker, Eleanor, 84, 87
Penn, Arthur, 129–130, 133–136, 138
Penn, Sean, 17, 19, 21
Post-traumatic stress disorder (PTSD), 11–12
Pretty Baby (1978, Louis Malle), 21
Prince, Morton, 5, 92
Prozac Nation (2001, Erik Skjoldbjærg), 17

Psycho (1960, Alfred Hitchcock), 8
psychoanalytical criticism, psychoanalytical critics, 29–30
psychopath, psychopathic, 4, 7, 8, 22, 25, 90, 221
psychopathy, 5, 219
Pushkin, Alexander, 3

Radio (2003, Michael Tollin), 18–19
railroad spine, 12
Random Harvest (1942, Mervyn LeRoy), 8
rape-revenge films, 21
Raw Deal (1948, Anthony Mann), 7
Reefer Madness (1936, Louis J. Gasnier), 12
La Reine Margot (1994, Patrice Chéreau), 37, 41–42, 44–45, 57–63
Reitman, Jason, 191, 193–194, 199–200, 205
Ricci, Christina, 17, 198
Richardson, Natasha, 162, 164–165
Rodin, Auguste, 39–41, 44–45, 53–56
Rush, Geoffrey, 15

Saboteur (1942, Alfred Hitchcock), 73–74
Sacks, Oliver, 2
Sanders, George, 73, 103, 218–219
Scandal in Paris, A (1946, Douglas Sirk), 218–219
Searchers, The (1956, John Ford), 174
serial killer, 32, 67, 101, 102, 109–110, 117, 122–125
Shadoian, Jack, 5
Shadow of a Doubt (1943, Alfred Hitchcock), 8, 204
Shine (1996, Scott Hicks), 15
Silver Linings Playbook (2012, David O. Russell), 15
Sirk, Douglas, 218
Sleepers (1996, Barry Levinson), 21
Slender Thread, The (1965, Sydney Pollack), 14

Snake Pit, The (1948, Anatole Litvak), 4, 9, 158–159, 163, 167
Sniper, The (1952, Edward Dmytryk), 101, 102, 109–123, 125
sociopath, sociopathic, sociopathy, 2, 7, 8, 19, 193, 199, 213, 219, 224, 227–228, 230
Spellbound (1945, Alfred Hitchcock), 4, 8, 31
Spider (2002, David Cronenberg), 4, 157, 160–168
Spotlight (2015, Tom McCarthy), 21–22
Still Alice (2014, Richard Glatzer), 10
substance abuse, 12, 14, 17, 30
suicide films, 13–14
Superstar—The Karen Carpenter Story (1987, Todd Haynes), 14–15

Taxi Driver (1976, Martin Scorsese), 194, 200
Theron, Charlize, 191–192, 195–200, 202
Three Faces of Eve, The (1957, Nunnally Johnson), 4, 32, 79–80, 89–97
trauma, traumatic, 4, 8–9, 28–29, 32, 44, 48, 84–85, 93, 96, 125, 173–187, 191–192, 194, 198–199, 222
Truffaut, François, 38–39, 43–44, 47, 49, 51–52, 61

Up In the Air (2009, Jason Reitman), 194–195

Valley of the Dolls (1967, Mark Robson), 12–13
Vampires, Les (1915–16, Louis Feuillade), 4
Vertigo (1958, Alfred Hitchcock), 8, 113, 123
Vidocq, Eugène-François, 207, 215–219
Vidocq films, 218–219
Villeneuve, Denis, 173, 178

Warning Shadows (1923, Arthur Robison), 4
Wayne, David, 95
What About Bob? (1991, Frank Oz), 15
While The City Sleeps (1956, Fritz Lang), 32, 101–102, 103–109, 116, 119, 122–123, 125
White Heat (1949, Raoul Walsh), 7–8
Whitman, Stuart, 22, 25–26
Wicked Attraction series, 221
Wolf of Wall Street, The (2013, Martin Scorsese), 13
Wolf of Wall Street, The (novel), 13
Woodsman, The (2004, Nicole Kassell), 22, 26–27
Woodward, Joanne, 84, 94–95, 97
Wrong Man, The (1956, Alfred Hitchcock), 8
Wuornos, Aileen, 21, 191–192, 197–198, 213

Young Adult (2011, Jason Reitman), 32, 191–205

THE SUNY SERIES

MURRAY POMERANCE | EDITOR

Also in the series

William Rothman, editor, *Cavell on Film*

J. David Slocum, editor, *Rebel Without a Cause*

Joe McElhaney, *The Death of Classical Cinema*

Kirsten Moana Thompson, *Apocalyptic Dread*

Frances Gateward, editor, *Seoul Searching*

Michael Atkinson, editor, *Exile Cinema*

Paul S. Moore, *Now Playing*

Robin L. Murray and Joseph K. Heumann, *Ecology and Popular Film*

William Rothman, editor, *Three Documentary Filmmakers*

Sean Griffin, editor, *Hetero*

Jean-Michel Frodon, editor, *Cinema and the Shoah*

Carolyn Jess-Cooke and Constantine Verevis, editors, *Second Takes*

Matthew Solomon, editor, *Fantastic Voyages of the Cinematic Imagination*

R. Barton Palmer and David Boyd, editors, *Hitchcock at the Source*

William Rothman, *Hitchcock: The Murderous Gaze, Second Edition*

Joanna Hearne, *Native Recognition*

Marc Raymond, *Hollywood's New Yorker*

Steven Rybin and Will Scheibel, editors, *Lonely Places, Dangerous Ground*

Claire Perkins and Constantine Verevis, editors, *B Is for Bad Cinema*

Dominic Lennard, *Bad Seeds and Holy Terrors*

Rosie Thomas, *Bombay before Bollywood*

Scott M. MacDonald, *Binghamton Babylon*

Sudhir Mahadevan, *A Very Old Machine*

David Greven, *Ghost Faces*

James S. Williams, *Encounters with Godard*

William H. Epstein and R. Barton Palmer, editors, *Invented Lives, Imagined Communities*

Lee Carruthers, *Doing Time*

Rebecca Meyers, William Rothman, and Charles Warren, editors, *Looking with Robert Gardner*

Belinda Smaill, *Regarding Life*

Douglas McFarland and Wesley King, editors, *John Huston as Adaptor*

R. Barton Palmer, Homer B. Pettey, and Steven M. Sanders, editors, *Hitchcock's Moral Gaze*

Nenad Jovanovic, *Brechtian Cinemas*

Will Scheibel, *American Stranger*

Amy Rust, *Passionate Detachments*

Steven Rybin, *Gestures of Love*

Seth Friedman, *Are You Watching Closely?*

Roger Rawlings, *Ripping England!*

Michael DeAngelis, *Rx Hollywood*

Ricardo E. Zulueta, *Queer Art Camp Superstar*

John Caruana and Mark Cauchi, editors, *Immanent Frames*

Nathan Holmes, *Welcome to Fear City*

Homer B. Pettey and R. Barton Palmer, editors, *Rule, Britannia!*

Milo Sweedler, *Rumble and Crash*

Ken Windrum, *From El Dorado to Lost Horizons*

Matthew Lau, *Sounds Like Helicopters*

Dominic Lennard, *Brute Force*

William Rothman, *Tuitions and Intuitions*

Michael Hammond, *The Great War in Hollywood Memory, 1918–1939*

Burke Hilsabeck, *The Slapstick Camera*

Niels Niessen, *Miraculous Realism*

Alex Clayton, *Funny How?*

Bill Krohn, *Letters from Hollywood*

Alexia Kannas, *Giallo!*

www.ingramcontent.com/pod-product-compliance
Lightning Source LLC
Chambersburg PA
CBHW020646230426
43665CB00008B/332